GOLD, GRIT, GUNS

Cover of William Hazlitt's *British Columbia and Vancouver's Island*

GOLD, GRIT, GUNS

Miners on BC's Fraser River in 1858

ALEXANDER GLOBE

RONSDALE PRESS

GOLD, GRIT, GUNS
Copyright © 2022 Alexander Globe

RONSDALE PRESS
3350 West 21st Avenue, Vancouver, B.C. Canada V6S 1G7
www.ronsdalepress.com

Typesetting: Julie Cochrane, in Caslon 11.5 pt on 15
Cover Design: Julie Cochrane
Cover Image: Miners panning for gold. *Harper's New Monthly Magazine*, vol. 20, no. 119 (April 1860): 604. San Francisco History Center, San Francisco Public Library.
Paper: Rolland Enviro Print 60 lb.

Ronsdale Press wishes to thank the following for their support of its publishing program: the Canada Council for the Arts, the Government of Canada, the British Columbia Arts Council, and the Province of British Columbia through the British Columbia Book Publishing Tax Credit program.

Library and Archives Canada Cataloguing in Publication

Title: Gold, grit, guns: miners on BC's Fraser River in 1858 / Alexander Globe.

Names: Globe, Alexander, 1943– author.

Description: Includes bibliographical references and index.

Identifiers: Canadiana (print) 20200158244 | Canadiana (ebook) 20200158252 | ISBN 9781553805847 (softcover) | ISBN 9781553805854 (HTML) | ISBN 9781553805861 (PDF)

Subjects: LCSH: Fraser River Valley (B.C.)—Gold discoveries. | LCSH: Gold mines and mining—British Columbia—Fraser River Valley—History—19th century. | LCSH: Fraser River Valley (B.C.)—History—19th century. | LCSH: Gold miners—British Columbia—Fraser River Valley—Diaries. | CSH: British Columbia—History—1849-1871.

Classification: LCC FC3822.4 .G56 2022 | DDC 971.1/3—dc23

At Ronsdale Press we are committed to protecting the environment. To this end we are working with Canopy and printers to phase out our use of paper produced from ancient forests. This book is one step towards that goal.

Printed in Canada

In memory of my grandfather
Alexander Rankin Globe
gold miner and philanthropist
who improved the lives of miners
wherever he worked

CONTENTS

LIST OF ILLUSTRATIONS

Introduction

∞

GOLD RUSHES CONTINUE to fascinate us in the twenty-first century as much as they lured young men in the nineteenth century to dare to travel the world in search of wealth. The first frenzy turned 1850s California into a land of dreams where, for the first time ever, any adventurer could become rich, irrespective of birth. The world had never seen such fabulous amounts of gold: 17 tons in 1849, 68 in 1850, 126 in 1851, and 135 in 1852.[2] On June 11, 1858, the *Sacramento Daily Union* newspaper described the overpowering attraction and devastating reality for the hundreds of thousands of adventurers who risked everything to travel to California:

> Mining for gold, in either a newly discovered or old gold bearing section . . . is the most uncertain of all the numerous pursuits of man . . . [yet] the most seductive and irresistibly attractive. . . . Gold mining is a vast lottery, in which the blanks greatly outnumber the prizes; and this, too, without regard to the reported or real richness of the diggings. As in other lotteries . . . the names of the disappointed many

Emory's Bar in 2019

who draw blanks are suppressed. . . . Fortunate strikes are published, the exact amount gold taken out in so many days stated to an ounce . . . and the stimulating effect of such statements upon the minds of the generality of men is prodigious.[3]

Australia came next with the discovery of gold north of Melbourne during 1851. In 1858, some thirty thousand foreigners flooded the Fraser River in search of gold. The British government responded decisively by proclaiming British Columbia a new colony, which later guaranteed Canada a province on the Pacific coast. The immense fortunes made in British Columbia's Cariboo region during the 1860s are still memorialized at Barkerville, a restored town bustling with nineteenth-century shenanigans. The picture of hundreds of miners filing up a snow-covered mountain pass during Yukon's Klondike gold rush of 1896-1899 is seared into the minds of everyone who has seen it.

In the catalogue of a Royal British Columbia Museum exhibit on the 1858 Fraser gold rush, Kathryn Bridge comments that "Understanding the average person of that time remains a challenge for historians. . . . How do we learn about the lives of people of whom so little is documented?"[4] This current book focuses on ordinary miners during 1858 to recapture the transformative events that led to the creation of British Columbia. This study is anchored by the only four extensive miners' journals known to have survived from that year. Three are unknown to scholarship, while historians of British Columbia have cited only a few sentences from the fourth.[5] This is the first book to recreate the 1858 mining milieu exclusively from the participants' perspectives. Because the diaries offer previously unexplored material, they are quoted extensively rather than being summarized. That way, their own voices bring these men and their times back to life.

Miners who prospected on the Fraser River in 1858 concentrated on their quest for gold. The work took determination and stamina, while it cost hundreds of dollars to get to the mines. Once there, participants found themselves negotiating numerous conflicting claims.

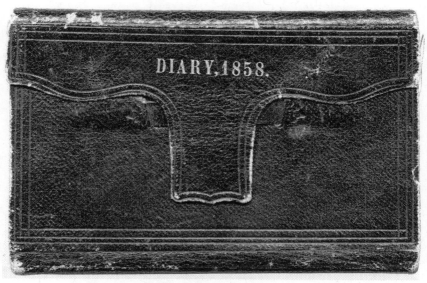

Pocket diary of the anonymous Canadian miner

Indigenous people wanted no trespassers stealing their gold or destroying their salmon fisheries. The Hudson's Bay Company insisted on a monopoly of trade. A lively black market presented mining supplies and bootleg smuggled north from Washington Territory. Colonial authorities in Victoria protected British sovereignty. The Imperial government in England placed global decisions above local desires. Americans assumed that the border could be expanded north of the forty-ninth parallel. Notions about the use of firearms differed as much then as now. The rhetoric of loyalty to the Crown and personal liberty under the Stars and Stripes did not always match experience on the ground.

— • —

Part A consists of four chapters outlining "The 1858 Setting." Chapter 1 presents a brief overview of "Victoria and International Tensions." At the start of the year, the place was a sleepy British Hudson's Bay Company trading post. The arrival of some thirty thousand foreign prospectors transformed it into a mining transfer point. The shrewd strategies of Governor James Douglas and the Colonial Office in London prevented American annexation of the area.

Chapter 2, "Travellers to the Fraser River and Their Expenses," details the conditions that encouraged people to join gold rushes, the physical and financial challenges of getting to the mines, the first detailed overview of shipping to Victoria and the Fraser River, road building in 1858, maps available for miners, the contents of miners' kits, the cost of provisions on the river, and the difficulties of keeping in touch with families through the sending of letters.

Chapter 3 presents the first comprehensive treatment of "Gold Mining Techniques and Regulations." Previously, just a few often contradictory details have found their way into print. The year started with individual prospectors digging up the gravel bars that formed the open air mines on the banks of the Fraser. Then they separated the gold from the rocky rubble through simple washing techniques. As the year progressed, large, efficient sluices started stripping the landscape. Effective extraction using mercury polluted the land and the river. Government regulations shifted as authorities abandoned failed attempts to impose unrealistic directives, then made pragmatic adjustments closer to American miners' demands.

Chapter 4 treats "Indigenous Resistance to Displacement." Everyone on the Fraser River in 1858 interacted with Indigenous peoples. By June, thousands of prospectors had forced them off traditional fishing spots and settlement areas so that the river's gravel bars could be mined. Once the salmon fishery failed in August, Indigenous resistance escalated into what has been termed the Fraser Canyon War or the Fraser River War. "Peace," always on miners' terms, required Indigenous surrender and displacement. Fortunately, the moderating leadership of miner Harry Snyder from San Francisco prevented a bloodbath.

Part B's four chapters focus on three miners and a merchant who wrote diaries on the Fraser in 1858. Months of online and on-site searching through dozens of libraries, archives, and museums uncovered many documents assigned to 1858, but most were short letters from that year or reminiscences written decades later. The only four extensive journals surviving from 1858 present the adventures of four courageous men in search of wealth to secure better futures. Their diaries contain detailed, spontaneous reactions to significant or everyday events happening at the moment rather than selective memories blurred by the passage of time. They unfold tales of dreams conjured, hardships endured, and fortunes won and lost. They even verbalize private feelings that most men of the period were unwilling to speak out loud. Fortunately, all four men had distinctive personalities and different experiences.

George Leach Slocumb (1830-1890) was the son of an Illinois state legislator and judge. Stymied by a depressed economy, at age twenty-two he joined the fifty thousand optimists who crossed the continent on foot in 1852 to make their pile in California. He never had a lucky strike. On April 20, 1858, he sailed north on the *Commodore*, the first steamer to arrive at Victoria with a large number of argonauts. Fortune also eluded him on the Fraser. Most miners suffered similar despair in 1858. Without a claim that paid living expenses, Slocumb's savings disappeared until he returned to California broke on December 8. What makes Slocumb's diary distinctive are the numerous literary quotations that capture his psychological state at any given moment, like the musical score in a film. He explored his emotions more fully than most men of the period dared. His diary also has the best description of how the Fraser gold rush impacted the towns of Washington Territory during 1858.

George Wesley Beam (1831-1866) quit Illinois in 1854 after his father's death left his mother destitute. He trekked across the continent with relatives to pioneer as farmers on Whidbey Island in Washington Territory, around a hundred kilometres (sixty miles) south of the forty-ninth parallel. When he heard about sensational gold strikes on the Fraser early in 1858, he relied on friends with California experience to teach him how to mine gold. Pushing off on July 15, Beam and his friends canoed across the Strait of Georgia and up the river. He was the only diarist who chose this option, typical of Washington residents. Beam's diary focuses outwardly on work, providing the most detailed record of 1858 mining practices that has surfaced. An ardent patriot, Beam was thrilled with the rumour that "the forty Ninth Parilell runns north of Fraziers River."[6] Like most Washingtonians of the day, he wanted Indigenous people cleared off the land—killed, even, in retaliation for their raids. He had been permanently scarred by the Indigenous beheading of his first cousin in 1857. On November 13, he returned to Whidbey Island with around a thousand dollars.

Otis Parsons (1831-1875) was a Connecticut native who established a stabling and merchandizing business in California around 1850. Knowing that big profits could be made in new mining areas, he sailed from San Francisco to Victoria on July 2, 1858. He stepped forward on August 3 when the government called for five hundred volunteers to build a hundred and thirteen kilometres (seventy miles) of road from Harrison Lake to Lillooet Lake, then on to Anderson

Lake. That was the government's largest public works project in 1858. It is described in detail here, because the undertaking has received much less attention than the legendary Cariboo Road up the Fraser River into the Interior. Parsons' journal records the road cutters' day-by-day triumphs and frustrations. By December he started wholesaling and retailing supplies to prospectors and settlers between what is now Pemberton and Lillooet.

The final diarist was an anonymous anglophone from Canada West (now Ontario). Neither his birthdate nor death date is known, but a photograph of him shows a strong, determined man in his twenties. After working in the California gold mines for a number of years, he arrived in Victoria by steamer on July 12, 1858. His diary reveals a personality very different from the Americans of the other diaries. His colonial demeanour made him comfortable with Vancouver Island officials, and they helped him in ways unavailable to Americans. The gold commissioner in Victoria told him about the most promising diggings and gave him a letter of introduction so that William Manson, the Hudson's Bay Company agent at Lytton, became his first mining partner. The Canadian respected the strength of his Indigenous packers and called them by their names, Stin-oop and Kam-uck. He was the only diarist who braved the arduous trek up the Fraser to Fountain, just north of Lillooet, which was then the northern limit of gold mining. He earned over a thousand dollars in two months.

The ninth chapter looks forward to "Perspectives beyond the End of 1858." The most important political outcome was the proclamation of the Colony of British Columbia at Fort Langley on November 19. Victoria and the Fraser River were transformed irreversibly by the gold rush of 1858. Mining had arrived and was clearly going to expand. California prospectors kept heading north along the Fraser River searching for the motherlode, where large nuggets would be found. The first significant discovery came in summer 1859 at Horsefly, near Williams Lake. A series of similar discoveries started the legendary Cariboo Gold Rush, the subject of many books.

The ten thousand people who remained in Victoria and on the lower Fraser River needed more developed infrastructure. Governments responded by extending existing projects and formulating long-range plans. The British government kept ships safer by updating marine charts for Victoria and Esquimalt harbours, the Strait of Georgia, and the Fraser River up to Yale. The colonial government updated town surveys for mushrooming Victoria and Esquimalt. Settlement on the lower Fraser River was encouraged with the survey of building lots in Langley, Hope, Yale, and Port Douglas. Ambitious surveys produced maps recording mineral and agricultural opportunities in mainland British Columbia. Ongoing projects developed better roads into the Interior. First Nations also received special attention. Governor Douglas set aside huge tracts of land as reserves so that Indigenous peoples could maintain their traditional ways of life.

— • —

Forty-seven ships are mentioned in the diaries. They sailed in the orbit of Victoria, San Francisco, the Fraser River, and increasingly interdependent Puget Sound in adjacent Washington Territory. Those vessels were the essential carriers of passengers, their baggage, food, a wealth of other domestic and commercial goods, construction supplies, local as well as international news, personal mail, business communications, government communiqués, and naval plus army personnel. Simply put, a good knowledge of shipping is crucial to understanding the infrastructural challenges and achievements during 1858.

Because existing sources about shipping in 1858 were so incomplete and unreliable, the first exhaustive survey of 1858 Customs House records, newspapers, the log book of the Hudson's Bay Company steamer *Otter*, and other sources was undertaken. A comprehensive overview emerged in a census of over sixteen hundred sailings of 276 vessels.

One result is a stand-alone book-length study entitled *Ho for*

Fraser River! Shipping in 1858 between Victoria, the Fraser River, Puget Sound, and San Francisco. Details about the forty-seven ships mentioned in *Gold, Grit, Guns* are not buried in references that would be difficult to find, but are collected in "Appendix 1: Ships," which can be consulted whenever needed.

— • —

Faced with four unexplored diaries from 1858, I decided to give them the agency of their own nineteenth-century voices rather than fit selections into traditional third-person histories or theoretical debates. The goal has been to show how people of that era understood their own roles and their relations to others, using their own words. To bring readers close to the tumultuous events of 1858, the diaries are juxtaposed with a variety of competing contemporary voices from that year.

Additional sources include the thoughtful diaries and self-flattering or pleading official letters of Governor James Douglas to the Colonial Office in England. The government in London sometimes sent instructions that contradicted him. The latest scoop in newspapers from Victoria, Puget Sound, and California could convey accurate information, speculation, or idle gossip. Their opinionated editorials were written to influence public and government action in a variety of different ways. A few other diaries and letters of the period clarify some obscurities, and a few books rushed to market in America and Britain capitalized on early interest. The technology and language of 1858 may sound quaint in our digital age, yet some of the issues seem as familiar as this morning's news.

The racist attitudes of many whites who lived in 1858 are very offensive, particularly after the Black Lives Matter protests of the summer of 2020 that encouraged Indigenous Canadians to speak out more forcefully against systemic abuse. Chapter 4, on "Indigenous Resistance to Displacement," highlights the atrocities. They need to be exposed in all their painful, destructive power, not forgotten as if they never existed. The words of many American officials and miners of that time reveal their aim of racial containment or even elimination. Terms such as "Indian menace," "Indian wars," "Indian reservations," and "white settlement" showed which way the cards were stacked. That systemic racism became naturalized and set unfortunate precedents for the containment of Indigenous people in B.C. and the rest of Canada from Confederation onward. Among the worst legacies were the later Indian residential schools, whose scars have been especially deep, as detailed in the 2015 report of the Truth and Reconciliation Commission. During news coverage in the summer of 2021, many Canadians were shocked, and grieved over the news about thousands of secretive burials of Indigenous children at those places.

My use in this work of such terms as Indigenous, First Nations, Stó:lō, and Nlaka'pamux indicates respect. Some people in 1858 showed similar esteem. The Canadian miner praised the efforts of his Indigenous guides. English Colonial officials encouraged all people suffering racial discrimination to immigrate to British Columbia. Governor Douglas welcomed African-Americans and Chinese people north from California and usually did his best to protect Indigenous peoples from destruction. All of those people used the word "Indian," a term that was standard back then but has now become problematic.

The challenge with sources from 1858 is that the word "Indian" is used frequently. The context will tell which of a range of meanings that word has in any given quotation. In 1858, some called for genocide. Others had the courage to stand against indiscriminate killing and devised strategies of resistance. An example of giving Indigenous people agency occurred in late May on the Fraser River when American miners were trying to get rid of them. Governor Douglas visited the river and took "an Indian highly connected . . . and of great influence, resolution, and energy of character, into the Government service," then appointed "Indian magistrates" there.[7] The final paragraphs of Chapter 9 voice hope that a more participatory future is emerging for Indigenous people in British Columbia.

— • —

Many unfamiliar sources from 1858 are quoted throughout this book. A multitude of notes identify every source. That way, the research trail can be followed whenever an interesting detail strikes a reader. The notes help determine what can be established, replacing guesses in some previous sources.

The vocabulary of the nineteenth-century sources often extends beyond the riches of the *Oxford English Dictionary* and *Webster's Third International Dictionary*. In those cases, the four-volume *Imperial Dictionary of the English Language* (1883) and several dictionaries of slang have proved indispensable.

Many illustrations present a comprehensive visual record of 1858. The often published photographs made in the Cariboo during the 1860s have been avoided, because they show more developed mining technologies in a different landscape. Unfortunately, pictorial material produced on the Fraser River in 1858 is very limited. Life-threatening trails prevented all photographers from lugging their bulky and heavy equipment to the surface mining bars that year. Only a few paintings and drawings left a visual record of the area. Illustrations that get close to 1858 include a few sketches of landscapes in books, maps, portraits of miners, pictures of the politicians whose decisions affected their lives, photographs of diary pages, pictures of some of the ships and canoes the miners used, and later photographs of undeveloped areas. Mining techniques are illustrated by engravings from 1850s California, since most 1858 miners spent years there and brought those methods north.

PART A

The 1858 Setting

James Douglas, chief factor of the Hudson's Bay Company and governor
of the two colonies of Vancouver Island and British Columbia

CHAPTER 1

Victoria and International Tensions

ᴄⱽᴼ

Should the . . . gold on Frazer river [be as] rich
in that metal as California . . . we may even witness the
revival of the old northwestern boundary dispute.
—Sacramento Daily Union, *May 25, 1858*[1]

AT THE BEGINNING of 1858, Fort Victoria was a tiny outpost of the British Empire. James Douglas, chief factor of the Hudson's Bay Company, administered operations west of the Rocky Mountains with a few hundred "servants."[2] He had laboured effectively for the Company during thirty-seven years, increased profits, maintained discipline, and built strong trade relations with Indigenous people. The Company's early nineteenth-century commerce was founded on fur. By 1858, Fort Victoria's economy had diversified to include salmon, sturgeon, whale oil, dogfish oil, herring, cod, oolichan (a fish so oily it can be set alight), isinglass (fish gelatin used in glue), grain, peas, potatoes, turnips, butter, cheese, wool, flour, cranberries, salt, lime, bricks, coal, lumber, and cedar shingles. Indigenous people contributed inexpensive labour. One prized blanket that retailed at twelve dollars on the Fraser River or five dollars in San Francisco could be had for forty palisade logs, two tons of coal (worth $28–$30 wholesale at San Francisco), two thousand shingles, half a month's farm work, twenty-four gallons of cranberries (worth $30 wholesale at San Francisco), or five barrels of herring.[3] On May 30, 1859, those arrangements would change with the expiry of the Crown Grant for the Hudson's Bay Company's exclusive trade with Indigenous people.

Fort Victoria was also the capital of the Colony of Vancouver Island, created in 1849 to protect British sovereignty on the Pacific coast in the wake of the American annexation of Texas in 1845, Washington and Oregon in 1846, and the area from Texas to California in 1848. The thousands of prospectors flooding into California after gold was discovered in 1848 prompted the British to declare ownership of Vancouver Island in case Americans turned their sights north, as they had during the treaty negotiations that established the border at the forty-ninth parallel in 1846. The British Parliament saved money by appointing the Hudson's Bay Company as the colony's custodian for a period of ten years, until 1859. James Douglas was named the colony's second governor in 1851. A census of Vancouver Island on December 1854 counted just 774 white residents (232 in Victoria, 151 in coal town Nanaimo, 178 on Hudson's Bay Company farms, and 213 scattered elsewhere).[4] The 25,873 Indigenous residents were usually left to themselves unless they attacked white settlers. Douglas was often praised by his two masters, but occasionally he was asked to implement policies that he found distasteful. Occasionally, too, he found ways of ignoring directives.

Early in 1858, Victoria presented a stark contrast to rollicking, wealthy San Francisco. Alfred Waddington, a Victoria and San Francisco merchant, recalled:

> no noise, no bustle, no gamblers, no speculators or interested parties to preach up this or underrate that. A few quiet gentlemanly behaved inhabitants, chiefly Scotchmen, secluded as it were from the whole world . . . As to business there was none, the streets were grown over with grass, and there was not even a cart.[5]

Fort Victoria with Songhees longhouses across the harbour

A gun blockhouse of Fort Victoria

— • —

A few Americans trickled over the forty-ninth parallel in 1856 and 1857, searching for rumoured gold.[6] By February 1858, 800 ounces of gold collected by the Hudson's Bay Company reached the San Francisco mint. The mint superintendent spread the news about what he thought would be the next big gold rush, telling a friend, James Moore, about the Hudson's Bay Company hoard, which was "coined as a souvenir of the first gold found."[7] Moore and some friends sailed north and found gold on March 23, 1858, at Hill's Bar, across the Fraser River from Fort Yale (now Yale, B.C.).[8] That mine became a magnet. Diggers there regularly made a handsome $50 per day. By July 1858, one American's claim had yielded about $1,000. Hill's Bar produced a reputed two million dollars in gold before it was worked out.

Fatefully, on April 25, 1858, the steamer *Commodore* landed at Fort Victoria with 450 passengers from San Francisco. Douglas observed to the Colonial Office and Hudson's Bay Governor in England that these newcomers:

> are all well provided with mining tools, and . . . there was no dearth of capital or intelligence among them. About 60 British subjects, with an equal number of native born Americans, the rest being chiefly Germans, and a smaller proportion of Frenchmen and Italians. . . . They are represented as being, with some exceptions, a specimen of the worst of the population of San Francisco; the very dregs, in fact, of society. Their conduct while here would have led me to form a very different conclusion, as . . . there was not a single committal of rioting, drunkenness, or other offences, during their stay here.[9]

Most of the thirty thousand prospectors who came to the Fraser River in 1858 arrived at Victoria and Esquimalt harbours by steamers or sailing ships from San Francisco—sixteen thousand by the end of June and eight thousand more in July.[10] An additional six thousand came from Puget Sound or overland up the Cowlitz or Columbia rivers from Oregon. Many were American, but British subjects,

Esquimalt Harbour

Frenchmen, Germans, Italians, Hungarians, Poles, Danes, Swedes, Spaniards, Mexicans, African-Americans, and Chinese also came.[11] London author William Hazlitt heard that even "men who can't speak a word of English are going, accompanied by interpreters."[12] Grocers, butchers, bakers, dry goods and mining tool merchants, clothiers, lumbermen, jewellers, printers, booksellers, barbers, hoteliers, bartenders, auctioneers, and land agents arrived to serve the thousands of prospective customers.

Douglas welcomed African-Americans and Chinese north because he thought that they would be good British subjects and he wanted to help them escape racial intimidation in California. Many settled near Victoria, but others returned south because they preferred more open American lifestyles. Lord Napier, the British minister to Washington, D.C., wrote to American officials on July 30, 1858, that the British government would value "the claims and services of the Indians, Negroes, Half-castes of all complexions or Asiatics, who, maltreated or excluded in the United States, will again repair to a land, we trust of irreproachable equality and freedom with instincts of affection towards the British Crown."[13]

Victoria was no longer just a Hudson's Bay Company fort, but grew quickly. The Earl of Albemarle wrote that it soon looked:

> like a regular mining town. . . . Groups of men with rough beards and hair swagger and stagger about. The prevailing costume consists of a red or blue flannel shirt, and a pair of trousers stuck inside Wellington boots. . . . An axe, a [thirty-eight-centimetre long] bowie-knife, and a pair of "Colt's" [hand guns] stuck ostentatiously into a rough leather belt, are the necessaries of life, tobacco and strong drinks its luxuries. Rough songs from rougher throats fill the air, at least so much of it as is not filled with oaths; quarrelling goes on in every language under heaven. The shops display spades, picks, shovels, pans, blankets, and rockers, all ticketed "for the mines." There are more drinking saloons and bowling alleys than dwelling houses: the former are built of rough lumber, most of the latter are simple tents. . . . Placards and Newspaper bulletins are outside nearly every house with the latest news from the mines.[14]

Providing goods and accommodation to tens of thousands of newcomers proved challenging. Fortunately, abundant supplies were readily available from nearby Puget Sound or San Francisco. The Hudson's Bay Company profited handsomely by selling American imports, though it kept prices low so that miners would not starve.[15] Victoria was a duty-free port, unlike California state and Washington Territory towns. Opportunistic San Francisco merchants set up Victoria branches, at first in tents, and profited handsomely. Waddington noted that "the five or six stores that were first established did as they pleased."[16]

Some building supplies reached Victoria from San Francisco as early as May. However, lumber at Victoria spiked to $100 per thousand board feet, even though Puget Sound sawmills were exporting millions of board feet at $19 per thousand board feet. (A board foot is one square foot one inch thick.) When the price fell to $50 around July 17, the building boom began.[17] Alfred Waddington wrote that "in six weeks 225 buildings [went up], of which nearly 200 were stores." By September, wood buildings numbered 344. Victoria had expanded to four miles across, with much of the countryside "covered with tents."[18]

Eating places were initially set up in tents. Hotels followed slowly as building materials became available. For those who wanted permanent housing, the Hudson's Bay Company sold lots 18 by 36.5 metres (60 by 120 feet) for $25 to $75 each in spring, then on June 21 offered a new set for $100 apiece.[19] Speculation drove building lot prices up to $1,000, then $5,000, while half lots rented from $250 to $400 per month. Eager for scandal, Whatcom's *Northern Light* newspaper reported that some "old Sacramento friends have made $100,000 selling lots to each other at Victoria!"[20]

— • —

Governor Douglas let free trade reign in Victoria, but on the Fraser River he did not want the Hudson's Bay Company monopoly or British sovereignty undermined. In 1857 he had already imposed a monthly licence fee of twenty-one shillings on miners, imitating Australian practice. That translated into five American dollars, payable in coin only, which quickly became the currency on the river.[21]

A worn American half dollar used by the anonymous
Canadian miner on the Fraser River in 1858

Beginning in March, an increasing number of Americans arrived on the Fraser River in canoes and other vessels to search for gold. The invasion reminded Douglas of the loss of Washington and Oregon to the United States during border negotiations in 1846. By British Parliamentary charter, the mainland was officially administered by the Hudson's Bay Company, not the British government.

Acting in his capacity as chief factor of company operations west of the Rocky Mountains, Douglas sent the British naval steamer HMS *Satellite* to Point Roberts on May 15 "as an imposing display of force" to stop boats from entering the river. By May 20, it was anchored on the south arm of the river's mouth, ensuring that all entering vessels had a licence for sailing issued by the Hudson's Bay Company and that everyone had a mining licence costing $5 a month. Meanwhile, British naval survey steamer HMS *Plumper* guarded the Fraser's north arm. At the beginning of August, the Hudson's Bay Company's brigantine *Recovery* replaced the British vessels near future New Westminster, at a point where the Fraser still flowed in a single channel.[22] Despite these attempts at vigilance, many Americans in canoes boasted that they never bought a licence.

In May 1858, Douglas proclaimed that ships "should carry the Hudson's Bay Company's goods into Fraser's River, and no other," and that the Company was to be paid "two dollars head money for each passenger carried into Fraser's River."[23]

In June, sufferance documents listing every ship's cargo taxed at 10% were issued at Victoria and could be inspected at the entrance to the Fraser. Steamers had to pay $12 more for the documents while canoes paid $6.[24] Regular shippers to the Fraser River were infuriated, because the tax had to be paid before each and every voyage at Victoria, where clearance fees added another $10 for foreign vessels, $5 for small boats, and $3 for British vessels every time.

Americans met those arrangements with outrage. An editorial in San Francisco's *Daily Alta California* bristled at $5 mining licences being required for a person taking "a tour of pleasure or business . . . even though he may return in three days."[25] Sufferance fees and repeated Victoria clearance tolls were equally unpopular, even though they resembled San Francisco practice. To avoid trade restrictions and river taxes, goods were smuggled over trails from Whatcom, Washington. Americans gleefully pointed out that the Hudson's Bay Company's monopoly was due to run out in May 1859.

Dissatisfaction from Fort Victoria residents and Canadian colonists had led the British Parliament to convene a select committee on the Company's fate in 1857. It recommended the termination of Hudson's Bay Company holdings. Its lands across British North America should be settled, and the Crown Colony of British Columbia be created on the mainland.[26]

Sir Edward Bulwer Lytton, secretary of state for the Colonies, was faced with delicate challenges. Britain did not want to antagonize its most important trading partner, the United States, over a wilderness that contributed little economically to the empire. It did not, however, want to lose the Pacific coast, which might also threaten possession of the vast lands that stretched east across the Prairies to what is now Ontario. The new British Conservative government also favoured free trade and the termination of monopolies. Those goals were achieved when Parliament created the Colony of British Columbia on August 2, 1858, and on September 2 withdrew the Hudson's Bay Company's trade monopoly. At the same time, Lytton was drafting legislation to dismantle the British East India Company. In 1857, rioters across India had protested the monopoly's greed and merciless army. From 1858, India was ruled by a British-appointed governor general answerable to the Colonial Office.

Lytton praised Douglas's vigilance in protecting British interests, but countered several conflicts of interest. He reminded the governor that the Hudson's Bay Company's privilege extended only "to the exclusive trade with the Indians," and that "it is . . . contrary to law . . . to make any Government regulations subservient to the Revenues or interests of the Company." With a stroke of the pen, the head tax and prohibition of freight other than the Hudson's Bay Company's disappeared. At the same time, "it is necessary to maintain the principle,

Sir Edward Bulwer Lytton, the British minister for the colonies

that the navigation of Fraser's River itself above the mouth is open in law to British vessels only. American or other foreign vessels ... should be required to take a licence."[27]

Douglas's edict that nobody be allowed up the river without a mining licence was emphatically dismissed: "Such licence can properly be required of intending diggers on the ground, but not of persons merely seeking to land on the territory."[28] As for foreign newcomers, they were to be welcomed, not discouraged:

It is no part of [Her Majesty's Government's] policy to exclude Americans and other foreigners from the Gold fields. On the contrary, you are <u>distinctly instructed to oppose no obstacle whatever</u> to their resort thither for the purpose of digging in those fields, so long as they submit themselves [to the local authorities]. . . . I need hardly impress upon you the importance of caution and delicacy in dealing with those manifest cases of international relationship . . . which might easily lead to serious complications.[29]

What sweetened the sense of loss as Douglas watched the habits and achievements of decades of Hudson's Bay Company service slip away was his appointment as governor of the new Colony of British Columbia, concurrently with his position as Governor of the Colony of Vancouver Island. A condition was his cutting all ties as employee or shareholder of the Hudson's Bay Company.

Douglas must have been horrified by a final suggestion by Lytton:

ascertain what Americans resorting to the diggings enjoy the most influence or popular esteem, and . . . open with them a frank and friendly communication as to the best means of preserving order, and securing the interests and peace of the Colony [of British Columbia. Also, find] amongst the immigrants, both British and foreign, some persons whom you could immediately form into a Council of Advice.[30]

How could foreigners advise a colonial governor when their views were "anti-British"? Douglas replied ambiguously to Lytton that he would "gladly avail myself of such aid, should it be at any time attainable."[31]

— • —

Possible U.S. annexation of the Fraser River interested both the American public and government. On July 8, 1858, the *Sacramento Daily Union* announced that "The recent discovery of golden treasures on the Pacific slope of British America has induced the vain idea, with some, that [the American] Government can easily acquire the whole" coast as far north as Russian America (now Alaska).[32] A month earlier it had published a rant titled "'Fifty-Four Forty' and Fraser River," referring to the southern border of Russian America.[33] President James Polk was castigated for not securing the entire region north of the forty-ninth parallel during the border negotiations of 1846. Others quoted in that newspaper argued that common economic interests and a shared geography would lead to an inevitable, peaceful "annexation to our glorious Union of all the British Possessions" in North America. Douglas was alarmed that American settlers were already taking up Washington Territory land grants on the disputed San Juan Islands next door to Victoria. Britain also claimed the archipelago, where the Hudson's Bay Company had lucrative farms.

Doctor A.A. Riddel in Toronto urged the Colonial Office to encourage western settlement, because some "American papers advocate its being at once settled by American Citizens, so as ultimately to be admitted as a State."[34] Californians in Victoria "with time on their hands and whiskey in their bellies spoke openly of fulfilling the American dream of '54-40 or Fight!'"[35] A Sacramento lawyer at a gathering in Fort Yale argued that "no man could say where the 49th parallel was ... and it was more than probable Fort Yale was most likely on American Soil."[36] The governors of California and Washington Territory wrote the U.S. federal government questioning whether Douglas had any authority on the Fraser River.[37] A private letter that Douglas forwarded to London suggested that an armed invasion of British Columbia had been planned, although he stood firm that "no other power can wrest it from our grasp."[38]

California outlaw Ned McGowan aggravated Governor Douglas when he had the steamer *Pacific* in Victoria Harbour fire its guns to celebrate the Fourth of July. Some speculated that he would foment an invasion of the Fraser River by the American troops which were flooding into Washington Territory to quash Indigenous unrest there. Later McGowan wrote how he and other miners at Hill's Bar:

had arranged a plan, in case of a collision with the [British] troops, to take Fort Yale and Fort Hope . . . and retreat into Washington Territory—only twenty miles distant. This would . . . bring on the fight and put an end to the long agony and public clamor . . . that our boundary line must be 'fifty-four forty or fight.'[39]

McGowan's actual "war" ended in December as a petty mining dispute with a small fine after a trial by Judge Begbie.

As chief factor during the border settlement in 1846, Douglas had watched Hudson's Bay posts south of the forty-ninth parallel disappear. Dismayed by the number of American interlopers and their anti-British attitudes, he appealed to the Colonial Office for British naval and military assistance on April 8 and several times later. It took two months, though, for each official letter to reach London, more time for government discussions, and another two months for a reply to return. Five months vanished as Douglas waited for answers.

Lytton took seriously Douglas' news that tens of thousands had arrived on steamers from San Francisco, via "roads from Bellingham Bay, [the Cowlitz River and other valleys leading from Oregon to the south end of Puget Sound at] Nisqually, and by way of the Columbia River."[40] Colonial Office requests for troops had to pass through the Foreign Office, the War Office, and the Admiralty. On August 16, the Admiralty finally decided to inform Rear Admiral Robert Lambert Baynes at Valparaiso, Chile, that "the greatest importance is attached to the presence of a naval force off Fraser's River. . . . Every possible assistance . . . should be given to support the authority of the Governor of the Hudson's Bay territory."[41] On September 2, Lytton informed Douglas that ships had been sent.

Rear Admiral Baynes arrived at Esquimalt on October 17 with 715 sailors and eighty-four cannons on HMS *Ganges*.[42] By then, some eight thousand miners had left because low gold yields were nothing like the 150,000 ounces found during the first eight months of the California rush.[43] Earlier, most miners had concentrated on digging for gold rather than revolution. Even an American contributor to the *Daily Alta California* newspaper commented: "I never saw a mass so idle nor so orderly as these are."[44] An American invasion did not materialize. As Douglas reflected, "The evil will thus work its own cure without interposition on our part."[45]

— • —

The American federal administration became increasingly curious about the Fraser district as the year wore on. On August 2, 1858, Secretary of State Lewis Cass appointed a special agent to report on the extent and quality of the British gold fields, the number of British settlers, the British naval and land forces, the treatment of Americans, the location and number of "Indians," what roads had been built from adjacent American territory, and many other details.[46] The vast range of intelligence to be collected suggests the bear-trap mind of President James Buchanan. He had been secretary of state during the 1846 border negotiations.

Two sentences in the 1858 instructions imply that annexation was being discussed: Americans "in a foreign country . . . must remember that they are subject to its laws and to all the lawful regulations of its authorities. Whenever these regulations are onerous and oppressive, their own Government, you will renewedly assure them, will not fail to take the necessary steps to procure their modification or repeal."[47]

President James Buchanan

American action elsewhere varied from forced treaties to takeovers. From 1845 to 1849, President Polk added most of the American land mass west of the Mississippi through war with Mexico and negotiation with Britain. In 1858, Buchanan sent an expedition to punish Paraguay for firing on an American Navy ship surveying the Rio de la Plata. That foray ended in a forced apology from Paraguay and a commercial treaty advantageous to the United States.[48] The U.S. and Britain had earlier quarreled over Nicaragua.[49] An American citizen became president there in 1856. In 1867, the American government purchased Russian America for $7.2 million. That area became Alaska. In short, annexation was a real possibility.

John Nugent

John Nugent, editor of the *San Francisco Herald*, was chosen as the special agent to report on affairs in Victoria and the Fraser River from September 20 to November 17.[50] Buchanan had been impressed with his skills as Washington correspondent to the *New York Herald* in the 1840s. In protest, the *New York Times* retorted that a "man better calculated to stir up broils could not be found."[51]

Much of Nugent's government-printed report detailed facts about the mines, the failure of most Californians to earn enough to pay their expenses, and a predictable rant against the Hudson's Bay Company. He concluded that British possessions on the Pacific would ultimately become American, "but in the meantime their intrinsic value either of locality, soil, climate, or productions, does not warrant any effort on the part of the American government or the American people towards their immediate acquisition."[52] The spy's verdict forestalled invasion any time soon. Nugent's finest moment came when he helped seventy-four destitute miners on the Fraser to return free of charge to San Francisco, on the promise that the government would reimburse the Pacific Mail Steamship Company.[53]

Nugent inappropriately meddled in colonial affairs when he demanded that American lawyers should be allowed to represent Americans in the Victoria court and when he personally presented mining complaints from Americans at Hill's Bar. In a paid notice printed in the November 16 *Victoria Gazette* newspaper, he asserted that Americans abroad should first take their grievances to local courts. He continued with the inflammatory suggestion that if they were unsatisfied, "the Government of the United States . . . [will] intervene for the redress and protection of its citizens in British

Columbia and Vancouver's Island, I am authorized and instructed to give them the most emphatic assurance . . . [as] in Nicaragua."[54]

The *Victoria Gazette* editors castigated Nugent: "we dissent from the conclusions of the document, and disapprove its tone. . . . We are firm in the belief that nine-tenths of the Americans in the two Colonies disagree with the conclusions of his present manifesto."[55] When Nugent's report was printed in 1859, Victoria's *British Colonist* editorialized, "Had a similar address been issued by the British Consul at San Francisco . . . he would probably have been insulted or shot before night, and the California press would have blazed with indignation."[56]

Of course, Britain did not abandon the Pacific Northwest. It was a stroke of luck that during the middle of Nugent's controversial visit, on October 17, HMS *Ganges* sailed into Esquimalt with 715 British sailors manning eighty-four cannons. Military and Department of State officials in Washington, D.C. could not brush off the implications of such a dramatic U.K. Navy presence with a few smooth phrases.

By the end of 1858, Governor Douglas's initiatives, the arrival of *Ganges*, the British creation of the Colony of British Columbia, mediocre gold returns on the Fraser, and flagging American curiosity ensured that Vancouver Island and British Columbia remained part of British North America.

CHAPTER 2

Travellers to the Fraser River and Their Expenses

∽

Many have exhausted their means in getting here.
—*James D. White at Whatcom, June 25, 1858*[1]

THE MAIN EVENTS of the Fraser River gold rush of 1858 are well known, but questions about details abound. What kinds of people flocked there? What conditions drove them to make such expensive and arduous journeys? What social changes resulted from those argonauts' attitudes and actions? How did miners journey to Victoria on Vancouver Island, the closest landfall to the mines? What transportation was available to travel to the Fraser River mines north of Fort Hope (now Hope, B.C.)? What craft were available on the river itself? What costs were involved? What maps were available? What equipment did a miner need? What items could be purchased on the river, and at what price? Was communication with the outside world possible? And what means were available to return home?

— • —

Since earliest recorded times, the rich have prized gold for its beautiful colour, rarity, workability, and resistance to corrosion. In antiquity,

Detail from the first edition of Victoria merchant Alfred Waddington's
Correct Map, April 1858

miners were short-lived slaves working in dangerous conditions. The gold pillaged in Central and South America during the sixteenth and seventeenth centuries was flaunted by Spanish kings and churches. All of that changed in the middle of the nineteenth century, when Californian and Australian discoveries suddenly put golden dreams within reach of ordinary men. Gold returns pumped over a hundred million dollars into the 1850s economy every year, including $165 million in 1857.[2] Today, that would be worth more than $16 billion dollars, with current gold prices almost a hundred times higher than the $15 to $18 an ounce common in 1858.

Imagine the incentive those figures offered to the 1850s shoe-maker from Ohio who for twenty years had "never earned over one dollar per day," or around $300 per year.[3] Most North Americans then worked ten to twelve hours a day, six days a week. As Henry Thoreau wrote in 1854, "The mass of men lead lives of quiet desperation." The average worker "has no time to be anything but a machine. . . . Why should they begin digging their graves as soon as they are born?" Wealth came to a very small number: "a few are riding, but the rest are run over."[4]

Wages in San Francisco were higher than most of North America during 1858, but so were expenses. Apprentices and unskilled cartmen earned $2 to $3 a day, while bricklayers, carpenters, jewellers, and shipsmiths earned between $5 and $8 (between $600 and $2,400 annually *if* they were lucky enough to work for 300 days). Monthly wages between $35 and $75 ($420 to $900 annually) were made by brick makers, lumbermen, and mill sawyers; highs between $100 and $150 a month ($1,200 to $1,800 annually) went to barbers, butchers, engineers, and mates or pilots of vessels.[5] Atlantic coast wages were lower, and Canadian ones even less. At Kingston in Canada West (Ontario from 1867), blacksmiths and carpenters earned from $1.25 to $2.20 daily. Farm hands took in $16 per month with board or $200 to $250 per season without board. Boat engineers made $40 to $70 per month when water was ice free.[6] Dreams of wealth from gold lured such men from home.

Many Americans who had been impoverished by industrialization left for California's gold fields. Artisans who had once made a good living could not compete with inexpensive goods mass produced at new factories that paid low wages. Sons of farmers whose land was too small to subdivide faced bleak options. Worldwide famine and political unrest drove thousands from home. Many left Ireland, where a million people died in potato famines between 1845 and 1852. After European revolutions were crushed in 1848, thousands fled from France, Germany, and Hungary. The poor in China were reeling from famine, farms that could not sustain growing families, and wars with European powers from 1839 to 1860.[7] For such people, success in the gold fields meant financial autonomy and the time to enjoy their dreams. A New York City native wrote, "You know that I am in the prime of life. . . . I can hardly make a living here. . . . Labor is *capital*" in California.[8]

During the early 1850s, supplies of new bullion seemed endless. California banks eagerly extended credit for leveraged business investments, real estate, and luxury goods. When prices fell in the mid-1850s and borrowers could not repay their loans, financial institutions suddenly discovered that they did not have enough cash on hand for daily transactions. Two hundred San Francisco business bankruptcies in 1855 toppled most of the city's banks that year.[9] The 1857 failure of an Ohio bank led to a worldwide collapse. In the United States and what is now Ontario and Quebec, 5,123 businesses failed, representing $299,801,000 of losses.[10]

Recovery was painfully slow and typically jobless. Wealthy men in Canada lost around a third of their wealth. In Gananoque, retired tycoon John Macdonald was worth £3,695 in 1856, but only £2,176 in 1860. His heir, William Stone Macdonald, dropped in wealth from £7,550 in 1856 to £5,770 in 1861.[11] A Toronto doctor wrote to the London Colonial Office in June 1858: "Owing to the great commercial depression in Canada, thousands of the working classes are idle, and there is no prospect of an early improvement."[12]

By 1858, easy gold had been worked out of California, and independent miners were being replaced by a capitalized industry where men worked for low wages on large, exposed sites blasted apart by water cannons, or in dangerous underground tunnels. California earnings had declined from highs of $20 or more a day for lucky miners in the early 1850s to just $5 in 1853 and $3 by 1860.[13] Early in 1858, California newspapers reported that prospectors on the Fraser River were making from $20 to $50 per day.[14] A predictable stampede for better opportunities soon followed.

— • —

Nineteenth-century gold rushes transformed the lives of their participants and the structure of their communities. The industrial revolution of the eighteenth century had already created a more educated and independent class than was possible for unschooled farm workers tied to land that others owned. A typical nineteenth-century gold miner was literate enough to be informed about distant events, driven by declining circumstances, self-reliant enough to want to improve his economic standing, a quick learner in the mines, young and strong enough for the bruising physical labour, and endowed with the collaborative skills needed for many short-term partnerships. Most were independent enough to resist regulation. Even though miners knew they did not own the land, they resented having to pay government fees to mine. Governor Douglas dismissed such adventurers as freewheeling American raiders. However, British and Australian gold miners rioted against similar government regulations at Ballarat, Australia, in 1854.

Australian miners created a society "on a larger economic scale, with larger ideas, larger demands, larger and more sophisticated connections with the great world, and with more diverse skills than" had existed in 1850, as J.A. La Nauze has concluded.[15] The same could be said for gold rush California, which made San Francisco one of the wealthiest, best supplied cities in the world. Until 1858, the few hundred residents of Vancouver Island depended on the autocratic Hudson's Bay Company for their meagre livelihood. The thousands who settled in Victoria that year brought new skills, their own capital, entrepreneurial projects, and cries for responsible government. The colony's governor, James Douglas, rankled, but laissez-faire ideas were also sweeping Britain and its government.

For Douglas, Scottish settler James Yates, owner of Victoria's Ship Inn, was a trouble-maker.[16] He signed petitions for open trade and governance independent of the Hudson's Bay Company. His appeals pestered Douglas and reached the Colonial Office in England, which sided with change. Fraser River prospectors were like their Australian counterparts. David Goodman sees them as "self-seeking, self-regulating, morally and emotionally autonomous, transnational . . . gold diggers [who] were the citizens of nineteenth-century liberal modernity."[17]

— • —

As in every business, miners could profit only if earnings were higher than expenses. California newspapers recommended that adventurers to the Fraser should budget at least $300 for six months, which is what many men earned per year in the United States. Another newspaper warned: "those that come with less than $500 . . . find themselves in a bad fix."[18] The anonymous Canadian miner (of Chapter 8) used over $600 to reach Fountain, on the Fraser River near Lillooet. After paying up to $70 for ship passage from San Francisco, he bought $279.53 of supplies at Victoria, then paid over $60 to reach Fort Hope with his overweight cargo. Once there, he hired four Indigenous guides to pack his supplies for over two weeks at $224 or more: each man earned at least $4 per day for fourteen days.

The Canadian mined enough gold to cover his expenses on the river and take a thousand dollars out. By contrast, poor George Slocumb (of Chapter 5) had only $200 before he booked his passage in San Francisco. He spent a quarter of it on a steamer to Victoria, then found himself constantly on the precipice of disaster. Often unable to pay the high cost of food, he foraged for whatever could be found to eat. George Beam, who was lucky enough to be living in Washington

Territory, cut costs to around $100 by purchasing four months of inexpensive foodstuffs and mining supplies before canoeing from Whidbey Island to the mines above Fort Hope (Chapter 6). Given the floods on the Fraser that prevented mining for most of the summer, it is no wonder that many Puget Sound and California newspapers urged those who had jobs to stay where they were.[19]

— • —

For almost everybody, the most expensive single item was ocean passage to Victoria. From April 20 to September 30, 1858, 24,078 passengers packed into steamers and sailing vessels at San Francisco.[20] First off the mark were 420 people who boarded the steamer *Commodore* on April 20. It took more than a month, however, before California prospectors and shipping agents could respond fully to overblown newspaper accounts. May saw just 1,875 passengers on six sailings. Then June 4 to July 10 were the five weeks of heaviest emigration from San Francisco (19,241 passengers on fixty-two sailings), followed distantly by July 10-August 10 (1,837 passengers on fifty-two sailings).

Arrivals at Victoria Harbour and nearby Esquimalt Harbour jumped dramatically from eight vessels in May to twenty-six vessels in June and fifty-nine in July. Even though passenger demand fell sharply, August was the heaviest month, with ninety-nine vessels, a few making more than one trip. By that point, a constant flow of supplies was required for the tens of thousands of people in the north. Demand for cargo continued through September (sixty-six vessels), October (fifty-nine), November (fifty-one), and even December (fifty-one), because more than ten thousand prospectors overwintered at Victoria and on the mainland. From June to December, over a million and a half dollars of goods were brought to Victoria.[21]

Throughout 1858, 142 steamers and sailing ships carried passengers and cargo from San Francisco to Victoria and Puget Sound, which was a closer staging point for access to the Fraser River. Because so many people wanted to go north, shipping agents scrambled

Two ships for Victoria overloaded at San Francisco in 1858

to find any vessel that would agree to sail once or twice. Fortunately, numerous Puget Sound captains were eager for money-generating voyages, and San Francisco harboured hundreds of vessels.

The most obvious candidates were 104 American vessels. Most served the coast of California, bringing large amounts of produce, meat, seafood, lumber, and coal to the state's 538,002 residents—some 60,500 in San Francisco.[22] They could easily be diverted for one or two lucrative sailings, with profitable cargo and passengers paying from $25 to $60 each.

The most intriguing vessels were the thirty-eight long-distance traders attracted by San Francisco's immense wealth. Some vessels had earlier sailed to Central and South American ports in Mexico (a voyage lasting 16 to 28 days), Nicaragua, Panama (17 days), Peru, Bolivia, and Chile (63 days). Others arrived from the Atlantic, including Boston (160 days), New York (109 to 140 days), and Philadelphia (163 days). Still others sailed the Pacific, from Russian America (now Alaska), Honolulu (16 to 25 days depending on the winds), the Society Islands (halfway to Australia, 32 days), Japan (30 days), Hong Kong (50 to 59 days), Tahiti (42 to 63 days), Sydney, Melbourne (86 to 104 days), Manila, and even Calcutta (104 days). These vessels happily set aside upcoming sailings to overseas ports because profits for even a single trip to Victoria were high.

Most steamers took from three to five days to reach Victoria from San Francisco. Half the sailing ships took ten to fourteen days, though unfavourable weather slowed others to between fifteen and thirty-three days.[23]

The fares were relatively high, given the typical annual income of $300 in North America. The cost of passage rose steeply during periods of greatest demand. Ship owners charged as much as possible and managed to pocket over half a million dollars in five months.[24] Fares on sailing ships ranged from $25 to $60.[25] Steamer steerage cost from $20 to $32.50. For the steamship *Commodore* on April 19, 1858, George Slocumb's steerage ticket cost $25, but he "stood it only about six hours and paid $20 more for Cabin Ticket." His ship had its legal complement of 420 passengers, with bunks in steerage. Cabin fare for the June 13 sailing of *Panama* rose from Slocumb's $45 to $66.75.[26]

Steerage conditions could be suffocating. The problems came with making a freighter that usually held coal or clams into a vessel carrying people, or else cramming up to four times the legal limit into passenger vessels. The July 1 sailing of *Sierra Nevada*, which was licensed to carry around 500 passengers, had an illegal over-limit of nineteen hundred, as emphasized by the *San Francisco Herald*: "every possible available space was occupied with persons ... [including] the upper deck."[27] On July 12, the anonymous Canadian miner was on *Oregon*, stuffed with an illegal overload of "1500 passengers most standing berths only."[28] Standing berths resembled vertical coffins two by two feet, stacked "in three tiers, one over the other," where passengers could rest at night, as explained in the *Sacramento Daily Union*. In the morning, the wood panels were taken down by sixty crew members.[29]

Access to outside decks was forbidden on many sailings. The stench in enclosed holds must have been overpowering, with few provisions for seasickness or natural functions. A very few vessels boasted much better conditions. For example, *Georgiana*, a clipper ship registered at New Granada (now Panama), boasted "between-decks upwards of eight feet in height, with side ports and thorough ventilation," as did British clipper bark *Robert Passenger*.[30]

People farther afield than California started leaving home after August, when news of the Fraser River gold rush finally reached them. By October 13, two thousand hopeful prospectors had arrived in San Francisco from Canada and the Atlantic states.[31] The fastest routing from New York took twenty-two to forty-two days by steamer to Panama, across the isthmus on a new fifty-mile railroad costing $25, then by steamer to San Francisco. At least three more days to Victoria completed approximately 9,770 kilometres (6,100 miles). First class from New York to San Francisco cost from $300 to $600, while second class was $250 and steerage $150.[32] Freight and hotels added to costs. It took three-and-a-half to six months to sail the 20,900 kilometres (13,000 miles) from New York around South America to San Francisco.

Australians were next, sending two sailing ships in mid-August 1858. *Orestes* arrived first, reaching Port Townsend with just fifty Melbourne passengers on November 16.[33] *Norton* followed with five hundred more Melbourne passengers. Even so, the gold fields of

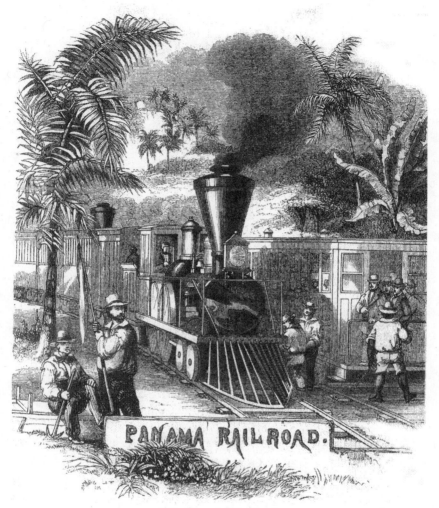

The Panama Railroad

Australia were still productive enough to discourage most from leaving on an expensive goose chase. Hong Kong cargo ships accepted a few passengers in August and September.[34]

England lay even farther away, so it took until September and October 1858 for the first dozen ships for Victoria to be announced. A London *Times* newspaper advertisement optimistically promised steam passage from England to Victoria in under forty days, taking the shortcut across Panama by a new railroad.[35] Most sailing vessels that voyaged from England around the tip of South America to Victoria took around eight months; steamers would have been faster.[36] Fares from the U.K. to Victoria by steamer via Panama were $350 to $500 first class, $200 to $350 second class, and $130 third class. Steamers around the tip of South America were only a bit less expensive: $300 to $370 first class, $175 to $260 second class, and $125 third class.[37]

— • —

To the dismay of travellers, costs did not end on arrival at Vancouver Island. Smaller vessels could land in Victoria Harbour, where disembarking fees were probably assessed. Large ships had to go to the deeper waters of nearby Esquimalt Harbour. From that second port, passengers were faced with paying $5 either to Indigenous canoeists who took them to a trail on shore, or for small craft that ferried them to Fort Victoria. Freight transfer from ship to shore cost another $8 per ton—$5 for weight plus $3 for unloading.[38]

The overland trail from Esquimalt to Victoria was rough in May 1858 but was improved as time wore on. By July 17, an express wagon costing a dollar left Victoria hourly from 8 a.m. to 4 p.m. and returned from Esquimalt hourly from 9 a.m. to 5 p.m.[39] Freight in small enough quantities to fit in the wagon added to the cost.

— • —

In Victoria, hard decisions had to be made about traversing the 190 kilometres (120 miles) to Fort Hope (now Hope, B.C.), the start of the open-air mines on the Fraser River's gravel bars. Provisions there were expensive and heavy flooding prevented mining on the Fraser. Consequently, some returned to California quickly—around 140 in May and June, followed by 1,374 in July.

For those who remained in Victoria, Indigenous canoers had the skill and equipment to ensure a successful journey to Fort Hope.

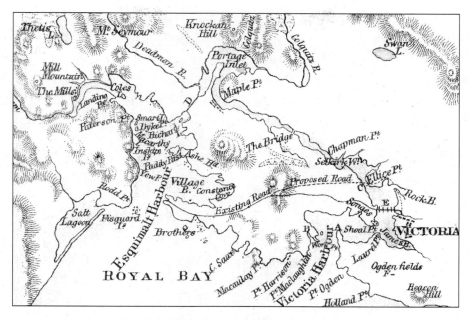

The trail from Esquimalt Harbour to Victoria

However, some prospectors dared crossing the dangerous Strait of Georgia in boats they built themselves for between $50 and $100. Since these craft were "small and badly constructed, and as a general thing, still more badly navigated, [many] met with . . . disasters, often of a fatal character," according to Henry de Groot, a California newspaperman who settled in Victoria. Ominously, they resembled "coffins" to Victoria doctor John Helmcken.[40] Some of the miners went to Bellingham Bay in Washington Territory and obtained canoes there. It was considerably closer to the Fraser and avoided most of the open water.

Once Puget Sound residents heard about the discovery of gold at Hill's Bar on March 23, hundreds left their jobs to try their luck. Some vessels took them to Point Roberts or Semiahmoo Bay near the international border close to the Fraser River. The steamer *Sea Bird* provided reliable service on April 16, 18, 24, 26, and 30. Point

Roberts proved so strategic that merchants James and Fitzpatrick of Whatcom opened a mining supplies store there in May.

On April 13, 1858, schooner *A.Y. Trask* was the first recorded vessel to take prospectors right into the Fraser River, as far as Fort Langley. It repeated the same trip on April 27, when the mail steamer *Columbia* reached Port Townsend from San Francisco with as many as 250 passengers. On May 9, Puget Sound schooner *Wild Duck* completed a trip from Fort Langley. These American incursions led Governor Douglas to position a naval guard at the entrance to the Fraser from May 15, as detailed in Chapter 1.

Throughout the summer, other small craft made trips upriver, including Puget Sound schooners *C.S. Kidder* and *H.C. Page*, and California steam tug *Ranger No. 2*. On July 17, the iron-sided Victoria-based schooner *Alice* attracted some prospectors by taking "20 skiffs [row boats] and canoes . . . on deck, for 10 miles inside the mouth of Fraser River, free, with allowance of six men with 200 lbs. freight, at $10 per passenger."[41] But larger vessels with more regular service were required to serve the thousands who wanted to travel up the river.

As early as May 1, 1858, diarist George Slocumb heard about plans to put the Hudson's Bay Company's steamer "*Otter* to run to Langley and flat bottomed boats up" the river from there.[42] *Otter* proved the most important vessel for the 1858 gold rush. It made at least eighty-six voyages to Puget Sound and the Fraser River.

Governor Douglas did not press *Otter* into transporting miners, because it was tending to crucial Company business running all the way to Fort Simpson near the border of Russian America (now Alaska). During May, he also resisted helping interlopers who compromised British sovereignty. In any event, *Otter* was of limited use, because it could carry only 250 people, "crowded on the upper deck, without food or shelter, and the deck covered with coal dust."[43] As the year wore on, it did transport some prospectors, but it played a much more important role in supporting government initiatives, such as the governor's trip to Fort Yale during May and June to investigate disturbances between miners and Indigenous people, several trips from August through October transporting workers and supplies for the Harrison-Lillooet road building project, Governor Douglas's September trip to Fort Yale to deal with the aftermath of the Fraser Canyon War, and the November trip to Fort Langley to proclaim the Colony of British Columbia and install Douglas as its governor.

On October 30, the *Beaver*, the other Hudson's Bay steamer in the area, returned to Victoria from its annual seven-month cruise north to Fort Simpson. It then shuttled prospectors, cargo, and settlers from Victoria to Fort Langley five times during November and December.

More spacious boats had to be found to handle over twenty thousand prospectors and merchants who wanted access to the mines. On June 5, official sufferance papers to enter the Fraser River were issued to the American steamer *Surprise*, which was leased through shipping agents Forbes and Babcock, a Hudson's Bay Company subsidiary in San Francisco.[44] It carried 400 passengers and their gear from Victoria and Bellingham Bay in Washington to Fort Hope. It made at least ten trips upriver, usually as far as Fort Hope, before it was sent back to San Francisco on August 14. It was replaced by California ocean steamer *Wilson G. Hunt*, which arrived at Victoria on August 16. *Hunt* made at least eight trips from Victoria to the Fraser before business declined and it returned to more profitable California runs on October 7.

On June 8, the ocean steamer *Sea Bird* was leased from a Puget Sound company. It had served there reliably earlier in the year, but its draught proved too deep for the river, and it grounded on a shoal near the Fort Hope from June 24 to September 2. After returning to Victoria, it was destroyed by fire on September 7.

Three flat-bottomed rear paddlewheelers proved more suitable for the river, because they could crawl over some shoals and run up banks to load. Eager for profit, Captain James Ainsworth brought *Umatilla* to Esquimalt from Oregon on July 13, 1858. On its initial voyage to the Fraser River, it was the first vessel to reach Fort Yale (July 21). Its

The Hudson's Bay Company steamer *Otter*

second trip took it to the head of Harrison Lake on July 24, another first. It made at least thirteen trips before being shipped to San Francisco on October 18 so that its owner could return to the lucrative Sacramento River trade. *Maria* arrived at Esquimalt from Sacramento River on August 9 and spent the rest of the year ferrying passengers and cargo on the river. *Enterprise*, championed as the most comfortable of the lot, reached Esquimalt from the Columbia River on August 19. It steamed from Victoria to Fort Hope and back at least eleven times between August 31 and November 21. After customs disallowed it crossing the Strait of Georgia during the winter, it sailed between Fort Langley and Fort Hope until the Fraser River froze. Profits could be astronomical: the steamer *Surprise* made $50,000 in just nine weeks.[45]

Despite incentives for profit, some American captains shied away from the risks posed by the Fraser's strong currents and dangerous shoals. They also wanted to avoid the nuisance of expensive visits to

Victoria to pay habour clearance tolls and sufferance fees to enter the Fraser River for every single voyage. As an alternative, Puget Sound vessels dropped cargo and passengers at Point Roberts, on the border near the mouth of the Fraser River. The *Otter* joined them regularly from Victoria. River steamers would then carry passengers up the Fraser from Point Roberts. Those who disembarked at Semiahmoo (now Blaine, Washington) could trek for two days over the twenty-six-kilometre (sixteen-mile) trail to Fort Langley.

By September, Governor Douglas was unable to stifle private enterprise because of the number of captains eager for profit and orders from the Colonial Office to allow Americans upriver once they paid sufferance fees and taxes on cargo. The *Victoria Gazette* reported "the opening of the river to traders" around the beginning of September.[46] Boats already on the river took full advantage of the new freedom. On October 7, the steamer *Enterprise* advertised a trip from Victoria with "a full cargo of miscellaneous merchandise for traders at Forts Hope and Yale."[47] Plentiful supplies led to dramatically lower prices on the river by the end of the year, but not until profit-grabbing freight costs were reduced after Governor Douglas complained.

Steamer travel up the Fraser from Victoria or Point Roberts cost more than a basic steerage fare from San Francisco. The *San Francisco Herald* warned that it was a whopping "$40 to $60 per man. Thus passage $24; License $5; freight $4 to $7; meals $1 each, berths $1 each night. The trip requires two days."[48] Each passenger was allowed 200 pounds of mining kit and provisions. More freight cost 2¢ per pound, or $40 per ton, from Victoria to Fort Hope, and 1¢ per pound, or $20 per ton, for the twenty-four-kilometre cartage of cargo by canoe from Fort Hope to Fort Yale.[49]

Returning from Fort Hope in the summer cost the same $20 by steamer as coming up, but the price plummeted in November to $10 from Fort Hope and $5 from Fort Langley as winter approached and demand vanished.[50] The current made the downriver journey much faster, and miners brought nothing back except for gold and a few clothes. The *Daily Alta California* did miners a service by pointing

Drawing of Point Roberts on May 21, 1858, by Alexander Grant Douglas

out that the cheapest return was $2 to $4 for a place "in canoes that carry fifteen to twenty persons, and are two days to Victoria or Bellingham Bay."[51] Those who returned to California by ship faced more gouging, as the *Sacramento Daily Union* was quick to point out. On July 12, the *Cortes* steamed back to San Francisco at a price of "thirty dollars. One poor fellow only had twenty dollars, and . . . was ordered back by the kind-hearted purser, and told to keep off."[52]

By August, "there were about 5,000 unemployed adventurers [in Victoria]—2,000 at least, of whom . . . were 'flat broke'—without a dollar," according to Olympia's *Pioneer and Democrat* newspaper.[53] Two hundred impoverished miners at Whatcom threatened to seize the steamer *Panama* to travel back south.[54] "At Fort Hope, a Frenchman who peddled poultry in Sacramento, and made a good living by it, became short of food and in despair took his rifle and blew his

brains out," mourned the *Sacramento Daily Union*.[55] Urban Hicks and his companions welcomed a starving "nearly naked and bare-footed" hard-luck case as a hired hand. That destitute fellow "had been the head bookkeeper in a large wholesale grocery establishment, and was a young man of fine education and social standing" in San Francisco.[56] Luckily, he earned enough to pay for a ticket home.

— • —

Until a road was completed on the Fraser's east bank between Forts Hope and Yale in September, that twenty-four-kilometre (fifteen-mile) journey had to be made by water. Indigenous guides assisted miners with large canoes they paddled for seven to nine hours against a punishing current of ten to fifteen kilometres per hour. Early morning travel avoided strong afternoon winds. Melting snow increased afternoon river flows. The fare was $2 or $3 going up river, every

Fraser Canyon trails were treacherous

passenger being required to paddle and pole. The fare down was just $1 dollar, with the current doing most of the work.[57]

One voyager described the boats as "less than 20 feet long, and not more than 3 wide, and scarce thicker than my hand. . . . One of the Indians sat in the stern of the boat, and the other in the bow, both on their knees and facing the bow. . . . The boat leaked badly . . . and one of us was obliged to bail constantly."[58] Some described canoes "requiring to be 'warped' up by means of ropes in the hands of men on shore, and shoved ahead by others standing waist deep in the cold water, with no other clothing save an undershirt."[59] A disgruntled traveller complained that "the boatman should have paid us; for we actually pulled him and his canoe to Fort Yale."[60]

A white man at Fort Yale in July 1858 boasted that Indigenous men there would serve "faithfully as guides or boatmen for a small amount of money or cast-off clothing. A penny whistle or a brass button takes wonderfully."[61] A less condescending report set the cost for long journeys at a dollar a day per guide. Others going upriver from Fort Hope in May "paid $2 per day." On May 24, Governor Douglas noted that Indigenous "wages are from 3 to 4 dollars a day" at Fort Hope. Above Spuzzum on June 12, other guides cost "$3.50 per day, each." On July 17 near Boston Bar, Indigenous trekkers "charge four dollars a pack. The men pack from 70 to 80 lbs. and the [women] from 100 to 130 pounds." As miners boasted about their gold, the price rose to $5, then as high as $8 per day.[62]

Proceeding above Fort Yale was perilous, whether by river or land. Hundreds of rash men in canoes braved the "Jaws of Death" in the Fraser River Canyon above Fort Yale and "Hell's Gate" below Boston Bar. As miner Urban Hicks pointed out, they usually met "with disaster and death. Large canoes and boats would be caught in the whirl, be upended and disappear, only to be seen again miles below all in splinters. . . . The Indians refusing to go on it, ought to be sufficient caution for white men."[63] Alfred Waddington warned about the equally dangerous Fraser Canyon "foot trail, along hair breadth ledges and over gaping precipices."[64] There a contributor to the *Daily Alta California* saw men "crawling upon all fours under overhanging rocks—again clinging carefully to bushes . . . without daring to look into the waters that boiled a hundred feet below."[65]

— • —

The greatest infrastructure challenge of 1858 was building roads to access the upper Fraser River. Immediately north of Fort Yale, the only safe passage was by trails developed by the Hudson's Bay Company in the 1840s. The Douglas Portage ran for 37 kilometres (23 miles) due north of Fort Yale in a valley west of the river's cliffs.[66] Several applications by locals to improve that trail were presented to a government that had too few financial resources to cover all needs, however urgent.[67] On August 18, 1858, the *Victoria Gazette* reported, a meeting of dissatisfied Fort Yale miners decided to embark on road building themselves. One hundred men present "resolved to render the trail . . . practicable for [pack] animals."[68] On August 27, miners started using the Douglas Portage after Indigenous warriors had been pacified during the Fraser River War (as will be described in Chapter 4). By September 7, the trail was in excellent condition. Governor Douglas found enough money to pay for bridges, which were completed by October 12.[69]

A canoe ferry crossed the Fraser at Spuzzum. The old Hudson's Bay Company brigade path then avoided the treacherous precipices of the river canyon by ascending a steep hillside to the Anderson River, whose valley led down to the Fraser just south of Boston Bar. The 70 kilometres (44 miles) from Spuzzum to Lytton were "full of big logs and difficult places to travel, though mules manage to pass on it," as the *Victoria Gazette* observed.[70] Significant improvement of that route would have to wait, but by September, provisions were being packed from Yale to Lytton for "fifty cents per pound, . . . thus preventing many who are anxious to go."[71]

September 1858 saw accounts in the *Victoria Gazette* about the survey of "a fine stage road" built by miners on the east bank of the Fraser from Fort Hope northward, with a ferry to Fort Yale.[72] That road replaced the difficult canoe passage against strong river currents between Forts Hope and Yale. The most ambitious scheme of 1858 avoided the Fraser Canyon and winter snow. The government sponsored the building of roads from the head of Harrison Lake to Lillooet Lake and from that lake up to Anderson Lake during August and September. Private ferries, roads, and bridges completed the way to Cayoosh (renamed Lillooet in 1860) on the Fraser River. That saga is the subject of Chapter 7.

Although far from perfect, these projects were impressive achievements that manifested Douglas's tenacity in creating infrastructure to open a colony that would remain loyal to British interests.

— • —

The rush to the Fraser mines encouraged the publication of maps of the area, whatever their quality.[73] The first was a large single sheet produced in April 1858 by Alfred Waddington: *A Correct Map of the Northern Coal & Gold Regions*. Not enough reliable surveys were available to cover such a huge area accurately. Vancouver Island and the surrounding waterways are based on readily available marine charts. The area from Harrison Lake to Seton Lake is included, but details are out of scale. Bridge River plus the Big Falls are placed too far north, and the herring-bone tributaries of the Fraser north of Bridge River are inaccurate. The extent of gold shown on the map represents wishful thinking.

In May 1858, Alexander C. Anderson drew on his decade-long surveys for a much more accurate *Map Showing the Different Routes of Communication with the Gold Region on Frasers River*. It appeared in his short *Hand-Book and Map to the Gold Regions of Frazer's and Thompson's River*.

No other 1858 books had good maps. Sketchy plans did little more than suggest where the Fraser River lay in Robert Ballantyne's *Handbook to the New Gold Fields*, Kinahan Cornwallis's *The New El Dorado*, John Dower's *New British Gold Fields*, William Hazlitt's *British Columbia and Vancouver's Island*, and Elias Smith's *Guide Book to the Gold Regions of Fraser River*.

Curious Californians would have devoured the sketches printed in local journals. They all placed the Fraser and Thompson Rivers reasonably well. The *Correct Map* in *Hutching's California Magazine* on May 20 included an inset of the Fraser River up to Fort Langley

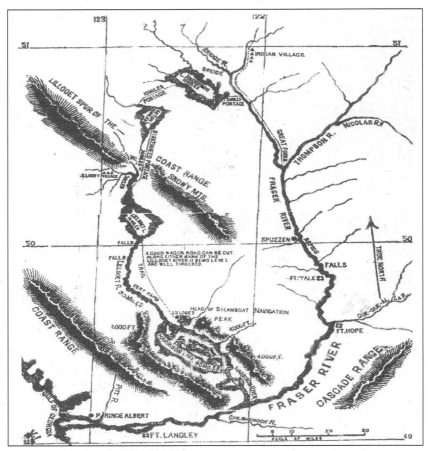

The Map of the Harrison and Lillooet Route to the Upper Fraser

based on an accurate source, but did not show the Gulf or San Juan Islands, had an inaccurate representation of Harrison Lake to Seton Lake, and foreshortened the distance to the Rocky Mountains. The version in San Francisco's *Daily Evening Bulletin* of June 7 indicated the worst rapids on the Fraser, but placed Lopez Island on the wrong side of Orcas Island, misnamed Sumas Lake as Shuswap Lake, and did not include the lakes north of Harrison Lake. The *Daily Evening Bulletin* of August 2, 1858, capitalized on news of road construction for its *Map of the Harrison and Lillooet Route to the Upper Fraser*. However, it reversed the names of Anderson Lake and Seton Lake, and had a distorted scale.

Once prospectors were on the river, maps were seldom needed, since other miners and Indigenous people who were treated with respect were there to consult.

— • —

Detailed information about miners' kits lies scattered in just a few places. On Puget Sound Bar north of Fort Hope, George Beam saw a "great Many [miners] passing up and down with packs on their backs and pick, pan, and shovel in their hand." At Fort Hope on May 31, 1858, Douglas recorded what he saw: "flour, pork, tea, sugar, coffee, nails, . . . Coarse clothing, woolen shirts, shirts—blue & gray, stockings, quicksilver, men's leather boots, rocker irons [metal pieces for mining equipment], long-handled shovels, American wood axes, molasses, saleratus [baking soda], yeast powders, sheet iron, wash pans."[74] His notes pinpointed articles that the Hudson's Bay Company could order for sale.

The most helpful record is a "List of Outfits for Four Men, Six Months" on D. McGowan's *Map Exhibiting the Routes to Pike's Peak*, where gold was discovered south of Denver, Colorado.[75] It included mining tools, cooking implements, food, and other items. Thoughtful examination indicates how each item was useful—even necessary. However, the total weight per man would be daunting.

■ TOOLS:

4 Steel Picks w/handles	$5.00	4 Shovels	3.00
1 Pit Saw	7.00	2 Axes	2.00
1 Hatchet	.65	1 Saw File	.25
2 Gold Pans	1.50	1 Chisel	.30
1 Auger	.25	1 Hand Saw	1.00
1 Drawing Knife	.50	25 lb. of Nails	1.25
2 lb. Quicksilver and retort	3.00	2 Gimlets	.15
Sheet iron for Long Toms	.75		

■ CAMP FIXTURES AND FURNITURE:

8 Pair of Blankets	$24.00	1 Camp Kettle	1.00
4 Tin Plates	.30	4 Spoons	.15
1 Coffee Pot	.50	1 Camp Stand	1.00
4 Cups	.35	1 Dipper	.15
1 Large Spoon	.15	1 Large Fork	.15
1 Frying Pan	.35	1 Dutch Oven	.70
1 Bread Pan	.30	1 Coffee Mill	.40
1 Wooden Bucket	.25	4 Knives	1.00

■ PROVISIONS

6 Sacks of Flour	$18.00	6 lb. of Tea	4.50
400 lb. of Bacon	40.00	100 lb. of Salt	1.00
100 lb. of Coffee	11.00	6 lb. Ground Pepper	1.00
1 Ten Gallon Water Keg	1.00	2 Bushels of Beans	2.00
100 lb. of Sugar	7.00	25 lb. of Rice	1.50
2 Bushels of Dried Fruit	2.50	1 Box of Soap	1.00
250 lb. Pilot Bread [biscuit][76]	12.50		

■ UNPRICED SUNDRIES

3 Gallons of Brandy; 12 lb. Gunpowder; 20 lb. of Lead;
10 lb. of Shot; 2000 Gun Caps; 2 dozen Boxes of Matches;
15 lb. of Candles; 1 Whet Stone, 30 lb; of Rosin.

The total expense of $159.35 amounted to approximately $40 for each of the four men, plus unmentioned firearms.

— • —

The cost of provisions on the Fraser rose exorbitantly away from the coast because of high shipping fees and merchants' greed. A recurring estimate of day-to-day living expenses in the mines (not counting the tool kit and cost of a mining claim) was $5 a day, even though meals were simple.[77] In the field, "boiled coffee, sweetened with brown sugar, and without milk, pork and beans, and the favorite slapjack [pancake], is the regular diet," so the *Victoria Gazette* explained.[78] In July, such a meal at Fort Hope cost a dollar, and a cup of coffee 50¢.[79] Prices did, however, fall quickly over the year as better roads were built.

TABLE 1: PRICES ON THE COAST AND FRASER RIVER 1858[80]

ITEM	STEILACOOM PUGET SOUND JULY 9	FORT HOPE JULY 17	LYTTON AUG. 20	FOUNTAIN* OCT. 10	BRIDGE RIVER† DEC. 9
Flour	$9 per 100 lbs.	$18 per 100 lbs.	$45 per 100 lbs.	$80 per 100 lbs.	$50 per 100 lbs.
Bacon	25-35¢ lb.	65¢ lb.	$1 lb.	$1.50 lb.	75¢ lb.
Sugar	20¢ lb.	40¢ lb.	75¢ lb.	—	60¢ lb.
Coffee	18½¢ lb.	50¢ lb.	—	—	60¢ lb.
Beans	10¢ lb.	18¢ lb.	50¢ lb.	$1 lb.	45¢ lb.
Nails	$8.50 keg	50¢ lb.	$1 lb.	—	—

*via Fraser Canyon / †via Harrison Route

— • —

Communication with the outside world was possible by letter, but at a high price. For decades the Hudson's Bay Company had carried non-employees' letters at $1 for the first half ounce and 25¢ for each additional half ounce.[81] By July 1858, American Billy Ballou was operating an express service on the Fraser and Thompson rivers running as far as Kamloops and Cayoosh.[82] Using steamboats, canoes, mules, and men, he always managed to deliver letters to their destination. Express agents collected fees for letters and distributed mail at the mining sites, as Urban Hicks did on Puget Sound Bar. Because so many vessels sailed south from Point Roberts, Ballou easily expanded his express service throughout Puget Sound at unknown cost.

For other destinations, a half-ounce letter from the Fraser River was assessed several separate fees:[83]

• An express fee for Billy Ballou's transport to Victoria and possibly Whatcom: 50¢ from Forts Hope and Yale, $1 from Lytton, and $2 from more distant places.

• 5¢ postage paid at Victoria to the post office of the Colony of Vancouver Island.

• 25¢ to Freeman's Express (Ballou's original partner) or later to Wells Fargo Express for shipping from Victoria to San Francisco and probably for locations in Oregon. The cost of shipping from Victoria to Washington Territory has not yet been found.

• Additional pre-paid United States postage of 3¢ for Washington, Oregon, or California; 10¢ to the U.S. Atlantic coast (carried on steamers via Panama); 15¢ for Canada West; 29¢ for Great Britain; and 33¢ for Australia.

• Pre-paid charges to any United States Express company involved.

George Beam would have had to pay at least 50¢ to send a letter to his friends on nearby Whidbey Island. Most men would have had to pay about $2.45 to send a letter by express from Fountain to Canada West, but the anonymous Canadian miner spent only 45¢ because gold licencers carried his letters free of charge to Victoria.[84] Collect mail was common in those days. Miners typically felt isolated and welcomed communications from distant friends and relatives. George Beam craved for news from Whidbey Islanders even if he had to pay for their letters. He wrote that they "probably think I can't raise the tin to pay the Express. . . . I will dig of Nights to pay if they will send them along."[85]

Ballou also offered other courier services. Miners could save trips for provisions by paying Billy a carrying charge. He regularly conveyed small items of mining equipment such as mercury retorts. For a dollar, the news-hungry could buy a copy of the *Victoria Gazette* or San Francisco's *Daily Evening Bulletin* or the *Daily Alta California*.[86]

Competition was soon offered by Wells Fargo, the largest and most reliable California Express. After hearing about Ballou's initiative in gold rush country and his partnership with Freeman's Express, they opened a branch in Victoria by July 1. The first office was

A letter sent from New Westminster, British Columbia,
to California in 1859 or 1860

located "in the bar-room of a hotel, where letters to go [to San Francisco] are placed in open cigar boxes, accessible to all, and those received are laid upon a table."[87] Within a few weeks, the firm moved into a permanent building that added banking. A *Victoria Gazette* advertisement guaranteed letter delivery, offered banking services, and promised that gold would be "shipped and insured at lowest rates."[88] Naval commander Richard Mayne wrote with assurance that "I have never known a letter sent by them miscarry."[89] Wells Fargo engaged J. Horace Kent and H.F. Smith for an express up the Fraser

River. They competed with Ballou all the way up to Kamloops and Cayoosh.[90]

Once British Columbia became a separate colony, postmaster Alexander C. Anderson established post offices at Fort Langley, Fort Hope, and Fort Yale, soon followed by New Westminster and other places.[91] The charge was 5¢ per letter within the Colony of British Columbia, plus an additional 5¢ if the letter continued to the separate Colony of Vancouver Island. That price was not high, but most agreed that the expensive express companies offered more reliable and speedier delivery.

CHAPTER 3

Gold Mining Techniques and Regulations

⤳

Very good day—$50. One man
took out two thousand.
—*Canadian miner's diary, September 17, 1858*

GOLD IS A NOBLE METAL, found in nuggets and flakes between 70 and 90% pure. One of the rarest elements, it accounts for only 0.0011 parts per million of the Earth's crust. Even in promising locations, luck is needed to hit pay dirt. One estimate has 2.5 tonnes of debris removed for every gold ring, a yield of only 0.00015%. Current production runs under three thousand tonnes annually. If all the world's 205,238 tonnes of gold stock were gathered together, it would form a cube only twenty-two metres in each direction.[1]

Gold occurs frequently in the California and British Columbia mountains because of tectonic activity.[2] Erosion exposing underground veins releases gold, which is then carried long distances by glaciers or rivers. The farther it travels from the motherlode, the smaller it becomes. By 1857, Indigenous people on the Thompson River were bringing gold to the Hudson's Bay Company, once they learned its value. As a company agent told the Canadian miner, women and

Noon on the Fraser River

small children "use stout sticks to pry the rocks and dirt and use their baskets to winnow the larger nuggets from the stones."[3]

Those techniques would not work on the Fraser between Hope and Yale. Severe abrasion through the turbulent canyon created "flour" or "float" gold which settles into sediments where the river slows or forms an eddy. The most productive mine on the Fraser in 1858 was Hill's Bar, "located on the lower arm of sharp angles in the river, at the upper end of which is a strong current, and at the lower end a strong eddy," as a perceptive miner detailed to the *Daily Alta California*.[4] Urban Hicks remembered that "in California the heads of bars were always found to be the richest."[5]

— • —

The Fraser between Fort Hope and Fort Yale was quickly covered with California-style surface placer mines.[6] The term "placer" (rhymes with "passer," not "racer") derives from the Spanish word *placer*, "sand bank." Miners dug and washed away boulders, stones, sand, and clay with simple shovels, picks, pans, and rockers, leaving only gold. The skills were easy to learn, but "severe and arduous," according to a miner's accounts of California work. It consisted of:

> prying and breaking up huge rocks, shovelling dirt, washing it with wet feet all day, and sleeping on the damp ground at night, with nothing above but a thin covering of canvass, or a leaky log roof. . . . Getting dressed took no time. . . . A pair of damp overalls, a pair of socks, a pair of . . . heavy rubber boots. Flannel shirts we slept in. Then a splash of cold water from a tin basin and a swipe with a comb.[7]

Breakfast was a gulp of coffee, some slapjack pancakes, and possibly a bit of salt pork.

The archetypal image has a dishevelled miner crouching with a stamped metal pan ten to eighteen inches across the top, with sides sloping down at thirty degrees to the bottom. Miners filled their pans with gravel and water. Large stones were hand washed to loosen dirt that could contain gold. Clay was broken up manually, and the grit tipped out of the pan. Since gold is much heavier than the surrounding debris, the nuggets, flakes, and fine "flour" settled to the bottom of the pan with heavy black sand. Most of that black material could be blown away or winnowed when dry. Pans were actually used less for full-scale mining than for prospecting a site. If there was nothing or only a speck of "the colour," the miner would pass on. A hard-working miner could examine a third to a full cubic metre or yard in a ten-hour day. Prospectors' pans were also used for washing clothes, mixing flour cakes, and feeding the mules.

The rocker, or cradle, had a handle fitted on a rectangular box with curved pieces attached to the bottom. Gravel and earth were shovelled onto a metal sieve on top that caught large stones. Some cradles placed a sloping piece of canvas or wood under the sieve to break the fall of what fell through. Buckets of water were poured in as someone rocked the equipment back and forth to wash the grit down and out. Wooden slats called riffles were nailed to the bottom,

Miners panning for gold

Miners rocking for gold

which slanted down to an open end. The gold and heaviest sand settled against the riffles. The finer the gold, the less the slope and flow of water required. The residue was then panned out. Early in 1858 most mining took place on the banks of the Fraser, an inexhaustible source of water. Two or three people digging, pouring, shaking, and dumping could rock two to six cubic metres per day—up to eighteen times as much as through panning. Abrading gravel called for regular replacement of wooden parts. Intensive rocking left small stacks of tailings beside the river.

Long Toms replaced the short top of a rocker with a trough four to eight metres long and around thirty centimetres wide. Ditches were dug to bring a constant stream of water so that three or more miners could spend all their time loosening ground with picks, shovelling it into the trough, washing clay away, and discarding stones. At the lower end was a sheet of iron with holes about a centimetre wide. Under that, a two-metre-long wooden box with riffles caught the gold. The dregs were panned or winnowed out. Several miners could examine up to thirty cubic metres of material in ten hours—five to ten times the volume of rockers and up to ninety times of a pan. The term Long Tom originated as military slang around 1812 to describe a cannon with a particularly long range. The word "tom" was widely used to describe brute strength and sexual potency. The expression was transferred about 1839 to the mining trough, which was cannon length and shot rocks through.[8] What a simple improvement on panning and rocking!

Sluices up to several hundred metres long had complex sieves, false bottoms, and riffles custom-designed for each location. They needed unlimited flows of water from high elevations—ideally an astonishing 8,000 litres per minute (1,760 Imperial gallons per minute).[9] The tremendous pressure created by that amount of water separated gold from rocks and sediment. Sluices out-produced Long Toms but damaged terrain. Some miners dug canals up to 160 kilometres long that could change water flows permanently. Landscapes were clear-cut for lumber to build sluices and repair damage from punishing

Miners winnowing gold from lighter sand

Miners at a Long Tom

abrasion. The first sluice on the Fraser was built in July for rich dirt in the woods below Hill's Bar.[10] During his September trip to the river, Governor Douglas noted that "at Hill's Bar ... rockers are making from 1 to 5 oz. to the man a day; and sluice digging 36 oz. a day to 6 men."[11] Sluices and Long Toms left large tailings of rocks.

On the Fraser in 1858, early government regulations protected the lakes and streams that Indigenous people relied on for water and fish: "Sluices as yet can only be operated by water raised from the river with wheels."[12] When Urban Hicks arrived from the Washington Territory on August 13, he started building two twelve-metre-high (thirty-nine feet) water wheels to service sluices on Puget Sound Bar.[13] Standing as high as a modern four-storey building, they rested on large flatboats that cost $450. He used lumber from a recently opened Yale saw mill costing $90 per thousand board feet when prices on the coast were just $12. On September 21, the first wheel "upset" several boats, with a complete loss of provisions. On October 6, the wheel was "in operation with troughs that lead the water to the top of the Bar," but then the river fell too low on October 7 to turn it. Hicks persevered until it worked on October 27, only to have the sluices blown down in a storm. Hicks and his partner "employed two sets of hands and ran night and day. . . . We paid $4 per day and $5 per night and board. The first run of about forty hours we took out about $900." Even with earnings that high, food and other expenses were crippling. Hicks wrote: "[I] returned home at the commencement of winter with just about as much as it had cost me to go and come."

Californians pressed aggressively for change. By July 20, 1858, Assistant Gold Commissioner Richard Hicks at Fort Yale (not related directly to Urban Hicks) reversed early government policy and issued licences for flumes and ditches from lakes and tributaries.[14] One company employed sixty-eight men to build a three-kilometre ditch from a lake to service sluices at American and Santa Clara Bars. The cost was $5,000. Another ditch at Hill's Bar cost $4,000.[15] By November, twenty-one "ditch companies [were] all busy getting the water in

Long sluices

A river water wheel servicing a sluice

from the lakes and creeks along the river, some of them employing as many as 100 men."[16] The longest ditch serviced a thousand claims. In September, Douglas "was particularly struck with the ingenious contrivances for distributing water.... Small streams had ... been diverted from their course, and conveyed in skillfully graded ditches, even from a distance of 3 miles.... The owners of the ditches charg[ed] a certain sum per inch.... The sluice is far [sup]erior as a means of washing gold out of the soil, to the cradle."[17]

The dry terraces or benches between Lytton and Lillooet, rising 200 metres above the river, are ancient river banks formed when glaciers melted after the ice age. As early as 1857, dry digging there uncovered nuggets. The anonymous Canadian miner was sluicing at Fountain, north of current Lillooet, by October 5, 1858. Alfred Waddington noted how, in November, "a party of Italians . . . open[ed] a very considerable water ditch for sluicing, and all around the Fountain, six miles above the Big Falls, miners are doing remarkably well."[18] High government fees eventually made many of those canals unprofitable, though they remained to irrigate farms at a later date.[19]

— • —

Mercury has been known as quicksilver for thousands of years, because it forms a liquid at room temperature.[20] It amalgamates with every metal except iron and platinum, making storage difficult. It is measured by the flask, a steel or iron vessel that holds around 34 kilograms.[21] Gold is one of the heaviest elements, its specific gravity being 19.3, while mercury's is only 13.56.[22] When clean, gold sits on top of clean mercury. It eventually wets and sinks, forming a pasty grey amalgam. Almost everything else slips off the surface. Only mercury could recover large quantities of the Fraser's flour gold through amalgamation.

In May 1858, Governor Douglas observed that "quicksilver [is] required urgently" near Fort Hope.[23] Private enterprise remedied that situation quickly. During June and July, at least 141 flasks (4,797

Fine flour gold of the type found on the Lower Fraser River
was best captured through amalgamation with mercury

kilograms) of quicksilver were shipped from California to the lower
Fraser River. Quantities reached 186 flasks (6,324 kilograms) by the
end of September, but there was not enough supply to reach Lytton
by August. Mercury cost around $1.43 per kilogram (65¢ per pound)
in San Francisco and Whatcom but ran up to $20 and $30 per kilo-
gram on the Fraser.[24]

Rockers could use up to 5 kilograms (around 10 pounds) of mercury daily. Sluices needed a large start-up, say 40 kilograms (88
pounds) or more for long ones, then 20 kilograms (around 40 pounds)
daily, and more for large ones.[25] Canvas or carpet could be smeared
with mercury and fitted in rockers or sluices. A more expensive but
more efficient method uses copper plates 1 metre by 1/2 metre (3 feet
by 1-1/2 feet). They are cleaned with nitric acid and smeared with
mercury. A copper-mercury amalgam forms that gold running over
the surface binds to.[26] George Beam's party paid $5 for each copper
plate acquired at Fort Hope in October 1858. Many fine particles of
gold were captured, but 10% to 30% of the mercury escaped to pollute
the ground and rivers.

To recover the gold, miners scraped the amalgam off the canvas or copper plates, which could release harmful fumes. Some miners then pressed the material through a cloth or chamois leather. Mercury droplets squeezed through, leaving a gold-mercury concentrate inside. Next, the quicksilver was boiled off over an intense fire at 356.7 degrees Celsius, leaving gold *doré* behind.[27] Novice miners reached for pans or cups and watched the fumes escape. Californians also baked amalgam in potatoes. Many fell sick from mercury poisoning after breathing escaping gas.

Retorts made this process much safer. The simplest retort was a sealed, angled pipe. The end containing the amalgam was heated, and the mercury vapour rose away from the gold residue. The gas condensed inside cool stretches of the pipe, and liquid mercury ran into the far end. Retorts were relatively safe if they remained closed until the mercury gas became liquid again. During one day in October 1858, reported the *Victoria Gazette*, one sluicing company took out "12 pounds [5.4 kg] of amalgam, which is equal when properly retorted to 6 pounds [2.7 kg] of pure gold."[28] As letter-bearing expressman Billy Ballou passed up and down the river in July 1858, he offered retorts for sale, and possibly even quicksilver.[29]

George Beam and his friends began their work being very naïve about the dangers of mercury. On October 17, one of his party "retorted Some four hundred Dollars," around 26.6 ounces of gold at $15 per ounce.[30] Two to three times that amount of mercury fumes could have escaped.[31] That was an extremely dangerous level since current U.S. standards allow just two parts of mercury per billion in drinking water, just one part of methylmercury per million in seafood, and just one microgram of organic mercury per cubic metre of air.[32] The miner must have opened the retort too soon or it leaked, since he was too sick to work for three days. On the fourth, he was still "unwell but able to work" lightly. Beam installed copper plates in three rockers, and was thrilled to see "they work very well." Unfortunately, he did not clean up thoroughly. The next day he "was quite sick" and remained off work for four days.[33] Californians at risk from mercury fumes created by other miners would have quickly taught novices safer methods.

The Puget Sound Bar neophytes had time on their side. Their main exposure was occasional and limited to around twenty-nine days—from October 17 until they left for the coast on November 14. The body has enough resilience to flush moderate, short-term exposure that causes nausea, abdominal cramps, diarrhea, muscle aches, fever, chest tightness, a cough and shortness of breath. Long-term exposure produces irreversible damage when blood carries mercury into the brain. Symptoms include hand and tongue tremors, excessive shyness, irritability, depression, drowsiness, loss of memory, insomnia, hallucinations, delusions, mania, loss of sight, loss of hearing, mouth gingivitis, kidney damage, cancer, birth defects, and early death.[34]

— • —

The government tried to control mining activity, to prevent a "scene of lawless misrule" as Douglas put it, by issuing licences that also raised much needed revenue. The Colony of Victoria in Australia had previously introduced this system. When Americans started trickling north up the Columbia River looking for rumoured gold in 1857, Douglas proclaimed in December that nobody could prospect without a licence costing ten shillings ($2.50) per month, payable in advance at Victoria. A month later it rose to twenty-one shillings ($5).[35] However, overland arrivals had no desire to make a long and expensive detour to spend money on a scrap of paper. Most of the tens of thousands who arrived by ship simply ignored the regulation.

As Douglas had intuited earlier, "it will be impossible to levy such a tax without the aid of a military force."[36] Even the presence of enforcement ships *Plumper*, *Recovery*, and *Satellite* on the Fraser proved ineffective. By June 25, 1,500 licences had been issued, rising to 3,500 by July 10, collecting $12,625 by June 30.[37] But by July 10, 21,966 had arrived on ship from San Francisco and thousands more had come overland. Most miners boasted that they had never paid the obnoxious tax. There were too few fee collectors because the

NOT TRANSFERABLE.

No. ————.   185. .

THE BEARER, —————, having paid to
me the sum of TWENTY-ONE SHILLINGS, on
account of the Territorial Revenue, I hereby
License him to dig, search for, and remove
gold on and from any such Crown Lands,
within the Couteau and Fraser River Districts, as shall be assigned to him for that
purpose by any one duly authorized in that
behalf.

This License to be in force for three
months, ending ——————, and no
longer.

Received   ——————
Received   ——————
Received   ——————

_Regulations to be observed by the Persons digging
for Gold, or otherwise employed in the Gold
Fields;_

1. This License is to be carried on the
person, to be produced whenever demanded
by any Commissioner, Peace Officer, or other
duly authorized person.

2. It is especially to be observed that this
License is not transferable, and that the
holder of a transfered License is liable to
the penalty for misdemeanor.

3. No mining will be permitted where it
would be destructive of any line of road
which it is necessary to maintain, and which
shall be determined by any Commissioner,
nor within such distance around any store,
as it may be necessary to reserve for access
to it.

4. It is enjcined that all persons on the
Gold Fields maintain a due and proper ob-
servance of Sundays.

5. The extent of claim allowed to each
Licensed Miner, is twelve feet square or
144 square feet.

6. To a party consisting of two miners
twelve feet by twenty-four, or 288 square
feet.

7. To a party consisting of three miners,
eighteen feet by twenty-four, or 432 square
feet.

8. To a party consisting of four miners,
twenty-four feet by twenty-four, or 576
square feet, beyond which no greater area
will bei allowed in one claim.

A Fraser River mining licence in July 1858

wages were so low, and Americans like Beam refused to pay. A proposal to tax each sluice at $5 a month would probably have been just as unenforceable.[38]

Miner Urban Hicks, who had extensive government experience in Washington Territory, gave an earful to Gold Commissioner Richard Hicks:

> He claimed that the tax went to maintain the Victoria police, not one of whom were on the river at that time. I pointed out to him that had it not been for Yankee enterprise these mines would probably have never been discovered; that their discovery . . . greatly augmented the trade and wealth of the town of Victoria; that the American miners needed no police protection or interference; [and] that we were abundantly able to take care of ourselves. . . . It was a shame, if not robbery, to compel the poor miner to pay a license to mine before he had discovered whether there was anything to mine. Not one in a hundred who reached the country was able to find half the amount it cost him to get there.[39]

After many similar encounters, the gold commissioner recommended reducing or discontinuing the fee, owing to "its effects in exciting feelings of irritation and dislike of the Government, and provoking antagonism to the public officers." Richard Hicks excused 881 destitute miners between Fort Yale and Fort Hope from paying anything.[40]

After reviewing these details, Colonial Minister Lytton in London reminded Douglas that miners in Australia had rioted over similar taxes. In response, the government there changed the licensing period from a month to a year and imposed an export duty of two shillings and six pence on each ounce of gold. Those changes collected much more money for the government.[41] Douglas's calculations indicated that an export tax could raise as much as £100,000 annually.[42] Even so, he preferred a licensing fee, which became annual rather than monthly in 1859.

To those, like George Slocumb, who expected free access and unlimited services:

The amount of Taxes here amounts to an imposition, viz. Miners License $5.00, $6.00 for Clearance of Boat [each time], 10 per cent on Invoice of Merchandise. $7.50 for Ground Rent for Tent and $5.00 per month for chopping wood or 20 cents a cord. . . . The wood choppers here are indignant. It takes off some profit and the wood cut is nothing but dead pine, useless to the Company.[43]

All ignored the facts that roads and other "increased expenses of the government had to be paid somehow or other," and that taxes in the British territory were much lower than in California, as Waddington pointed out.[44] The following table from the *Victoria Gazette* compares fees in the various districts.[45]

TABLE 2: TAXES, FEES AND DUTIES 1858

ITEM	CALIFORNIA	VANCOUVER ISLAND	FRASER RIVER
Import duties	15-30%*	None	10%
Entering vessels	Foreign $11.60	Foreign $10 British $3	$12
Tonnage dues	5%	None	None
Pilotage	Compulsory, $10 per foot in, $8 out + 5%	Optional, $2 per foot	No pilots
Head money	$5 in, $6 out	None	$2 in until Nov.
Poll tax	$2 per male	None	None
Mining licence	Foreigners only $4 per month	None	$5 per month†
General taxation	3% on "property real and personal," and on business	Liquor only	Liquor only

*Duty also charged on exported goods that were re-imported
†In 1859, $5 per year

— • —

Allowable claim sizes changed over the year as the government bowed to pressure from independent Californians who preferred to establish their own regulations on each different site. At the start of 1858, the colonial government specified that one miner could hold a claim just 12 by 12 feet (144 square feet). Two miners were allowed 12 by 24 (288 square feet), three could have 18 by 24 (432 square feet), and four miners could stake 24 by 24 (576 square feet).[46] The metric equivalents fall between 13.4 and 53.5 square metres.

In principle, the *Victoria Gazette* reported, the small claims were "to keep the miners, for the present, in as compact bodies as possible in order to insure their being readily supplied with provisions, and for the purposes of protection against" Indigenous attack.[47] Alfred Waddington articulated the objectionable practical problems:

> there were twice too many miners for the ground occupied. . . . Moreover many of these claims, which were only 20 feet square, could be worked out in a week, and there was no elbow room to take up others.[48]

George Beam and his party were lucky to arrive early enough to stake claims without purchasing costs at Puget Sound Bar on August 10. Those claims remained productive until he left for home on November 13. When Beam hired new men, the group could stake additional claims. In June, Urban Hicks and three partners took out four claims at the head of Puget Sound Bar. Even though two of the party left with their canoe to make money by freighting, the remaining two miners kept all four claims.[49] By contrast, the anonymous Canadian miner was more solitary, seeking one claim after another farther and farther north on the river. His necessary mining partners changed often.

Despite their individualist tendencies, the miners themselves did not want a free-for-all. They followed long-standing California practice by forming mining committees to regulate the bars they worked on. The terms have survived for three of them:[50]

TABLE 3: BAR REGULATIONS 1858

HILL'S BAR MAY 21	FORT YALE BAR JUNE 27	PUGET SOUND BAR AUG. 26-SEPT. 14
Claim size: 25 feet river front, extent back disputed.	Claim size: 25 feet river front extending to high water mark.	Claim size: 25 feet river front, extending back to the mountains.
Two claims could be held by each miner, one by purchase and one "by pre-emption" [that is, on unclaimed land].	Only one claim could be held by each miner.	Two claims, one by location [meaning unclaimed land?] and the other by purchase or gift.*
Claims had to be worked for one day in three, except in case of sickness.	Claims had to be worked for one day in five, except in case of sickness or public business.	
Thieves would be punished and expelled. First Nations could not be hurt or sold liquor.		Disputes settled democratically via miners meetings.
A captain and two others guarded the bar.	An elected recorder kept public records at fifty cents a claim.	An elected recorder kept public records at fifty cents a claim.

*After Sept. 14, only one claim

Miners' initiatives induced the pragmatic colonial government to increase claims to more reasonable sizes. The official "Instructions of Assistant Gold Commissioners" of July 13, 1858, allowed 25-foot frontage per licensed person, extending back to at least high water level on large rivers. In small creeks and ravines, 25-foot claims could run up both sides to the top of gullies. Claims for dry diggings away from streams were to be 20 by 20 feet (400 square feet). In actual practice, claim sizes fluctuated, ranging from 25 x 25 feet at Mormon Bar to 25 x 30 feet at Canada Bar.[51] On Prince Albert Flat south of Yale, deep diggings measured 25 feet frontage by 500 feet long.[52]

The July 13 official instructions stipulated that licence books had to record "descriptions of the localities allotted, with the names of the parties . . . [and] a rough chart of the ground."[53] Disputes were to be settled quickly by government officials, so that "disputants may not have the temptation to redress their grievances themselves."[54] The last directive was wishful thinking, given both the small number of officials and the unquestioned authority that miners' own committees had in the mines. In 1859, the government decided to give B.C. miners greater latitude: "Mining boards, having a power to make byelaws, with the consent of the Gold Commissioner, may be formed whenever 100 or more registered free miners are found in any district."[55]

— • —

No nineteenth-century gold miners gave any thought to the long-term environmental impact of their work. For over half a century, gravel bars and river banks along the Fraser and its tributaries were stripped of plants and one to three metres of earth. Vegetation grew back haphazardly decades later, leaving many areas prone to erosion. Boulders and large stones were left on the shore, but an estimated one million cubic metres of sediment were thrown into the stream every year for fifty-eight years. About half of it was sand and small stones that strong currents washed away within a year. The rest was coarser gravel that moved downstream very slowly.[56] Erosion caused by clear-cut forestry and agriculture added to the problem.

The finest sediments caused immediate crises. A recent study of Alaska placer mines found that just one mine discharged 244 milligrams of sediment per litre of water into a stream. Above the mine, there were only 0.7 milligrams of sediment per litre of water. The fish and insects downstream were only a tenth as plentiful as those above, with many fewer species. Fish gills were severely damaged by particulate abrasion.[57] Large quantities of sediment also lowered oxygen levels in water.[58] On the Fraser River in 1858, mining waste depleted the salmon fishery. Even worse, tailings and water diversions turned many spawning creeks into dry beds.[59]

During July, at a site opposite Cayoosh, Indigenous guards with guns forced miners off "their favorite fishing grounds," because "mining in the river muddied the water so as to prevent them from catching salmon," according to Whatcom's *Northern Light* newspaper.[60] Indigenous residents made the same conclusion at Fort Yale according to the *Daily Alta California*: "They know that the salmon will not run in dirty water, and when they fail, what are they to live upon?"[61] On August 14 at Fort Yale, they were convinced that "the 'Bostons' and their steamboats had stopped the salmon," as reported in the *Daily Evening Bulletin*.[62]

On September 26, the anonymous Canadian miner went to a traditionally rich fishing ground just north of Cayoosh: "*Fished below falls but nothing.*" In September, the *Victoria Gazette* reported on the "Scarcity of Salmon.—Whether it is from Indian indolence or piscatory migration that salmon have suddenly become scarce in this region, we are unable to say."[63] A December letter from Port Douglas on Harrison Lake reported that Indigenous people who lived there "are in a bad condition, being already short of food of their own providing."[64] In April 1859, the first judge of British Columbia, Matthew Begbie, reported from Cayoosh that "it was admitted on all hands that many hundreds of Indians had died of absolute starvation during the winter. The Indians said that the salmon had failed them."[65]

The larger aggregate thrown into the river by nineteenth-century mining and tree cutting created longer term problems. That mass is still working its way downstream at the rate of one to six kilometres per year, and may continue to do so for as long as three hundred years.[66] The first Admiralty survey of the Fraser River 1827 was published in 1849 as *Fraser River from a Drawing by Mr. Emelius Simpson*. Naval Captain George Henry Richards resurveyed the area extensively in 1859 and 1860 for a new Admiralty chart titled *Fraser River and Burrard Inlet*. During the thirty-three years between the 1827 and 1860, the main channel remained relatively stable on the south side of the river—up to seventy-one feet deep along Sea Reach. In 1860, Richards noted that "vessels of 18 feet draught may enter the Fraser near high water."[67]

The next full survey of the river in 1884 was recorded on a revised edition of the *Fraser River and Burrard Inlet* chart. The old shipping channel had "considerably shoaled" and been replaced with a "New Channel . . . carrying" only eight-foot-deep ships.[68] The 1890 survey showed that the southern channel along Sea Reach had silted in with new marshes and islands, while a deeper channel had been cut along the north side of the river. Recent studies have shown the river bed rising because of aggregate deposits west of the City of Mission. That phenomenon may have helped cause the devastating floods of 1882, 1894, and 1948. Dredging could alleviate flooding potential but would compromise fish habitat.

The impact of heavy metals associated with gold mining is more difficult to assess. Historically, mercury has proved lethal in many places. As early as the second century BCE, the mercury mines at Monte Amiata, Italy, caused such widespread destruction to farms, vineyards, forests, and fish that they were closed by Roman Senate decree.[69] During the nineteenth century, vegetation and cattle near retorts in California languished or died, and people who passed by occasionally found themselves salivating excessively. Miners' wives could be poisoned after repeatedly washing their husbands' mercury-laden clothing.[70] More recently, thousands of abandoned mine sites in Canada have been compromised with mercury and other toxins which have poisoned wildlife and humans—especially Indigenous people who hunt and fish downstream.[71]

Methylmercury is the most dangerous form of the element, because it is easily absorbed by fish and the humans who eat them. For years, heart-rending stories have flowed out of the Grassy Narrows First Nation in northern Ontario. The area suffers from pollutants released by a pulp mill at Dryden in the 1960s. Fish at Grassy Narrows contain up to 150 times the safe dose of mercury recommended by the U.S. Environmental Protection Agency. In 2016, for example, five-year-old children were suffering severe cognitive arrestment. A *Toronto Star* newspaper feature reported that "they can't talk, they talk gibberish."[72]

Little research has been conducted on mercury pollution in British

Columbia.[73] For a start, naturally occurring background levels of mercury are higher in B.C. than elsewhere. Even where toxic sites are well known, mining companies and the government have not shown consistent interest in spending the millions necessary for cleaning them up. A number of scientific and informal studies indicate enduring mercury contamination in the lower Fraser River region. Accounts written in 1858 and 1859 describe extensive gold prospecting along the Lillooet River, which flows into the north end of Harrison Lake. That activity is confirmed by residues in the river's delta, which has levels of gold 2,000 times higher than in fresh water elsewhere and of mercury 200 times higher than typical.[74] On the Fraser River, beads of mercury can be found today by digging a few feet into Emory's Bar, south of Yale.[75] Core samples taken from the Fraser delta show elevated levels of mercury in sediments laid down between 1894 and 1910.[76]

The miners of nineteenth-century British Columbia continue to leave their footprints on the Fraser River.

A family of the Songhees
Indigenous people

CHAPTER 4

Indigenous Resistance to Displacement

∞

Missourians . . . think as little of an
Indian's life as they do of a cat.
—Daily Alta California, *September 2, 1858*[1]

THE YEAR 1858 WAS a watershed when Indigenous people faced increasing displacement. Prospectors who set up mines on traditional fishing spots saw only individuals who could be driven away because they were outnumbered. But without fish, entire Indigenous communities faced hunger or even starvation. The miners' diversion of streams unwittingly took away another resource crucial for Indigenous daily life and spawning salmon. Age-old traditions were disrupted when settlements were forced to move or even destroyed by vigilantes. The crisis escalated into the Fraser Canyon War, which is the focus of this chapter.

When prospectors arrived on the Fraser River, they met people of the Stó:lō (Coast Salish) First Nation from the Salish Sea to a point above Fort Yale. The *Stó:lō Coast Salish Historical Atlas* unfolds their life powerfully. The Nlaka'pamux (Thompson, Knife, or Couteau) inhabited the Fraser Canyon north of Spuzzum, where turbulent rapids, including Hell's Gate, made access very dangerous.[2] For thousands of years they had pursued a life of fishing, hunting, and gathering that required large tracts of land.

Annie York, an Indigenous resident at Spuzzum, and Dr. Andrea Laforet, formerly of the Canadian Museum of Civilization, collaborated on a detailed study of traditional Indigenous life near Spuzzum. Women gathered berry and root crops found in the mountains. They prepared different diets "for infants, pubescent boys, pubescent girls, pregnant women, fathers expecting a first child, people in mourning, menstruating women, and all women."[3] Multiple wives were common because adult women left food tasks during menstruation, pregnancy, and child rearing. Men fished from specific rocks handed down through families. No one could fish there without the owners' permission. Salmon, the only food that could be eaten by anybody at any time, was dried on racks for winter. Other fish were caught in mountain lakes and streams. In autumn, men hunted deer, bears, mountain goats, marmots, rabbits, porcupines, and birds. Men constructed canoes and the long plank houses (40 or more metres, or 120 feet) where extended families lived and worked. The diarists followed Californians by calling those settlements *rancherías*, the Spanish word for "a collection of huts, like a hamlet."[4] Palisades around buildings protected against raids. Warriors occasionally conducted full-scale wars. But most Indigenous skirmishes simply rounded up slaves, grabbed food and other valuables, or avenged previous insults and killings.

After Hudson's Bay Company posts opened at Fort Kamloops (1811), Fort Langley (1827), Fort Yale (1847), and Fort Hope (1849), beaver, marten, lynx, otter, fox, and fisher were traded for clothing, tools, and firearms. Wooden palisades protected the forts from attack. Indigenous acts of theft, insubordination, and murder were punished immediately and ruthlessly. More often, Company employees used non-violent strategies to maintain control. Sympathetic Indigenous people could be bribed or cajoled into informing about impending trouble.[5]

Trade could be stopped if Company property or employees were

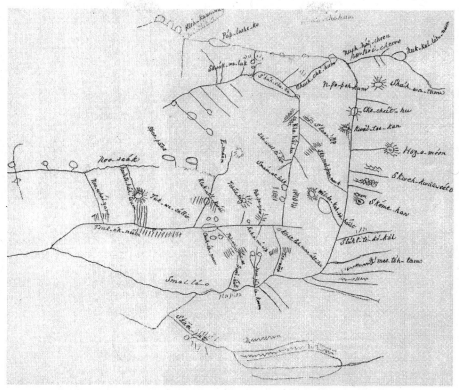

Chief Thiusoloc's sketch of river travel close to Mount Baker, Washington[6]

attacked. Marriages between employees and Indigenous women were encouraged to keep men sexually satisfied, discourage them from defecting, and promote the collection of valuable information. For the most part, the Company left Indigenous life as untouched as possible, because a robust wilderness meant more profits. Even so, resources were not infinite and eventually ran out.

Once the Company introduced alcohol it was impossible to remove the curse. Naval Lieutenant Richard Mayne wrote painfully about a reserve near Fort Victoria: "what with the drunkenness and the gambling . . . this village of the Songhies presents one of the most squalid pictures of dirt and misery it is possible to conceive . . . having lost what few virtues the savage in his natural state possesses, and

Photograph of Hell's Gate rapids by Bailey Brothers, ca. 1885

contracted the worst vices of the settlers." The Indigenous settlement across from Fort Langley fell into a similar state. When George
Slocumb arrived at Fort Hope on September 28, 1858, he fled the
tumult of drunken miners and Indigenous men.[7]

Indigenous people helped whites in many ways. They brought furs
and other goods to trade. In 1849, Governor Douglas encouraged
Vancouver Island settlers to engage Indigenous people, who were "not
only kind and friendly, but ready and willing to share their labours
and . . . bring in large quantities of the finest salmon and potatoes."[8]
Judge Matthew Begbie praised their willingness "to labour hard for
wages. . . . They have far more natural intelligence, honesty, and good
manners, than the lowest class . . . of any European country."[9] They
were strong, skilled packers and canoeists who transported people
and goods for the Company and 1858 miners.

A Stó:lō named Speel-Set piloted the first steamer from Fort
Langley to Fort Hope in June 1858: "He went aboard the *Surprise*
barefooted and wearing only a blanket. When he returned he came
as 'Captain' John dressed in a pilot['s] cloth suit, white hat and calf
skin boots, the proudest Indian in the country," according to Jason

Songhees Indigenous longhouses opposite Fort Victoria

Allard, son of the Hudson's Bay Company agent at Yale.[10] Over time Speel-Set amassed $2,000.

The power balance favoured the Company, yet Indigenous people also gained much. They bargained for trade items shrewdly. Metal pots, blankets, clothing, rifles, knives, and other tools made life easier. Trinkets and tobacco provided luxuries. New wealth strengthened their culture. On the coast, trade, the arts, and ceremonial life flourished on Indigenous terms.[11]

— • —

Most Americans brought unquestioned ideas of their government's "Indian" policies with them. The strategy of manifest destiny focused on white settlement of the continent from the Atlantic to the Pacific, not the preservation of Indigenous peoples. As American pioneers moved west, they aggressively settled the Indian Territory that had been set aside for Indigenous people displaced from the east, suppressed resistance through "Indian Wars," and created smaller and smaller reservations.[12] The hundreds of thousands of Americans who flooded into California during the 1850s devastated the Indigenous population by forcing inhabitants off desirable land, shooting those who resisted, and introducing new diseases. The numbers dropped from over 300,000 in 1769 to 85,000 in 1849, and then to 16,500 by 1880.[13] Populations in B.C. also dropped, but the meagre available statistics are difficult to interpret.[14]

Isaac Stevens (1818-1862), a West Point graduate involved in the Mexican-American War of 1848, was appointed governor of the new Washington Territory and its Superintendent of Indian Affairs in 1853. He hoped Puget Sound would be the terminus of a trans-American railroad to facilitate trade with Asia.[15] However, the four to five thousand white settlers were outnumbered by twelve to twenty thousand Indigenous people also desiring fertile land by the best rivers. Stevens imposed treaties in 1854 and 1855 that exchanged vast lands for small reservations and some cash. Mixed-race descendants of Hudson's Bay Company employees had their prize-land properties seized. The one concession to Indigenous people was continued fishing rights.

Late in 1855, eastern Washington Territory's Indigenous people rebelled because treaty compensations were not forthcoming and whites were trespassing on reservations.[16] Stevens vehemently opposed "any and all treaties made with [these hostile bands]:—nothing but death is a meet punishment for their perfidy. . . . The guilty ones should suffer, and the remainder placed upon reservations, under the eye of the military."[17] Seven hundred military troops were sent in. The conflict dragged on into 1858, when the sympathetic San Francisco *Daily Alta California* noted that various "tribes of Oregon and Washington Territories ceded . . . over sixty millions of acres . . . for two and a half millions of dollars . . . but the Indians have as yet received nothing in return."[18] The *Puget Sound Herald* mused how Hudson's Bay Company assimilation led to good relations, while American settlement led to brutal wars.[19]

The defeat of Colonel Edward J. Steptoe's 159 soldiers near Walla Walla, Washington, on May 16, 1858, by 1,500 Indigenous warriors drew a line in the sand.[20] Colonel George Wright led 1,500 U.S.

Army troops with the threat that he "did not come to talk." He crushed the revolt by September.

Given the continual bloodshed and dispossession, the Indigenous residents of British America tried everything they could to keep Americans away. In 1856 and 1857, Governor Douglas heard that Indigenous people living along the Thompson River "openly expressed a determination to resist all attempts at [others] working gold ... both from a desire to monopolize the precious metal," and from a resolve to protect the salmon they depended on for survival.[21] He wistfully reflected that:

> I am of opinion that there must have been some great mismanagement on the part of the American authorities, or it is hardly credible that the natives of Oregon, whose character has been softened and improved by 50 years of commercial intercourse with the establishments of the Hudson's Bay Company, would otherwise exhibit so determined a spirit of hostility against any white people.[22]

The American newcomers to the Fraser planted the Stars and Stripes on their Fraser River mining bars, which they named American, Boston, Fargo, Fifty-Four Forty, Madison, Mormon, New York, Ohio, Puget Sound, Santa Clara, Sierra, Texas, Washington, and Yankee.[23] Is it any wonder that the Stó:lō word for whites is *Xwelitem*, "the hungry people"?[24]

Until June, whites were outnumbered. In May for example, thirty whites working Hill's Bar across from Fort Yale yielded to the eighty Indigenous people living there. An "understanding was entered into, by which the miners agreed ... not to disturb them in their fisheries ... in the early mornings, and in the evenings," according to San Francisco's *Daily Evening Bulletin*.[25] The *Puget Sound Herald* noted that Indigenous people living near Sailor's Bar "impos[ed] a tax of a blanket or a shirt on each miner."[26]

Hill's Bar proved an early flashpoint because so many whites arrived to mine the flour gold that Indigenous people were unfamiliar with.[27] Around mid-May, according to the *Daily Alta California*, two

Salmon drying racks at an Indigenous site on the Fraser River

Indigenous men fishing for sturgeon on the Fraser River

to three hundred Indigenous people arrived, threatening "an exterminating fight. The Indian women thronged around the rockers in the way of the workmen, often interrupting their labours. It is estimated that the Indians took out at least $10,000 in gold dust." When rising waters drove the miners off the bar on May 22, the Indigenous people left "with a promise that they would return after salmon-time, and clean the miners all out."[28]

The commotion prompted Douglas to visit the Fraser from May 24 to June 1. He understood why the Indigenous residents "naturally feel annoyed at the large quantities of gold taken from their country by the white miners." Douglas told the miners, who were mostly "foreigners representing almost every nation in Europe," that they had no rights of settlement and "that the laws would protect the rights of the Indian, no less than those of the white man." Even more inflammatory was the transfer of law and order to Indigenous individuals. Douglas took "an Indian highly connected . . . and of great influence, resolution, and energy of character, into the Government service" and "appointed Indian magistrates" to settle difficulties between Indigenous people. This empowerment of Indigenous locals would have turned many American heads. Douglas wrote pessimistically to the Colonial Office in London: "The recent defeat of Colonel Steptoe's troops . . . by the Indians of Oregon territory, has greatly increased the natural audacity of the savage. . . . It will require, I fear, the nicest tact to avoid a disastrous Indian war."[29]

— • —

When tens of thousands of newcomers came flooding in, sometimes aggressively, Indigenous resistance escalated into violence between June and August.[30] An armed company of Americans coming up the Columbia River crossed the border at Okanagan Lake, destroyed an Indigenous cache of nuts and berries set aside for winter, and shot everyone in sight. Herman Francis Reinhart, a worldly-wise German prospector who witnessed this atrocity, observed that the "old California miners and Indian-fighters were the worst . . . [resolved to] clean out all the Indians in the land."[31] Indigenous residents on the Fraser also suffered, as the *Daily Alta California* pointed out: "Several Indians have been assassinated, others threatened, [their women] have been violated, and, sad to say, the aggressions have almost invariably been commenced by the Americans, who, at every trifle, draw their revolvers."[32]

Indigenous warriors fought back to protect themselves. The isolated Nlaka'pamux of the Fraser Canyon above Spuzzum mutilated white intruders, as newspapers reported, including the *Victoria Gazette*: "Decapitated, denuded corpses of unfortunate adventurers are daily picked up on the river."[33] On the Thompson River, an Indigenous woman attached to a miner told him to escape. Prospector Ned Stout and his friends managed to get down the river to Boston Bar, but "We had to fight our way through and we burn every rancherie and every salmon box that we could get hold of. They shot at us whenever they got a chance and we did the same."[34] Predictably, conditions worsened. The *Daily Alta California* reported how the ten thousand or so Indigenous people living on the river "have no fear of punishment; but the patience of the Bostons [Americans] is nearly exhausted. I have heard threats of a war of extermination."[35]

By August the situation was critical, because debris thrown into the river by some seven thousand miners compromised the fishery. Salmon were scarce and many traditional fishing spots were inaccessible. The *Daily Alta California* described the altered environment: "The whole river bank is lined with block houses, nearly all of which is impregnable to an Indian attack. . . . The underbrush and trees which would afford an ambush and hiding place, are cleaned away and burnt."[36] Retaliating Nlaka'pamux warriors stole miners' "provisions and clothing from them. They have gone as far as to take the very boots off a man's feet. . . . The Indians enter a man's cabin, or tent, and soil the floor or bed before the owner's eyes, taking any article of food or clothing . . . and threaten to kill if he does not leave instantly."[37]

Local residents and newspapers described how American "irregular troops started for vengeance, . . . the Stars and Stripes at their head."[38] On August 9, forty "well armed" miners left Fort Yale for the Thompson River, but stayed at Boston Bar "for the protection of those working there."[39] A rifle company of vigilantes also marched north to punish "those whom they *knew* were implicated in the murders and robberies that have been committed."[40] They were led by Captain Charles Rouse, a former Texas Ranger who was accustomed to killing Mexicans and Indigenous people. When they heard that two Frenchmen, Jean Le Croix and Pierre Sargoase, had been shot dead on August 9, they "commenced firing on the Indians, and killed nine" immediately, then twenty-five more in eight days.[41] The conflict was uneven: Indigenous warriors "were armed with the old Queen Anne flint-lock rifles; the miners with . . . good rifles" shooting three hundred metres, six times farther than the guns sold by the Hudson's Bay Company.[42]

Continuing raids prompted up to two thousand Indigenous people to meet at Spuzzum on August 12.[43] The danger was so great that the Stó:lō and Nlaka'pamux set aside their traditional enmity. The *Daily Evening Bulletin* described how those unexpectedly reconciled First Nations "said the 'Bostons' and their steamboats had stopped the salmon, and they were going to make friends . . . and then make war with the whites."[44] Rouse's destruction of buildings and goods at Spuzzum soon after that meeting strengthened their resolve.[45]

On August 14 at Boston Bar, 150 miners were involved in "a fight with the Indians . . . which lasted three hours, and resulted in the complete rout of the savages."[46] Seven were killed with only one white injury. Conditions were so unsafe by August 15 that "all the miners for twenty miles above the canyons had come down to" Spuzzum, having buried "their canoes with their provisions."[47] Around noon on August 17, over three dozen of Rouse's men arrived at Fort Yale with "the news that 180 men had gone up the river in two parties, one on each side, had attacked the 'Rancheria' [Spuzzum], killed . . . Indians and had captured a lot of guns."[48] Five chiefs were among the thirty-six casualties, while a total of three rancheries above the Big Canyon and two more below were incinerated, "destroying all of their provisions . . . of salmon and dried berries."[49]

Not all whites wanted Indigenous people cleared out. Captain J. Sewall Reed, a miner near Spuzzum, warned an Indigenous chief he had befriended of an impending destruction of his dwelling. The chief escaped. "Very early the next morning, Sewell was awakened by a visit from the old chief, with a present for him."[50] Not all Indigenous men attacked, as the *Daily Evening Bulletin* pointed out. Two chiefs from Spuzzum appealed that they "had often had the white man to eat with them. . . . Before the white men came here, they were poor and naked. When the salmon did not come, they starved; but now they had plenty of blankets, good clothes and food, and they knew that it was owing to the white men coming amongst them."[51]

— • —

On August 16, between 800 and 2,500 miners at Fort Yale met to address the crisis. Almost 200 men volunteered for five identifiable companies.

The Pike Guards had fifty-two members under Captain Harry M. Snyder. At Spuzzum they grew to eighty-two. They marched not under the Stars and Stripes, but with a white flag inscribed "PIKE GUARDS," the word "pike" referring to a miner's pick. Fortunately for the long term, they set out to prevent more deaths of miners, not to kill every Indigenous person they found. Snyder was a San Francisco stove dealer. Stymied by high water that prevented mining, he thought "for any one to start and come here now, I think it is a wild goose chase."[52]

The French, Italian, or Austrian Company of fifty to eighty marched under Captain John Centras. Mainly French, they seem to have banded together to avenge the killing of Le Croix and Sargoase. They co-operated with the conciliatory Snyder after the first treaty on August 17.[53]

The Whatcom Guard of twenty to thirty-three was led by Captain Graham. Whatcom was the Washington Territory county at the U.S. border and also a town on Bellingham Bay. This group acted out then current Washington attitudes about exterminating Indigenous people.[54]

The Madison Guard had forty-four men, possibly under Martin Gallagher. It may have been named for Puget Sound's Port Madison, the site of many raids by Indigenous warriors. This group fell in with Graham's exterminators.[55]

The Rough and Ready Rangers had between twenty and twenty-four men under Captain Galloway. True to their name, they joined Graham and shot indiscriminately whenever they had the chance.[56]

Harry Snyder led the Pike Guards: "by a unanimous vote I was elected their Captain."[57] He asked Ovid Allard, the Hudson's Bay Company clerk at Fort Yale, to lead all the companies and loan firearms.[58] Allard refused to be drawn into a scheme concocted by foreigners who had taken the law into their own hands. Snyder vented the criticism of many, including the *Victoria Gazette* editorials: "Why should the miners wait for the officers of the English Government to protect them in their just rights?"[59] Allard grudgingly agreed that the situation had become untenable for miners and ordered all Indigenous locals to hand in their firearms, perhaps more for their protection than the miners'. Without arms, the Indigenous men paddled down river.

The new mission differed from Rouse's scorched earth policy. Snyder set out with Chief Kowpelst (Copals) of Spuzzum to negotiate.[60] When Rouse had earlier brought him to Fort Yale, miners wanted to lynch Kowpelst, unaware that he had offered his life as a guarantee that his people had never attacked miners. Snyder realized the importance of locating an American that could speak Indigenous languages and found Mr. Batteice, without whom "I do not believe we would of seen one dozen of Indians." Also enlisted was the Hudson's Bay Company man William Yates, who spoke French and several Indigenous tongues.[61] Yates remembered how he was so trusted that he "was never troubled" by Indigenous people.[62] Yates left the expedition before Boston Bar; Batteice stayed to the end.

On August 17, three kilometres from Fort Yale, Snyder announced that he "endeavour[ed] to effect a peace with the Indians by peaceable means if possible, and only as a last resource to use force."[63] A vote gave "unanimous consent," and John Centras's French Company joined him. Near Sailor's Bar, thirteen kilometres north of Yale, Snyder had Yates explain "our object" to an Indigenous man they met. He "gave one yell" and seventy more appeared.[64] "A speech was made to them through the interpreter, to which their chief replied, and a treaty was made with them—a result which seemed to give great gratification."[65] Because this tribe had not "shot and robbed the whites," they were spared but also given "notice that the white men were in arms, and determined not to be further molested."[66] A white flag was given to prevent future attack. Ironically, the colour white that represented peaceful surrender to the Americans signified death, ghosts, and sickness to Indigenous people.[67]

Snyder's rhetoric and show of arms resembled Hudson's Bay Company strategies, and Kowpelst's presence sealed the deal. To give authority for the next negotiations, the local "Chief sent his son with us."[68] This pattern of Nlaka'pamux assistance continued up the river. It worked, because they trusted the other chiefs' assurances that the killing would end and knew that the alternative was American rangers shooting with better rifles.

Later on August 17 at Spuzzum, "another council was held with some sixty or seventy Indians . . . and an amicable understanding arrived at." More white flags were handed out. The 500 to 700 miners, "by an almost unanimous vote adopted Capt. Snyder's plan, and gave him nine cheers."[69] However, Washingtonians rankled. The Whatcom and Madison Guards insisted on genocide. Snyder was repelled that they "wished to procede and kill every man, woman & child they saw that had Indian blood in them. . . . My heart revolted at the idea of killing a helpless woman, or an innocent child."[70] Expressman Billy Ballou joined the cutthroats: "we had hand granades, & one thing & another. . . . We killed everything that looked like an Indian, dog or anything else; young ones, by George—shot them all. Col. Moore said 'Kill them all, little as well as big; nits make lice'."[71]

Crossing the river near Spuzzum on August 18, Snyder reached "the foot of the big canion."[72] Captain Graham's determination "to go to the lodges to kill Indians drove them into the mountains," as William Yates remembered.[73] Snyder, however, realized "that we would not be able to see any if we could not come to a better understanding with each other." After tense negotiations, Graham grudgingly agreed to "remaine where he was" until Snyder had made peace with the Nlaka'pamux near Boston Bar and sent a white flag back to Graham.[74]

Snyder ascended the old Hudson's Bay Company brigade trail leading up to Anderson River to avoid snipers.[75] At noon on August 19, they reached the Chinese camp on the Fraser south of Anderson River.[76] The Chinese, who were suspected of supplying Indigenous men with arms, were told to leave, though they could return to their claims when the trouble ended.

The first negotiation in Nlaka'pamux heartland would determine the expedition's fate:

> As this was the tribe who had given most trouble to the whites, a long talk was had. The Indians said that they "did not want war; that they had received bad usage from many white men—their women insulted," etc. The chief said that . . . with regard to the two Frenchmen, who had been shot, one of them had *first* fired his revolver at an Indian, but that now that his young men had seen all the warriors the whites had sent up, they would be afraid to do wrong in future. . . . They were very glad to hear there was to be peace.[77]

The respected chief and the show of arms had worked. Snyder sent the "white flag to Capt. Grayham: . . . the Chief's son [was] their guide."[78] On August 20, Snyder wrote a friend that this treaty "restores peace, and enables the miners to return to their" claims south of Boston Bar. He urged "forbearance towards the Indians."[79] Miners quickly returned to work there.

— • —

Meanwhile, on August 18, Graham immediately broke his word and returned to Spuzzum "to attack the Indians." Yates was sent with twenty-five others to find out "what he meant by not sticking to his promise." Graham snapped back to Yates that Snyder "was on his way to hell."[80] The Whatcoms and some Madisons set out to clear river-level trails on the west bank, while the rest of the Madisons and the Rough and Ready Rangers took to the east bank.[81] Horrified that white men were breaking Snyder's pact, the Nlaka'pamux removed bridging poles from the paths and fired guns on the Americans. Arrows with poison and anticoagulant were also shot.[82]

The Nlaka'pamux dislike of Graham intensified when Snyder's men brought word of the truce on August 20. The chief's son watched as Graham ordered "his men to take the white flag . . . and throw it away." One of Snyder's messengers "picked it up and slept on it the balance of the night," around fifteen metres from Graham's men.[83] Yates, who was in that party, remembered correctly that it "was moonlight but the moon was shut in sometimes by clouds." He also recollected that Graham had stationed "a guard."[84] Around midnight, "ten or twelve shots" were fired, killing both Captain Graham and his First Lieutenant, James Shaw.[85]

Contemporary accounts and modern reconstructions disagree about the extent of Nlaka'pamux involvement in this incident. Some think they played a central role. Near Graham, a man awoke when an "Indian . . . gun was pointed at his breast, he seized it by the muzzle, and turned it off, the ball grazing his shirt."[86] Since the Nlaka'pamux had made peace under duress, they would have been outraged when they saw Graham still relentlessly killing their people. The *Victoria Gazette* speculated "that Graham's party were followed . . . by the Indians, and that they had witnessed the treatment the white flag had received."[87] In the moonlight, sharpshooters could easily have picked off the sentries, killed the main troublemaker, then disappeared unheard. That would warn other miners who thought of breaking the treaties. Snyder later correctly mused that if Graham had "done as he promised to do he would now be alive."[88]

Indigenous grave on the Fraser River

Others think that Whatcom Guard members shot each other when they awoke, confused by gunshots. Yates remembered "fifteen or twenty shot to death or wounded" when "they commenced shooting among themselves in the dark. . . . A month or six weeks afterwards over thirty bodies of white men were picked up at Hope, . . . supposed to be the bodies of Captain Graham's men." They had been shot by American "dragoon pistols and five shooters," not the "old fashioned Hudsons Bay guns" the Nlaka'pamux owned.[89] This memoir provides a probable scenario of domino effects during nighttime confusion. Laforet and York even suspect "a garden variety homicide by one of Graham's companions."[90] However, the Nlaka'pamux had too much to lose if they did not eliminate Graham.

Shock waves went through Fort Yale on August 21 when news arrived that forty-three of Graham's party were dead. A few days later, the *Victoria Gazette* printed a sensational headline: "MASSACRE OF FORTY-FIVE MINERS BY INDIANS."[91] A "case of 20 muskets, which were in the H.B. Co.'s store, were demanded and given up to . . . 20 men [who] stood guard" at Fort Yale.[92] Fort Hope also went on alert: Donald "Walker (the Company's agent) would furnish twenty-five muskets . . . to be used exclusively in defence."[93] In the next issue, the *Victoria Gazette* printed a retraction: "The Story of the Massacre of the Forty-Three White Men Untrue!"[94] Gold Commissioner Richard Hicks at Fort Yale played down the situation to Douglas: just fifty men went up river, "the Indians challenged them to a fight," but the Americans concluded a treaty.[95] Ovid Allard wrote Douglas a more detailed and honest account.[96]

— • —

On August 20, Snyder made four more treaties, and on August 21 "made pease with 4 different Chiefs and camped within seven miles of Thompson River," at Siska.[97] He may even have made a pact at every fishing spot to protect future mining. After at least one treaty, "their young women" were offered in marriage at "forty dollars a head."[98] Along the way, several chiefs placated Snyder with "some beautiful specimens of gold."[99] The farther north he went, "the more intelligent the Indians appeared," especially Cexpe'ntlEm (Spintlum), "the war chief of all the tribes for some distance up & down Frazer River and . . . Thompson River."[100] From a stockade at Kumsheen (Camchin), near Lytton at the fork of the Fraser and Thompson, he ruled "near a thousand Indians."[101] Cexpe'ntlEm brought six chiefs and three hundred Nlaka'pamux down to Siska.

Snyder asked if they wanted peace or war. If war:

the whites would send ten times as many men up the river, who would destroy all of them; but they did not want to do it. "Spinkum" . . . [told] them that they now saw the consequences of their bad actions.[102]

With that preliminary understanding, Snyder marched on August 22 to Kumsheen, where he:

proceded at once to hold our grand council which consisted of Eleven Chiefs and a very large number of other Indians. . . . We stated to them that this time we came for pease, but if we had to come againe, that we would not come by hundreds, but by thousands and drive them from the river forever.[103]

Peace was concluded with two thousand Indigenous people. By early September, Snyder wrote, "everything has been peace and quiet. The miners go to and fro unmolested."[104]

Half a century after the war, anthropologist James Teit recorded a Nlaka'pamux memory of a debate when "Cexpe'ntlEm . . . made a treaty of peace with Governor Douglas." (If the chief actually thought that Snyder was Douglas, Snyder realized it would be strategically foolish to correct his error. Alternatively, this tradition could have conflated memories of Snyder's treaty at Kumsheen and Douglas's meeting with Cexpe'ntlEm at Fort Hope on September 5.) Hundreds of warriors met at Kumsheen for days:

Cuxcuxê'sqEt, the Lytton war-chief, a large active man of great courage, talked incessantly for war. . . . Cexpe'ntlEm, with his great powers of oratory, talked continually for peace. . . . With the arrival of Governor Douglas and the making of explanations or promises on his side, most of the people favoured peace; and finally Cexpe'ntlEm, on behalf of his people, allowed the whites to enter the country. . . . Had it not been for Cexpe'ntlEm, there would certainly have been a war with the whites, and much bloodshed would have resulted.[105]

Lack of provisions forced Snyder's speedy return to the Anderson River by August 23, to Spuzzum on August 24, then into Fort Yale at 11 a.m. on August 25, "half starved, woren down with fatigue and some of them bare-footed."[106] They brought two chiefs and three warriors from the canyon, who "were much impressed at the sight of the number of whites, which was one of the objects in bringing them." Despite Rouse's and Graham's aggression, Snyder had built such trust that the Nlaka'pamux accepted his pledge for their leaders' safety.

Indigenous survivors whose settlements had been destroyed "brought salmon to Capt. Snyder's and Centras' parties" as peace offerings. They were relieved to be free of the danger that an American rifle company was "going to return and kill all that were left of them."[107]

A fitting memorial of the treaties was celebrated 160 years later, on April 14, 2018, at Lytton, when the great-great-great grandnephew of Harry Snyder met descendants of Cexpe'ntlEm at the Chief Cexpe'ntlEm Recognition and Reconciliation Storytelling Circle. As historian Daniel Marshall has commented, "Chief Spintlum, I would argue, is as much a father of British Columbia as (Gov.) James Douglas."[108]

— • —

When an August 1858 delegation from Fort Yale went to Victoria and complained that the Hudson's Bay Company had offered no protection to miners, Governor Douglas "informed them that . . . the Americans in arming themselves and going out against the Indians were guilty of *treason*."[109] For a second time that year, Indigenous problems prompted Douglas to visit the Fraser, from September 3 to 21. Because of the gravity of the situation, he took along thirty-three officers and men from the Boundary Survey Commission and Navy vessels, even though it was a "military force . . . absurdly small for such an occasion."[110] His dilemma was that Americans had made peace on their terms with Indigenous peoples.

Douglas had reached an uncharacteristic stalemate. He never reported the skirmishes in detail to London. He could not rescind Snyder's treaties without antagonizing both miners and Indigenous residents. He could not declare the entire Fraser River an Indigenous reserve, because he was outnumbered by thousands of gun-toting Americans. Also, Colonial Secretary Lytton had insisted that Americans should not be restricted. In May, Douglas had reported Indigenous grievances to the Colonial Office. Now he duplicitously replaced the larger picture with the stereotype of the "drunken Indian." He claimed he was "irresistibly led to the conclusion that the improper use of spirituous liquors had caused many of the evils they complained of."[111] He issued a proclamation forbidding the sale of liquor.

At least Douglas officially reported "visits [at Fort Hope] from the Chiefs of Thompson's River, to whom I communicated the wishes of Her Majesty's Government. . . . I also distributed presents of clothing to the principal men."[112] Only in his private diary did Douglas note that he gave Cexpe'ntlEm "a present and gave him a charge concerning the treatment of miners visiting his country. Reported to be a treacherous Indian, but it is prudent to pursue a conciliatory policy at present."[113] Ovid Allard probably did not have to remind Douglas of an 1848 event when Fort Yale was built at the end of a new Hudson's Bay Company brigade trail that ran over Nlaka'pamux land. Cexpe'ntlEm had briefly held Allard hostage to stop the intrusion.

Harry Snyder wrote about "a long conversation" he had on September 20 at Hill's Bar, where the governor "complimented me highly for the course I had adopted in restoring peace with the Indians," and offered him a government position. He declined the proposal: "As for the pay that officers get here, a man, to be honest would starve." Douglas was following Lytton's advice to search out Americans who could further the aims of the colonial government. Snyder could be trusted, because his methods resembled the Hudson's Bay Company tactics. Douglas did not mention this meeting in his official report. Douglas was also less than honest when he told Snyder he would "not interfere with any rules and regulations that the miners may have adopted." The governor had visited Puget Sound Bar five days earlier and announced that the local protocol of allowing two claims per miner would be reduced to just one.[114]

The governor addressed the residents of Fort Yale on September 12 in terms very different from the harangue in May, when he told foreigners they had no rights of settlement. He first welcomed British subjects, numerous enough to have named their mines Canada, Cornish, New Brunswick, Prince Albert Flat, Trafalgar, Victoria, Waterloo, and Wellington Bars. Following Lytton's instructions, he welcomed the American majority:

I am commanded to say to the citizens of that great republic which, like the mustard-seed, has grown up into a mighty tree, and gives shelter to the oppressed of all nations, that offshoot from England of which England is still proud—I am commanded to extend to you the right hand of fellowship and to give you a hearty welcome to our country.

Douglas continued by promising that town lots and twenty-acre farms would be offered for sale once the area became a colony. In the meantime, Gold Commissioner Richard Hicks was authorized "to permit the building of sawmills, to establish ferries, to open roads," and to develop "the resources of this glorious country."[115]

Privately, though, Douglas was witnessing his work of decades being dismantled. An American had settled "peace" treaties on terms that allowed miners to stay on claims that had dispossessed the Indigenous people whom Douglas desired to protect. Property was being offered for settlement to foreigners who had no concept of British institutions and little respect for Indigenous residents. Hundreds of Americans were setting up mining companies, lumber mills, and merchandising networks. Commercial development now eluded the Hudson's Bay Company, which the British Parliament was stripping of its monopoly. That venerable institution was now a minor player, unable to compete with American wealth and initiative.

As has happened so often, Indigenous people were lost in the shuffle. Their immediate concern was the destruction of the salmon fishery, which led to widespread starvation that winter. Snyder's treaties may have ended bloodshed, but miners now occupied many traditional fishing spots on gravel bars. They stripped the vegetation, dug banks away, and diverted lakes and salmon-spawning streams to service rockers and sluices. The Indigenous people living there felt betrayed by the Hudson's Bay Company and colonial authorities. As will be seen in Chapter 9, Douglas was able to set aside large tracts of land that protected traditional Indigenous life only after the confusion of 1858 had settled down.

PART B

The Diarists in Fraser River Country, 1858

The steamer *Commodore* (under its original name *Brother Jonathan*), the first ship to sail from San Francisco to Victoria with many miners

CHAPTER 5

George Slocumb's Failure

∽

Desperate—desperation itself.
—*George Slocumb's diary, September 23, 1858*

GEORGE SLOCUMB'S SMALL diary was written with pencil that smudged as pages rubbed together in his pocket.[1] Water damaged some pages, destroying a few passages. Slocumb details the fate of most of the miners who visited the Fraser River in 1858. He left San Francisco with too little money for subsistence and never established a claim. As a result, he was constantly hungry and unable to pay his way out. His sensitive exploration of the psychology of failure went far beyond what most men of the period dared to articulate. His curious mind and store of memorized poetry kept the demons partly at bay. His diary also provides a superb description of how the Fraser gold rush impacted Washington Territory towns during the summer of 1858.

George Leach Slocumb was born on September 7, 1830, in Fairfield, Illinois.[2] He, his two brothers, and four sisters enjoyed a life of privilege, as their father was a state legislator, senator, and a judge of honourable repute. George's education made him the best-read of the four diarists, constantly craving new reading material.

Marysville, California, which Slocumb visited en route to San Francisco

Uninterested in following his father's path of public life and sty-mied by the economic malaise at home, the twenty-two-year-old trekked overland to California in 1852, when gold production hit $81,394,700.[3] More than fifty thousand people made the five-month-long crossing from Missouri that year, despite thousands of deaths from cholera, malaria, scurvy, dehydration, starvation, and attacks by Indigenous people trying to prevent invasion of their lands. During the next six years, he eked out a living in the gold fields of Placer County. All the while, independent surface miners were being re-placed by low-wage earners working the company hydraulics or in underground tunnels. The financial crisis of 1857 crippled many Cali-fornians. In 1858, the Fraser River offered promises not seen locally.

The diary begins in April 1858 at Mountain Springs, Placer County, which the depressed economy made "*exceedingly dull.*" (*Italics indicate passages from Slocumb's diary*). He had been out of work "*since February last,*" around six weeks. He decided to scurry away on April

12 in "*a desperate effort to make my pile in British America in the mines.*"
He even "*promised to write an article*" on them for a Placer County
newspaper.[4] Since March, San Francisco's *Daily Alta California,* the
Sacramento Daily Union, and Auburn's *Placer Herald* had reported
sensational finds on the Fraser River. They had broadcast irresistible
news about "seventy pounds of gold" and stated outright that the
"Victoria, V.I. GOLD DISCOVERY CONFIRMED . . . Miners Making
$8 to $50 a Day!" On April 5, the *Sacramento Daily Union* issued a
note of urgency: "Tell your friends to come soon, if at all; as the river
will rise, and they cannot get up."[5] What further encouragement did
the jobless need?

Slocumb detoured almost 145 kilometres (90 miles) overland by
stage coach to Marysville, to enjoy some "*celebrated*" sights. After a
day, he "*engaged passage on the* [steamer] Cleopatra *for the City of
Sacramento,*" where he transferred to "*the Steamer* Goodman Castle *for
San Francisco,*" paying around $11 in fare.[6] He took "*rooms at the Ras-
sette House,*" a more respectable accommodation than many rowdy
Frisco dives.[7] Naturally gregarious, he "*wrote to Milt, my olden time
friend,*" asking for his mail and newspapers to be forwarded. If he had
any qualms about the journey, they would have been dispelled by the
Sacramento Daily Union's account that hundreds of workers on Puget
Sound had fled to the Fraser, where two men "washed out in one day
$213.75."[8] Slocumb withdrew his entire savings of $200, his whole
"*Wealth . . . all I have to show for six years hard labor in the mines.*" As
time passed, he wrote zeros over his nest egg until nothing was left.

Slocumb spent his last evening in San Francisco seizing the opportunity "*for enjoyment, for I fear it is my last show for a year at least.*"
He might have sought out a bar where he could drink and talk up a
storm, or a gambling hall, or a bordello in the Barbary Coast district
to have some "*Calicofornica.*"[9] At his lodgings, he decided to travel
with three other "*embarcadors*": Brown, Drew, and Kelly. Slocumb
"*believe*[d] *we are all tight*"—close friends and penny-wise.[10] However, the trio immediately swindled the cash-happy innocent. He
lent them $13.50 for blankets. Later he lost $13.50 to them while

playing cards, which were likely stacked. They cancelled their debt that duplicitous way.

When at leisure, Slocumb pondered the same set of themes: hope for a future home and family, self-doubt over perceived failures, longing for friends and family, and recollection of poetry that fit his current mood.[11] This time he resolved to *"only look on the bright side in future"* and to remember *"the parting words on leaving home from Father—'George be an honorable man, at all Times.'"* Even so, he was haunted by *"my many failures"* and paltry savings: *"Fortune it seems I have wooed thee in vain."* With satisfaction, he remembered *"friends & a Home in the west, fond parent to extend the hand of Friendship should the weary Son return"* to Illinois. He would never be a *"Cosmopolite,"* a wandering libertine. Something of a loner, he remembered Byron's long poem about a romantic wanderer, *Childe Harold's Pilgrimage*: *"Sometimes I feel that I'm in the world alone.'"* Byron continued, "Upon the wide, wide sea: But why should I for others groan, When none will sigh for me?"[12] Slocumb bid *"Farewell California. I leave thee with many regrets."*

— • —

On April 20, Slocumb boarded the steamship *Commodore* in San Francisco. His estimate of 420 passengers formed the first large contingent to head north. *Commodore* carried useful cargo: ninety-five packages of liquor, twenty-six cases of ale, 409 packages of groceries, twenty-five boxes of candles, twenty-seven packages of clothing, fourteen cases of boots and shoes, fifty-nine packages of mining tools, six cases of gunpowder, two boats, and five packages of "drugs" (in those days including items like baking soda).[13] Slocumb was not a happy traveller, falling *"Sea Sick"* the first two days. His steerage ticket had cost $25, but he *"stood it only about six hours and paid $20 more for Cabin Ticket. Money is nothing in comparing the Cabin & Steerage. I do not think I could live 6 days in such a place."*

Steerage below decks consisted of bunks set close together with no privacy. Thieves pounced on unsecured baggage. The stench increased with normal bodily functions and when travellers succumbed to seasickness. Only a sliver of deck space offered relief. By contrast, first class passengers enjoyed one of twenty-four cabins that had a bed, desk, wash basin, wall mirror, storage space for trunks, and locking door. These rooms lined a lounge about twenty-four by six metres, decorated like an "imperial palace." Seating invited socialization with each other and the ship's officers. Meals were good, and large outside decks offered bracing sea air.[14]

Among the voyagers were "*over 100*" African-Americans who faced increasing discrimination in California. Governor Douglas promised them equality in the British Colony. Included was the "*celebrated Archy*" Lee. A slave from Mississippi, he escaped into the care of free African-Americans in California. Kidnappings and hearings followed. On April 14, 1858, the Supreme Court of California declared that slavery could not exist in the state and that Archy was free.[15]

Ominously, "*a few of the San Francisco Vigilance Banished Buccaneers*" were also on board. In 1856, a San Francisco Committee of Vigilance seized power from city authorities to punish rampant crime, correct political corruption, and keep municipal power in the hands of businessmen instead of the Democrat party. Most of the men found guilty were Irish, Catholic, and Democrat.[16] Slocumb had a similar mix of biases. Later he hoped that Vigilance exile Billy Carr would "*get his due in*" Victoria, ranted against an Irishman, defamed "*Democratic . . . ignorance*" at Port Townsend, and bet on Republican Abraham Lincoln winning an election.

Troubling news came from two men who embarked at Port Orford, a tiny lumber outpost. They reported "*an Indian outbreak.*" The *Puget Sound Herald* elaborated that on March 15, "about a hundred 'bucks' . . . killed the Indian interpreter, Oliver Cantwell, and . . . we are uncertain whether more lives have been lost."[17] Slocumb found himself back in the Wild West.

— • —

The steamer "*arrived at Victoria about 4 o'clock p.m.*" on April 25, after six days at sea. Another passenger's account reached the San Francisco *Daily Alta California*:

> The good people of Victoria were at church when we arrived, and were perfectly astounded when they came out, and beheld between 400 and 500 Yankees, armed with revolvers and [fifteen-inch long] bowie knives. At first, they thought we were the vanguard of a filibustering [i.e., invading] army . . . but our conduct soon proved we were not fire-eaters. . . . With the dint of scraping and gathering together from their country larders, and raising the prices, we succeeded in getting enough to eat.
>
> The colored people . . . got into an unoccupied house, and . . . some of them have purchased lands, which they are going to cultivate. . . . They have nearly all got employment, and are going to become free and enlightened subjects (not citizens) of Queen Victoria.[18]

Slocumb took "*quite a comfortable room at Bailey's Restaurant. Board 1.25 per day. Oh what a pleasant place after my trip.*" In a *Victoria Gazette* advertisement, C.A. Bailey promised patrons comfort in Victoria's "Pioneer Hotel" at Yates and Government Streets.[19] Slocumb heard reports about "*Gold on Frazier & Thompson Rivers,*" saw "*3 or 4 oz. of Gold dust,*" learned that the Hudson's Bay Company monopoly "*expires in May 1859,*" and noticed "*the Indians here are quite large and do not resemble our California Indians. They think they are as good as a White Man.*" At the card game quito, his three sailing companions fleeced him out of "*$13.50 for Blankets purchased for them in San Francisco.*" At first he declined lending them $25 more for Fraser River passage, "*for fear I may need it.*" He later relented and "*Loaned . . . Wm. Brown, Victoria, $20.00,*" which was repaid. He fell for yet another sob story and forked out $6 for their hotel bill: "*They were really in need & I could not see Americans in distress.*" After the hotel bills were paid, he had only $100 left.

A Yankee abroad, Slocumb found displays of foreign patriotism offensive. He thought that "*a Midshipman about 14 years old . . .*"

giving orders" for the warship *Satellite* "*look*[ed] *bad to an outsider.*" He condemned an Irish baker who had too little bread for so many new-comers:

> *An Irishman in the Business wants wheat bagged in the . . . Old Country for bread. The American portion cursed him for it. . . . He brags how happy he is to be under his good flag once more. . . . I am an American, and "Never will I be humbugged by these down trodden Sons of Erin," may I shout if I ever get back where the Stars & Stripes wave o'er the free. Remember this in casting my vote—never to vote for an Irishman.*

In actual fact, American flour on the Pacific was poor. To produce superior bread, the baker quite rightly preferred a better product from Britain.

Slocumb missed the San Francisco newspapers: "*Oh what a bless-ing it would be to hear an Englishman crying* 'Alta, Herald, *etc., only 25 Cents and a few more left.*'"[20] The *Victoria Gazette* did not start pub-lishing until June 25, with San Francisco presses and editors. His initial American sense of superiority would have annoyed long-time residents of Victoria: "*the British are so slow & selfish, nothing like Americans in giving information to strangers.*" However, he quickly re-alized he was "*seeing many strange things worthy of note & think I will be gainer in point of knowledge.*" He "*visited Beacon Hill, the pride of the Victorians. It is a real beauty of a place, and one has a splendid view of the Straits of Fuca Entrance . . .* [and] *Mount Baker.*" He admired the "*beautifully modeled*" local Indigenous canoes: "*they dig them out & then fill them with water and heat rocks and throw* [them] *into the water until they get it to boiling and then make it into the shape they want. . . . They bury their dead in the trees.*"

The success and plight of the first African-American immigrants struck him:

> *I see the colored population have opened a provision store at this place and are selling quite cheap. I think I will patronize them when I start for the mines. There is quite a number of them going back. I think it is not the*

*Heaven they anticipated & I also think the British will be sick of request-
ing them to come to their soil, for they are not exactly "the kind" they supposed they were, and the poor fellows find the free passage tendered by
Hudson's Bay Co. will be a promise forever, and will never be fulfilled.*

The *Sacramento Daily Union* wrote of further dissatisfaction:

Some of the colored persons who started a colony at Vancouver
[Island], have come over [to Port Townsend] disgusted with British
liberty. . . . Although they enjoy all the political privileges of the
whites, still . . . John Bull is a good deal like the Abolitionists of the
New England States; he likes to prate about liberty, equality and all
that, but, as one of them remarked to me this morning, "he wouldn't
like a darkey for a brother-in-law."[21]

Once acclimatized, Slocumb found that the gentlemanly *"government officers . . . give Americans all the information possible in regard to
the Mines,"* and *"that the Englishman never runs down any Country. . . .
On the other hand you hear Americans giving the Britons (their laws, Customs etc.) every kind of abuse. How unkind!"* All the same, his hotelier
Bailey *"played me a real Yankee trick in my board bill, charged me $2 per
week more than agreed upon."*

After five days, he was *"getting very tired of Victoria,"* a *"dull"* place
with *"no Excitement whatever."* Memories of California proved hard
to shake for others as well. Mary Jane Megquier, owner of a San
Francisco boarding house, found thoughts of her New England
home stifling: "I have seen so much of things a little more exciting, I
fear I shall never feel perfectly satisfied with [Maine's] quiet ways
again."[22] Slocumb asked his friend Milt *"to send my letters & papers to
Port Townsend."* By May 3, there were *"very few Americans on the
Island. The Canoes that leaves on tomorrow takes all away except 'Yours
Truly.'"* He stalled, because Victoria residents talked of the dangers
of crossing the Strait of Georgia and he heard on May 1 of plans
"that H.B.Co intend putting on Otter *to run to Langley and flat bottomed boats up"* the river from there. Government planning delayed

that transport until June 5, when the ocean steamer *Surprise* started ferrying miners up the Fraser River.

Loneliness pressed in: *"This is my first tramp without seeing someone I have known in California or on the Pacific Coast."* Homesick, he *"wrote to Father the first time for years,"* because he was ashamed to admit his failures: *"I have often thought of home and friends. . . . Am I the same lov'd and remembered one as in those happy days when I knew not what it was to wander, and the family circle was not broken? Is any nomad mentioned in evenings around the old fireside?"*[23]

— • —

On May 5, Slocumb sailed, *"Sea Sick,"* to Port Townsend, probably on the small Puget Sound schooner *Mary Dunn.* Port Townsend had become the preferred American staging point for the Fraser mines, since all vessels entering Washington Territory had to clear its *"neat brick . . . Custom House."* When miners started arriving in multitudes, speculators drove building lot prices as high as $1,000 in June. A crash followed when the crowds moved on to Bellingham Bay, which was closer to the mines, or to Victoria once steamers left there for the Fraser River.[24]

Slocumb wrote more during his month at Port Townsend than anywhere else. He felt he could *"gain more information in regard to the diggins at this place than at Victoria."* The natural beauty took his breath away, particularly when *"evening"* colours shimmered over a calm surface, broken occasionally by swirling currents: *"What a beautiful sheet of water Puget Sound is. I have never seen anything to equal it, but its reputation is worldwide."* The town's *"Billiard Table & Bowling Alley, three or four Whiskey shops, and as many stores . . . presents more of a business appearance than Victoria."* Even so, *"I am not very favorably impressed with the place & I must say so far, I find it beats California Towns in their best days for rowdy looking hombres. . . . Notorious thieves"* and *"desperadoes"* crowded the place. The town contained only *"forty-nine houses, and several of these are dilapidated,"* wrote the *Daily Alta California.*[25]

Newspapers contained negative accounts. The *Pioneer and Demo-crat* concluded that "it would be difficult to find a worse class of population in any part of the world . . . [with] 'beach combers' and outlaws of every description."[26] These included gamblers who moved on to Bellingham Bay, Fort Hope, and Fort Yale as opportunity arose. The *Puget Sound Herald* spoke of makeshift lodgings: "One public house there [has] three hundred boarders, who are lodged and fed in a ten-pin alley."[27] The *Sacramento Daily Union* wrote about poverty and eviction: "There are some 200 men . . . living on the beach and subsisting on clams, and amongst them some hard cases. Governor Douglas, in order to get rid of them, paid many of their passages from Victoria to Port Townsend."[28]

Port Townsend was a rough and tumble town: "*I should suppose this was a Democratic place judging from the amount of ignorance displayed on all occasions by the Settlers . . .* [who are] *rude & ungentlemanly to strangers.*" One "*evening on the beach*" Slocumb saw "*Americans & Indians jumping—they had a high old time. All the Indians were drunk.*" When he asked "*whether there was not a law prohibiting the sale of Rifle Brandy to the Indians . . . a 'Beach Comber'* [replied] *that it was nothing to Strangers—'Where ignorance is bliss, 'Tis folly to be wise.'*"[29] One evening he was even attacked:

> *After supper an hombre caught hold of me, and I supposed he intend giving me hell, and I went for my revolver and told him I would shoot him if he put his hand on me. . . . He proved to be a drunken sailor looking for a fight.*

In the town,

> *You see no trees or flowering shrub in front of their doors and seldom a fence . . . and most of the Bungaroos have lived here for 4 or 5 years. . . . A dog & gun is all they want. . . . It is seldom I see a newspaper or book and . . . I consider them . . . barbarians.*

Echoing the Wild West term "buckaroo" ("cowboy"), the slang term "bungaroo" dismisses the locals as "bung," which means both "asses" and "drunkards."[30]

On May 12, Slocumb saw a mob of Californians bringing their kind of justice north:

I have to record the most disgraceful proceedings I have ever witnessed. Two Sailors, deserters from an English ship, stole a boat etc., were taken away from the proper authorities by a mob in Port Townsend. . . . They will not let them have a trial before the Judge on American Soil. . . . The mob consists of the Law and Order Party from Frisco.

That group tried to stop the 1856 Vigilantes. Soon, "*a file of Soldiers arrived from the fort, and the Sheriff arrested six of the mobites. Hurra for the Sheriff. . . . Those that were arrested have sworn vengeance against the Citizens generally, and I fear before this Law and Order Party of San Francisco is stopped in its mad Career that there will be blood shed.*" The inmates "*have their trial tomorrow.*"

The next morning, "*two or three of the mobites that were out on Bail have flown.*" On May 14, "*the mobites were bound over to appear before the Court in August. Bail $300. . . . They will have to go to prison.*" Slocumb thought a "*Vigilance Committee [is] needed here, to assert the Supremacy of the law.*" For his own safety, "*I intend leaving here as soon as possible. This is no place for . . . a stranger, when the citizens are afraid to speak. . . . They live in perfect fear of the mob.*"

In that rough town, Slocumb thought the "*Indians are certainly the best part of the population, and they are regular flatheads.*" In childhood their heads were bound to produce tall, cone-shaped foreheads. Yet he did not romanticize them. One day "*an Indian was killed by an Indian*" to avenge an earlier murder. The victim did not need to be the killer, but "*one of the same tribe. They do business up with the white man on the same principle, & if the white man would remember this, that if he kills an Indian & gets off that the next white man has to suffer, they would be more particular about using their Colt Revolver.*" When a dead body was fished out of the ocean:

it proved to be a Cloochman [that is, a woman, who] *belonged to a Buck Indian. She was old. He said she could not dig clams & get around, so he drownded her, according to the Laws of the tribe (Iamicoms). He can do so*

An Indigenous woman with conical head

with impunity. They buy & sell the women. . . . Here is Slavery of the worst kind. Where is Greely of the Tribune?[31]

Horace Greeley (1811-72), editor of the influential *New York Tribune*, supported the anti-slavery Republican party, formed in 1854. Slocumb sympathized with Greeley's anti-Democrat stance.

News about Colonel Steptoe's rout spread quickly. On May 16, "*I heard today of the defeat of Regular Soldiers at or near Walla Walla. The Indians killed 50 Privates & three Officers and took 2 mountain Howitzers. The war is fairly commenced.*" After three Indigenous people were killed at nearby Bellingham Bay, Slocumb cynically observed how politicians could benefit:

for the future, we may expect hell from the Indians. Who wants a chance? Blood and Glory. Here will be chances to get wounded just enough to send some lucky fellow to Congress. Well Yours Truly was never cut out to be a politician.

Slocumb's emotional life in Port Townsend proved a manic depressive roller coaster. One day he was elated by good news and tried out newly acquired words in the Chinook jargon used by white traders and Indigenous people: "*Today I have seen* hiyu [much] *Gold and feel that I yet have a chance to make a pile. . . . I'm bound to be a miner root hog or die—*'" meaning, no matter what, do or die.[32] Like many other whites in Puget Sound, he learned "Chinook, thus proving the studious character of our people [Americans] in strange places," as the *Daily Alta California* observed.[33]

He was brought crashing back to ground by dispiriting rumours "*of several persons being lost, going up & coming down Fraziers River*" or men from the mines who "*report it impossible to get up before July*" or "*1st August.*" The previous winter had seen a very heavy snowfall. Since the Fraser River drains more than a quarter of British Columbia's land mass, a heavy runoff persisted until late September. He was exasperated by the lack of work: "*I wonder was there ever a man so restless as I am, never happy unless employed? Dimes and Dollars, Dollars and Dimes, An empty pocket the worst of crimes.*" Those with enough money could return to San Francisco, like the "*50 . . . returned miners disgusted with the Country*" who left on May 12, probably on the steamer *Panama*. But even if he had enough cash, he was stymied: "*I know of no place in California to go to get employment and must play the string out now, make or break.*"

When Brown and company returned dispirited, with no earnings from the flooded mines, Slocumb concluded, "*I acted wisely and well in not going when they did.*" They also reminded him that on the Pacific coast he had found only con artists: "*I have not found a partner yet and fear I am hard to tent* [to live with]. *My experience in partnerships have given me lessons only to be worried by forming them, & in future I will be more careful. I have been a 'victim' to misplaced confidence very often, & my idea is in future to be as much on my own hook as possible.*" Indeed, he preferred solitude: "*My idea of happiness—a cabin, Books, and to be alone.*"

On May 11, Slocumb fell into unceasing, depressing introspection: "*I have had the Blues—the Horrors—and today I feel perfectly sick when I think that it will take me so long to reach the diggins. Two months to remain in this county with nothing to do, and then the 'dark uncertain future.' Why hell, it would run a minister mad.*" The word "*blues*" meant "sadness" and "melancholy." "*Horrors*" pushed into the territory of clinical depression and delirium tremens.[34] Slocumb could not afford regular heavy drinking, but did visit saloons occasionally.[35] He wrote so disjointedly on May 11, 1858, that he may have been drunk. The "*dark uncertain future*" conjured up brooding Hamlet, one of his favourite literary characters. With a chill, he realized his irreversible mistake: "*I must say I have rushed the buck,*" like some impatient hunter. "*I have not acted wisely in leaving for the new diggins in such great haste.*" Henry de Groot remarked that Americans "have . . . a *penchant* for acting first and deliberating afterwards."[36]

Lacking options, Slocumb was resigned to "*go and see the Elephant, and of Gold I shall have the exquisite pleasure of being well sold.*" He puns on the word "sold" with devastating irony. Successful prospectors could "sell" plenty of gold, but others found themselves cheated ("sold" out). The expression "to see the elephant" described experiencing some extraordinary phenomenon personally whatever the cost. In Victoria, Governor Douglas agreed. He told an assembly of miners that "After the trouble and expense we have had in coming here, we must go to the end—we must see the elephant."[37] A man at Fort Hope had "seen the elephant—tusks and tail. That though rough, he likes the appearance of him, and that as soon as the water falls, he shall return."[38] Bitterness transported Slocumb to sarcasm. He greeted 450 new arrivals on May 18 via the steamer *Commodore* like a circus barker luring suckers: "*Go in, lemons & get squeezed. You will be certain now to learn that you are too early. . . . The Elephant is on Exhibition and may be seen by paying about $100. Come & see him foolish California miners.*"

This time his homesickness latched onto pleasant memories of Mountain Springs:

> *I have so many pleasant memories of the past in regard to the pleasant town and liberal hearted citizens that I can never forget. "The Lord says,*
> > *You may break the vase if you will,*
> > *But the scent of the roses will hang round it still."*[39]

The scent from the broken vase touchingly evokes, in Proustian fashion, the impossibility of retrieving the past despite persistent and tangible memories.

— • —

On June 1, Slocumb left Port Townsend by an inexpensive sailing schooner. The next day he arrived "*Sea Sick*" at Bellingham Bay, disembarked at deep port Sehome, then walked "*a mile and a half*" to the wider shore at Whatcom (both towns are now part of Bellingham). Lack of accommodation forced Slocumb "*to become a regular Beach Comber*" tenting on the shore. Forests came so close to the water that newcomers had to camp in a long line on the beach.[40] "*A

Whatcom (now part of Bellingham), as George Slocumb saw it

plate of beans for dinner [cost] *50 cents.*" The *Pioneer and Democrat* listed the free fare: "clam-beds, salmon and berries."[41] Slocumb remained there three months but wrote only four pages in his journal.

Would-be miners were roaming around restlessly, often intoxicated, brawling, or firing guns: "*There is many drunk men in town & after going to bed last night I heard a free fight going on. Heard a pistol Shot and a general rush and it was all over.*" The *Puget Sound Herald* agreed that Whatcom "is seething and boiling with excitement of every kind. The gamblers, those vultures who ever hover about when there is a carcass to prey upon, are there." Waddington added "pickpockets, swindlers, and men of broken down fortunes." Hazlitt wrote: "all the riff-raff of San Francisco of both sexes congregated there and converted [Whatcom] into Pandemonium."[42]

When Slocumb first arrived in June, Whatcom contained just thirty-five log houses and his estimate of around 600 mostly itinerant residents. The town was mostly "canvas tents where large quantities of miners' supplies were promiscuously traded," according to the *Puget Sound Herald*. The *Sacramento Daily Union* contained a picturesque description of the mud flats with "timbers of tramways and broken wharves used by the Bellingham Bay Coal Mining company. Every conceivable kind of small sailing craft lined the shore." Prospectors with money purchased Indigenous canoes to paddle up the Fraser River. At the end of June, the numbers had swollen to around four thousand, so that the *"Town has grown since I have been here more than the most sanguine expected."* Development surged with new streets, a brick building, a large hotel built by Slocumb's former San Francisco host, M.A. Rassette, and a printer's shop where the *Northern Light* newspaper was published from July 3 until September 11.[43]

The Whatcom boom was driven by local merchants who hoped to reap huge profits by building a miners' trail to Fort Hope.[44] It would be 200 kilometres (124 miles) shorter than the water route around Point Roberts and up the Fraser. That way British fees could be avoided. Blazing and building the path proved difficult. A letter sent on July 5 to the *Sacramento Daily Union* told of the arrival at Fort Hope of "over twenty men who have crossed the trail . . . barefooted, their clothes torn to rags, and they half starved." The same paper described another arrival at Fort Hope, a man who had "waded through a swamp, with water up to his armpits—lost all he had except what he stood in." Another arrival at Fort Hope "was asked whether a mule could come through? The reply was 'Can a mule climb a tree?'" Even the local *Puget Sound Herald* agreed that "a trail from Bellingham Bay to the Mines is just about as practicable as a railroad to the moon." Slocumb concluded that *"the Bellingham Bay Trail is a humbug."*[45]

The sailing of the steamer *Surprise* from Victoria to Fort Hope on June 3 proved that the Fraser was navigable by riverboats. Whatcom real estate speculation collapsed by August, and many buildings were dismantled and moved to Victoria.[46] Waddington wrote, astonished: "Of all the extraordinary ideas that have been broached [in 1858], that of cutting a perilous, and finally impracticable, trail 120 miles long over high mountains and perpetual snows, in order NOT to make use of a navigable river close by, is about the most extraordinary."[47]

Slocumb procrastinated because *"the stubborn waters of Frasier continue to rise."* Strapped for cash, he leapt at the opportunity to be "*engaged in helping a surveyor survey the mud flat of the City of What-com and have made my regular $25, the first money earned by Yours Truly since February last.*" The job, overseen by the original town surveyor, Alonzo M. Poe, determined the location of the E Street wharf, 700 by 6 metres (2300 by 20 feet).[48]

Slocumb brooded for almost two months, internalizing his pain and writing nothing from July 4 to 22 or from July 24 to August 21. Tragically, his Mountain Springs friend David Majors was shot during an argument about a mining claim:[49]

> *only two months since I bid Dave adieu. He expressed the heartiest interest in my welfare, wished me in miner's parlance "a lucky trip" and to be re-membered as a friend. It is a sad thing to die in a strange land with no friend to smooth the dying pillow.*

On August 23, it was time to leave "*detestable*" Whatcom for the "*miserable hole*" of Semiahmoo (now Blaine) on the U.S. border. Slocumb splurged on the Puget Sound steam tug *Resolute*, landing at "*Semiahmoo on the Sand Spit*," where Drayton Harbor still offers deep moorage.[50] He hiked "*about a mile & a half*" to "*Semiahmoo on the Hill*," where the 26-kilometre (16 mile) trail to Fort Langley began.[51] "*This, should it ever become a City, will be a rich place for scoundrels. Commit a crime on either Side and flee to the Soil of Johny Bull or Uncle Sam to avoid Justice.*" He envied the thirty men from the U.S. Coast Survey steamer *Active* who were surveying the forty-ninth parallel with British colleagues:[52] "*These hombres on board and ashore see a high old time, to judge from the outside.*"

At Semiahmoo, Slocumb met a friend who had proposed going to the Fraser together: "*Went out on the Trail today to see Cutlar and find he has taken a contract*" to work elsewhere. "*Today I am out of partner-ship and will remain so in future.*" Hurt, he packed his kit alone for two days, "*about as hard labor as I have ever performed.*" He arrived at Fort Langley on September 1, "*worn out*" and sick with "*diarrhea.*" He remained until September 28, hostage to the flooding river.

— • —

Fort Langley, sketched on May 24, 1858, by Alexander Grant Dallas

Fort Langley had been founded in 1827 and rebuilt in 1840. It was named after Thomas Langley, a Company director in London. The chief trader from the beginning was James Murray Yale, whose name was used in 1847 for Fort Yale upriver. W. Wallace, a correspondent sent by San Francisco's *Daily Alta California* to report first-hand on the Fraser River, captured how it looked on August 6, 1858:

> There is something quaint and primitive . . . [about] these old establishments. Here, a stockade fifteen feet high, of upright posts, encloses ten acres in an oblong shape. At the four angles are bastions, with loopholes for guns. Inside are erected the different offices of the Company. The "Hall" stands in the centre, at the upper end, and commands a fine view of the whole. On either side . . . are the warehouses, offices, cooperage, blacksmithy, jail, out-houses and residences of the employees. There are fifteen of these . . . roofed with cedar bark, which is now green and brown with moss, and the timbers are all black with the exposure of years. Behind the "Hall" is the vegetable garden and orchard. . . . Behind is the great farm . . . where grain, hay, potatoes &c. are raised. Three or four hundred head of wild cattle [graze with] many horses.

The fort is built upon an elevated plateau [on the Fraser River]. . . . Opposite is a large [Indigenous] Rancheria. . . . Extending for many miles up the river, on both sides, are the scathed trees of the burnt forest. The fire . . . was set by the Indians.

Outside the fort are the salmon houses, where, last year, 5,000 barrels of this fish were salted. The Indians do the fishing, and in other years, they gave 12 salmon for a dollar. . . . They get a dollar for a salmon now. Mr. Yale says he cannot afford to eat fresh salmon at that price.

On the water's edge above is a camp of miners. . . . We found them all in good spirits—singing songs, cooking bacon and flapjacks and coffee, and all eager to learn the news from up the river. They don't believe the reports of other people. . . . Not even the ragged, hungry appearance of the crowd from Thompson and La Fontaine afforded an argument to keep one man back.[53]

— • —

At the fort on September 24, Slocumb saw five steamers docked— *Active, Enterprise, Maria, Otter,* and *Umatilla.* They brought reliable reports about coarse gold mined around Fountain, as well as news of progress and setbacks on the road being built north of Harrison Lake to the Fraser at current Lillooet. Hordes of perplexed miners were waiting anxiously to go up river or were:

returning by the hundreds. What in the Hell can it all mean? Their tales perfectly agree in regard to the mines being a perfect Humbug. I consider myself, if Humbugged, the worst Humbugged man from the Land of Gold and Pine.

Exasperated by unceasing illnesses, Slocumb thought of returning cheaply overland to The Dalles on the Columbia River, drawn by the beacon of his *"Brothers & Sisters with happy smiling faces."* His playful lapse into Chinook jargon did not mask the pain:

Wake nika Kuway gold illeha halo Kultus chicamin Dollar. Boston man hias cultus gold illeha. Boston man hyack clatana frisco. Nika clatana nanish spose halo chicamin. Wake closy nika clatana frisco hiyu mamoke. [Not me (find in) all gold country absolutely no gold dollar. Americans (find) absolutely nothing (in) gold country. Americans fast return (to) Frisco. I go see if no gold. (If) no gold, I go Frisco (for) much work.][54]

The anxiety caused by waiting encouraged male aggression co-loured by taunts about nationality:

There was a Bloody mess between an American and a King George [Eng-lishman] *man at this place. The King George man said the American did not have the regular spunk and was not gentleman. Boston knocked him down & kicked him. King George man said "Damn your Bloody eyes. If you will come out I'll try you three Bloody rounds. Damn your Bloody eyes for I am a Bloody good Englishman."*

The word "bloody," slang for "very" and "detestable," was intended to give offence. "Spunk," meaning both "courage" and "semen," brought into question male virility.[55]

The Vigilance Committee exiles "*Ned McGowan and Carr arrived*" at Fort Langley on September 1, bringing the chicanery of "*near 20 Gamblers*" intent on swindling miners.[56] McGowan's notoriety and charm created opportunities. At the mines, McGowan did not lan-guish like Slocumb. A Nicaraguan colonel gave him a claim on New York Bar opposite Fort Yale. He and two companions "got fifty dol-lars worth of provisions on credit" and tools "from a disgusted miner for ten dollars." At the end of the first day, they "drank up a bottle of bad schnapps, for which we paid two dollars and a half, and had real-ized ten cents! I pitched the rocker, pick, and shovel, etc., into a deep canyon." Seeing that "there was money in the country," McGowan moved to Hill's Bar, joining a legislator, police chief, and liquor merchant from San Francisco. He remembered that:

After three days' sluicing, we panned out $1,598. We went along at this rate for five or six weeks, when the snows and heavy frosts came upon us, and we had to stop mining for three months. But we had lots of money, plenty of grub, a good cabin, and agreeable compan-ions.[57]

Surrounded by Americans, Slocumb fell in line with views that the Hudson's Bay Company:

> *are dead set against the country improving. . . . The Governor is an old fogy . . . says foreigners coming into this country and making war with the Indians are traitors to the country. The protection guaranteed by the mining tax is all humbug. There is not a Soldier in the mines, and the miners are doing their own fighting and doing it well.*

Captain Snyder's Pike Guards had just marched up the Fraser Canyon, pacifying hostile chiefs. Indigenous people were no longer the noble savages of Victoria or better than Port Townsend's whites. Possible threats had to be contained: "*The Indians here are peaceable, as the term goes, and are learning to have respect for the Boston man for Sunday kicks and licks over the head with revolvers. Civilises the red scoundrels wonderfully.*"

— • —

After six intolerable months, news finally came from the mines on September 20, as reported in the *Victoria Gazette*, that "the *majority* of the bars pay better as the river falls."[58] Slocumb had saved enough for the exorbitant $25 fare on the *Umatilla* to Fort Hope. He arrived after two days on September 28. The Hudson's Bay Company fort looked out from a raised bank at a sharp bend of the river, surrounded by mountains. In mid-July, the *Daily Alta California* printed that within a mile of the fort stood:

> 232 cabins, tents and camps, containing 973 men and 2 women—one unmarried; 1 eating house; 1 "hot coffee" sign; 1 gambling hall, where rum makes men garrulous, quarrelsome and brave; 2 cobblers; 2 small trading tents. There are also 127 boats and canoes lying on the river banks.[59]

A large throng of men were "waiting for the water to fall." Bedlam descended at night:

Engraving of Hope

Whisky is sold to the Indians . . . in large quantities. As soon as dark-ness sets in, the night is made hideous by their wild whoops; being mad by drink, they fight and halloo till morning. . . . In one night, there were no less than four distinct fights in gambling houses be-tween whites, each lasting for five or ten minutes—long enough at any rate, for a half dozen men to be badly whipped. It is a wonder that no one was shot, as every man is armed with a big knife and a Colt's revolver.[60]

Slocumb was equally dismayed: "*I found Fort Hope one of the damndest places I have seen. California in no time can come up to the crowd I see this evening at the Saloons. Tonight I returned to the Steamer and will lodge on Board until I leave. The place is too heavy for me,*" that is, too stress-ful, too dangerous.[61]

Between Fort Hope and Fort Yale, Slocumb anxiously ricocheted from one gravel mining bar to another. At least he had enough savvy to visit the best-paying ones—Texas, Emory's, and Puget Sound Bar, where he "*commenced work for friend Baxter at $5.00 for day's diggings. Weakened and commenced working for 2 shillings 0 pence. It won't pay.*"

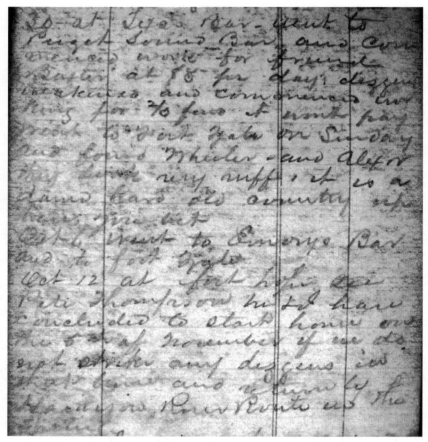

The diary page where George Slocumb realized on September 30
that two shillings would not cover daily expenses

Five dollars would cover the four dollar a day cost for grub, but two
shillings, or fifty cents, would not. Slocumb's *"clipper built"* frame and
depleted muscle left him too weak to dig gravel and toss rock.

At Fort Yale, Slocumb found friends *"look*[ing] *very rough. It is a
damn'd hard old country up here, you bet."* Back at Fort Hope, he and a
friend *"concluded to start home on the 5th of November if we do not strike
any diggins in that time, and return by Harrisons River Route in the
Spring."* On site, he had seen plenty of men making good money,

though he knew all too well that *"the high figures to be paid for Grub and the cold weather will be heavy on the uninitiated."* At Emory's Bar, an experienced Californian *"was putting on huge hills* [of gold]. *Supposed him to be the* Hias Tyee *of the Gold* Illihie," the "Big Chief" of the "Gold Country." The diarist lamented his own bad luck. For:

> *Yours Truly . . . "coming events, cast their shadows before."* Nika Hiyu chickamin hiass close Halo chickamin hias cultus—Nika Killipe California hiyu mamoke. Gold illihae. Wake Konsic clatana gold illiha California. [(For) me, much Gold (would be) very good. (But there is) no Gold, absolutely nothing. I return (to) California (for) much work (in its) Gold country. Never go to (Fraser) Gold country (from) California.][62]

Slocumb noted, miserably, *"At Puget Sound Bar have not succeeded in getting a claim. Chances decidedly against one, but think I may yet get my fins in, and make my pile."* If he had stashed away between $75 and $500, he could have bought a claim from a departing miner.[63] But he had:

> *not made more than $50 in the last six months, and should I have lived as I usually did in California I would have been broke months ago. A little money goes a great ways properly expended, and had I not met friends I should have more money. "Lord deliver me from my friends" is the prayer of the victimized.*

Hindsight proved a stark corrective to his misplaced generosity. At the end of his journal, Slocumb listed $40 of loans to others in the Pacific Northwest. Only $26 was repaid.

Swirling in the vortex of financial incapacity and no promise of work in either Fraser River country or California, Slocumb wrote the most touching passage in his journal:

> *News from California very discouraging. Reports say times were never as hard. I feel to be placed in a devil of a fix. Whether it is better to go back or nobly suffer in this cold inhospitable climate is a question that bothers me*

RETURNED FROM FRAZER RIVER.

Destitute miner

very much. One day I feel sure I shall start on Steamer day and today is
Steamer day and I am still here and am certain I shall start not today and
it may be so on the next Steamer day. I know not my intentions myself.
"There is a divinity that shapes our end,
Rough hew them as you will."

The quotation, meaning that some divine power guides us even when
we have bungled, comes from Hamlet's description of his "indiscre-
tion" and failed "deep plots."[64] Shakespeare's hero was tormented by
indecision, most notably in his hallmark speech, whose underlined
words Slocumb echoed in the passage quoted above:

To be, or not to be, that is the question.
Whether 'tis nobler in the mind to suffer
The slings and arrows of outrageous fortune,
Or to take arms against a sea of troubles,
And by opposing end them? To die, to sleep . . .[65]

On the Fraser, Slocumb was stifled by the impasse of constantly re-
peating indecision.

— • —

Three weeks of cold, torrential rain in November left him *"unwell for*
several days. . . . Here the climate is so inhospitable that man endangers
his health." Shortening days and the first snow forced Slocumb's *"de-*
parture for Frisco" on November 20. Two and a half weeks later, on
December 8, he reached San Francisco on the steamer *Pacific*. He
arrived *"with many misgivings. I do not know that I am superstitious,*
but I feel that I have acted very wrong in coming back to California.
Friends in time of need are scarce and I do not know that I have a right to
expect to find any." Back in Placer County, he actually *"found no*
Friends except twenty Dollars pieces. There is none other in this Section.
My surmises proved correct to a fault."

— • —

A mine tunnel in California

California miners gambling

Slocumb's journal for 1859 to 1863 documents typical troubles shared by thousands of gold seekers who missed one lucky strike after another in California and then adjacent Utah Territory. During those years, many became low-paid pawns of a capitalized industry as Slocumb did at the Comstock silver lode near Lake Tahoe: "*the capitalist reaps the reward in nine cases out of ten and the miner see himself 'froze out' for grub.*" With few social outlets and a life based on risk, he turned to gambling for release and hope: "*The fascination for gambling is so great with me that unless I keep away from the Halls I am sure to bet.*" He admitted that "*I have become so accustomed to excitements that no place lusts so well as a wild new country, and consider myself ruined for steady rational business pursuits in a civilized country and will still pioneer.*"

Even his love life suffered after a rejection by one of the few women available on the frontier: "*Should I ever get attach again, may the Crinoline be worthy of being loved and not be a strumpet, or fear my obituary. Well! And when will that be? Found Dead with Lady Luck, shot in the fracas.*" Still, he managed to step back from those dark thoughts and put his mortification to rest by striking out that passage.

The prodigal son returned to his family at Fairfield, Illinois, in time to celebrate his thirty-third birthday on September 7, 1863, and make the last journal entry. Back home he met eighteen-year-old Sarah, whose surname is unknown. She became pregnant, there was a shotgun marriage, and the couple fled to mining opportunities at Gold Run, Placer County, California.[66] There Slocumb finally realized his dream of a home where his six children were born. Around 1873 (aged forty-three) he relocated to rented accommodation in San Francisco, where he worked as a speculator and dealer in mining stocks. He was buried in San Francisco on March 28, 1890, at fifty-nine years, an advanced age according to a contemporary survey. He was survived by his children and widow.[67]

Photograph of diarist George Beam, ca. 1860

CHAPTER 6

George Beam, Entrepreneur and American Expansionist

∞

We see the stars and stripes up on the Frazier.

—*George Beam, letter of September 1, 1858*[1]

GEORGE BEAM WROTE his diary with pen in a large ledger at the end of every day.[2] His legible writing and immaculately clean book demonstrate his care over every small detail of his life. He is the only diarist whose work has previously been quoted by British Columbia historians, because of his patriotic glee that the Fraser River was definitely in American territory. Less predictably and even more important historically, his diary presents the most detailed account of mining practices to have survived from 1858.

George Wesley Beam was born in Sangamon County, Illinois, on October 22, 1831.[3] His father died on February 28, 1853, leaving a widow and son with few resources. She turned to her brother, Jacob Ebey, for help. He was considering leaving Illinois to join his son, Isaac Neff Ebey, who in 1850 had become the first permanent white settler on Whidbey Island in Puget Sound, Washington Territory. Isaac's 641.66-acre land claim looked over the ocean toward Port

Townsend, where he became collector of customs in 1853. The incentives for immigration were irresistible. Isaac had written home, "Whidbey's Island . . . is almost a paradise of nature. Good land for cultivation is abundant." In 1854, the U.S. government promised newcomers free land—160 acres for single men, plus 160 more if they had wives. What better relief could be found for the economic malaise affecting Midwest America? The Pacific Northwest was also free of the cholera that had claimed three of Jacob Ebey's children between 1849 and 1851.

From April 26 to October 12, 1854, Beam trekked across the continent with his uncle Jacob's family. Cousin Winfield Scott Ebey kept an informative journal along the way.[4] While travelling in the wagon train, Beam cut his name into a tree and cliff with Winfield, helped guard the animals, guided them across rivers, dealt with horse-stealing Pawnees, and saw the remains of whites massacred by Indigenous people who wanted no more intruders.

With his brother Isaac's help, Winfield became deputy collector of customs at Port Townsend. George Beam settled into farming on Protection Island in the Strait of Juan de Fuca, west of Port Townsend. He and the Ebey brothers prepared to fight during the 1855 "Indian War" but did not see active service. Puget Sound residents built blockhouses to defend against the greatest threat: constant raids by Indigenous warriors from Russian America.[5]

The event that shook Beam indelibly and permanently shaped his attitudes toward Indigenous people was the murder of Isaac Ebey on August 11, 1857.[6] In the previous November, Tlingit warriors from Sitka, around 1,200 kilometres (almost 800 miles) to the north, had raided Steilacoom to kidnap Indigenous people as slaves. During their repulse by the American navy, a chief was killed. The Tlingit returned the next year for revenge.

Whidbey Island was the first American landfall, since the British still controlled San Juan Island. Isaac Ebey's prairie provided easy access and swift escape. Once he was identified as an important figure, he was suitable compensation for the dead chief. When Isaac stepped outside on the night of August 11 to investigate a sound, he was shot dead and decapitated. The rest of the family and visitors escaped out a back window before the house was ransacked. After Isaac's scalped skull was displayed around the area, the Tlingits buried it on Smith Island, a small outcrop in Juan de Fuca Strait west of Whidbey Island.

Governor Douglas heard from Fort Simpson, where the scalp was shown off, that the perpetrators were "Russian Indians, and live at a place called 'Kooio,' a short distance from Sitka."[7] Douglas's intervention with Russian authorities led to the return of the scalp in 1860. The cost in trade was six blankets, a cotton handkerchief, a fathom (1.8 metres or 6 feet) of cotton, three pipes, and six heads of tobacco. The Ebey family buried the scalp with respect.[8]

— • —

A strapping six feet two inches, the twenty-seven-year-old Beam joined friends who adventured to the Fraser River from July 15 to November 18, 1858. Since March 5, Puget Sound newspapers had been reporting that "between Fort Hope and Thompson River . . . miners are getting out from $25 to $50 per day each" and proclaiming "GOLD DISCOVERIES CONFIRMED! RICH GOLD FINDINGS FOUND ON FRAZER'S AND THOMPSON'S RIVERS." The publisher of the *Puget Sound Herald* wrote that "in less than ninety days from the first publication of this news, ten thousand people gathered in Whatcom, several thousand found their way to the mines . . . [and] several townsite proprietors became insane through excitement."[9]

Winfield Ebey remained on Whidbey Island tending his ailing father, but his diary of 1858 records news he passed on to Beam. In March, a friend gave Winfield "glowing descriptions of the gold mines" and showed "$25 worth of Dust." That pioneer returned to the Fraser with his Métis paddling companion, taking "passengers at $20 per Head." Winfield had "no doubt there will be a rush." In April, "from 600 to 800 men are reported there & digging out an average of $15.00 per day. We are all getting the Fever." In early May,

Winfield continued, "George [Beam] & Mr. Engle purchased their 'Outfit' for the mines & expect to be O.p.h. [off] in about a week."[10]

Beam had never spent time in California but learned mining skills from twenty-six-year-old William Ballinger Engle and thirty-year-old Humphrey Hill, who had mined there. News of the swollen Fraser and the impassable Whatcom trail kept all at home for two months. Winfield Ebey noted that Hill showed Beam how to make "a 'Rocker' for his operation in the mines." Other Golden State veterans "returned from the Frazer River with plenty of gold" in June.[11] The *Victoria Gazette* of July 7 trumpeted the most profitable mining bars, which Beam explored when he reached the Fraser: Texas, Emory's, Hill's, Yale, and his ultimate choice, Puget Sound Bar.

Beam left much better prepared than George Slocumb. He and his experienced mining companions took four months' worth of affordable provisions from the coast. They also knew that either prompt action or cash was needed to stake a mining claim. On July 15, Beam, Engle, Hill, and long-time family friend John Crockett paddled north in a large canoe. Along the way they met other Puget Sound adventurers. Nothing equals the kaleidoscopic beauties of sky, rock, forest, water, and marine life there, but vigilance remained necessary. Winds can rise unpredictably. Strong opposing currents can make progress difficult to impossible. Pounding rain and whitecaps can capsize small boats. As the *Pioneer and Democrat* warned, the dangerous "Gulf of George [is] a wide sheet of water for small boats to

Indigenous canoe

venture on, as the winds have a fair sweep, and create a heavy sea. . . .
It cannot possibly be avoided."[12] More than once Beam's party wisely
stayed on shore for a day or two.

At the beginning of the trip, the group followed the "canoe passage" through inside waters between the islands and mainland. For
exposed stretches, they might have reinforced their canoes "with iron
bars passing on the inside from edge to edge . . . and 'slush boards,' at
least six inches high, on the sides" to prevent waves slopping in.[13]
Urban Hicks, whom Beam knew through the Ebeys, paddled with
three men from Olympia in a canoe which:

> was a splendid specimen of Indian architecture, twenty feet in length,
> made from a large cedar tree . . . and decorated with a long prow like
> a swan's neck, the edges of the prow studded with small marine
> shells . . . and gaily painted vermilion on the inside. It was well stan-
> chioned with ribs and thwarts and as tight as a drum. Four well made,
> light maple paddles and a large canvas sail constituted our propelling
> machinery.[14]

Beam's party stopped for a few days at Whatcom *"and looked at
the Fashions which improves the Place very much."* (*Italics indicate passages from Beam's diary*). Three thousand frustrated men were milling
around, patronizing the "hundred stores and trading establishments."
On July 18, the steamer *Sierra Nevada* was setting down hundreds
more eager passengers with the mining fever, and taking on the many
"badly busted and forlorn" men seen by Urban Hicks.[15] They expressed *"dissatisfaction . . . as regards the Mines and . . . are going back"*
to San Francisco.

Four other Whidbey Islanders joined the party at Bellingham Bay.
Charles Powell became Beam's most important mining partner. They
retreated from a *"wind which blew so hard that . . . we had to lay by all
day."* Beam stayed in camp with bloodthirsty *"Mosquitos."* Six of *"the
boys went down to Whatcom on a Spree,"* happy to throw off Whidbey
constrictions and relive rowdy California days in the throngs of the
young men there.

On July 22, a week away from Whidbey, the group pitched camp at Sandy Point, 20 kilometres (12 miles) north of Whatcom. Point Roberts beckoned, 48 kilometres (30 miles) and three more days distant on the horizon. On the sand spit, they met *"three other Canoes which makes our Company five Canoes and twenty Men, a Sufficient company for most any band of Indians if necessary to Pitch in,"* that is, fight back if attacked. Anxiety dogged Beam because of the murder of his cousin by Indigenous raiders. A rain storm forced a two-day layover in tents, south of Semiahmoo Spit (now Blaine, Washington). During this interlude, *"the boys [were] enjoying them Selves at a game of Poker and Seeing who Can growl the loudest."* When the weather cleared, they *"had a fine time in Crossing"* the exposed waters of Boundary Bay to the tip of Point Roberts. *"Our large Northern Canoe [was] loaded with John Cheerman,"* a phrase conveying the optimistic enthusiasm of new adventurers.[16] At *"Point Roberts City . . . Some of our Party done some trading"* at a Whatcom provisions outpost.[17]

The waters from Bellingham Bay north were filled with ships bearing passengers and cargo. Beam knew many of them by sight, from his vantage point on Protection Island and chats with customs collector Winfield Ebey. At Whatcom on July 18-19, Beam saw the California steamer *Sierra Nevada* and Puget Sound mail steamer *Constitution*. At Semiahmoo and Point Roberts on July 23-26, he caught sight of the U.S. survey brig *R.H. Fauntleroy*, the Puget Sound brig *Willimantic* delivering lumber for the new town, and the Puget Sound schooner *Rob Roy* on its way to Port Townsend with a deserter from the British navy steamer HMS *Plumper*, which was enforcing mining licences and ship tariffs at the mouth of the Fraser. The river steamer *Surprise* was towing the cargo-laden shallow-draught scow schooner *H.C. Page* to Fort Langley. The river steamer *Umatilla* was leaving on the first voyage to the head of Harrison Lake.

On July 26, eleven days out, Beam's group reached the mouth of the Fraser. It was an impressive *"half a mile Wide and larger"* with *"several outlets. . . . A great many Boats and Canoes [were] Passing up all the time and a good many Coming down the River. . . . It is the Worst place for Mosquitoes that I ever saw.*" Urban Hicks's party carried brushes "and at every stroke of the paddle brush[ed] the face and neck, and yet the blood trickled down each side of the neck from the ears and our faces were swollen from the bites." Indigenous people living along the river built platforms "about ten or twelve feet in height, where they lounged and slept, to get above the immense swarms of mosquitoes that rose from the surface of the water in clouds that fairly darkened the sun and stifled the breath."[18]

— • —

Beam's party had enough canoeing skills to slip through shallow canoe passages and evade the gunboat search at the mouth of the river. Beam defiantly refused to pay government fees during the entire trip. Urban Hicks also sneaked by and hired the son of an Indigenous chief to negotiate the currents, and "who was well known by all the Indians on the river, and his presence saved us from molestation and annoyance."[19]

It took the paddlers at least one unrecorded week to battle the strong river currents 160 kilometres (100 miles) up to Fort Hope. The *Sacramento Daily Union* reported that the July river was ice cold, "swift, tortuous and difficult of ascent," slowing even steam boats to "a mile in an hour, although puffing and wheezing and straining like an ever-driven, wind-broken horse."[20] Fort Langley offered a welcome break for a day or two.

Fort Hope contained "nearly 1,000 men lying idle, waiting for the waters to fall. . . . Trade was free, and there [were] a number of small stores in the village," according to the *Sacramento Daily Union*. Some merchants from nearby Puget Sound would have manned at least one of the new tent shops. Beam resumed his journal on August 5. He saw what everyone knew: "*the River is Still rising and very few Miners can work.*" Of the four to five thousand "men at and above Fort Hope—not more than one-half . . . are making 'grub' money."[21]

Between forts Hope and Yale, the *Daily Alta California* reported, one man "counted at the different bars on the river, 242 rockers and 8 sluices in operation," but not one man in ten was working.[22] Many "*discouraged*" miners were "*leaving and . . . selling off all that they have.*"

The swift current above Fort Hope impeded heavily laden canoes. The first stop was Puget Sound Bar, approximately a third of the way from Fort Hope to Fort Yale. The sweep of gravel was "large, and there are great numbers of men on it; a few of whom are working in the bank, under the great trees, and earning $2 to $4" per day, according to the *Daily Alta California*.[23] Beam felt comfortable there since it contained "*Mostly Men from the Sound, so it seems like home.*" Several "*from Seattle and from Steilacoom*" had given the place its name. His initial gold panning proved a disappointment: "*We went and Prospected some but found nothing to pay . . . but I think it will pay when the River falls.*" Was finding "*nothing*" caused by his inexperience, unable to see the fine flour gold? The only thing he could do was repeat what experienced men said: "*Miners say there is five hundred thousand Dollars in this Bar. I don't pretend to know anything about it.*"

A few days passed visiting Fort Yale, which boasted "two express offices, two doctors, one blacksmith shop, one gambling house and ten rum mills," according to the *Puget Sound Herald*.[24] Beam stopped at several mines, including Hill's Bar, Strawberry Island, and Victoria Bar. By August 9, the river fell enough for men to start working: "*They average four Dollars per day.*" Seeing returns that at least paid for food, Beam stopped searching and "*staked off a Claim on Puget Sound Bar*" on August 10.

While Beam rocked for gold, the name of the bar and familiar faces brought memories of home. So did the ever-present flag: "*We see the Stars and Stripes up on Frazier. . . . None never sees Johny Bull's flag. The Miners don't allow that.*" One "*old fellow up at Fort Yale hoisted the American Flag along side of the Fort and said the Man that took that down died.*"[25] Many Americans even assumed that the British northwest belonged to them. Beam was elated to hear that "*the Boundary Commission had said that the line between H.B. Ter. and the U. States*"

Run North of Fraziers River and gave us Fort Langley. You bet it done me some good."[26]

On the Fraser River, Beam's feelings about Indigenous people were impacted by the threat they had posed to Whidbey Islanders and the murder of his first cousin. On September 21, a boat capsized, "*and everything . . . went in the River. The Indian swam ashore with two sacks of Flour.*" Beam wrote no comment about how the Indigenous paddler saved a white man from drowning, only the self-interested note that "*I bought one barrel of Self-rising Flour at sixteen dollars,*" which he "*baked up*" that afternoon.

Beam was a safe distance from the Fraser River War during August. Even so, he heard unsettling second-hand reports. On August 15, "*the Indians up* [the Canyon] *is hostile and kill a greate many.*" He showed no awareness that Indigenous residents were defending threatened resources. A military veteran, Beam had supported the merciless U.S. army offensive in Washington. Why should things be any different on the Fraser? On August 17, Beam wrote:

Heard from Fort Yale today . . . [that] *three hundred marched up on Each Side of the River to the large Canyon and intends to kill all of the Indians they Can See and burn all of their Provisions and Property they Can find.*

More troubling intelligence came from the south on August 21: "*Down at Union Bar* [near Fort Hope] *they got five men out of the River that was Shot by the Indians. They had their heads Cut off.*" On August 26, "*Indians still hostile.*" Then suddenly, on August 28, the fighting was over: "*The Indians up Frazier River have made peace. Three of the Chiefs from Thompson River are at Yale and want Peace.*" Because mining could continue, Beam forgot about the conflict immediately.

Beam regretted that American responses were not monolithic. Most Washingtonians preferred killing Indigenous people, because they were still fighting for their land and their lives at home. By contrast, Californians had long since contained such threats, and some even saw two sides to the question:

Californians think and believe what ever the Indians say is all right. They think it is the Whites that is to blame and if an Indian yells at him he will run like the devil was after him and leave his Provisions and tools on the Bar. But Men from the Sound will go any where among them. They are not so brave when they find out that one is not afraid of them.[27]

Beam scorned Governor Douglas's ineffectiveness:

The Miners have sent Governor Douglass Some Strong talk about their protection from the Indians, but the Governor Can't do any thing. He has not the Power unless he will use his influence with the Indians.[28]

Nobody felt this dilemma more keenly than Douglas.

Apart from such excitements, simple pleasures gave relief from the gruelling physical labour. Once, *"Two women passed up to day. They look very fine you bet."* Another time he *"bought some potatoes,"* probably smuggled fresh from Washington Territory. Evenings were spent on whatever recreation the miners could provide for each other. One

Fort Yale, the most northerly post that many 1858 miners reached

time Beam and Powell went to hear Whidbey Islander Dr. Richard Lansdale *"play on the Violin and Sing."* Other nights he watched the boys play at euchre for a golden ring. On a more pious note, *"We had Preaching on the Bar to day and will have every Sunday so long as the Preacher remains on the Bar. The Minister belief is the Cumberland Presbyterian."* The Cumberlands emphasized revivalism over strict doctrine, sending preachers with little formal training to frontier areas.[29]

The chilly damp nights aggravated his arthritic joints: *"I have the Rheumatism very Bad. . . . I am quite lame to Night."*[30] California papers brought sorrowful news of the death of a friend, William Ferguson.[31] *"He was from the same place that I was and the Brightest young Man that I ever was acquainted with and would have been one of the Brightest Stars in the Nation, but* [for] *his untimely end by the hand of violence."* In Illinois, Ferguson was a presidential elector, then a state senator after he moved to California. The *Daily Alta California* reported how he died after a duel "growing out of some political controversy."

Letter writing brought on homesickness, particularly when folks back home balked at the dollar or two cost of sending replies. On August 20, Beam wrote to cousin Winfield, *"I can't do any thing, so I will scratch you a line. It is raining and has been very hard."* September 1 offered another *"opertunity of Sending you a line. I have not heard a word from the Sound Since I have bin up here."* October 8 found him even more despondent: *"I have wrote Several letters down but get no answers."* Despite the fact that he was working with long-time friends, he felt blue waiting almost three months for replies. On October 6 he finally *"received Some letters by Express, two from the States. I was greatly rejoiced to hear from My friends once More and hear that they are well."* Depressed by bad weather and isolation, on November 2 he finally *"received a letter from Whidby Island which gave me much pleasure for I had the horrors orfal."*

— • —

As summer passed into autumn, infrastructure on the river banks developed dramatically. Early on, miners lived in tents. On August 10,

Beam, Ben Powell, Charles Powell, and B.W. Johns "*Cleared away the Brush to set our Camp.*" Little time passed before Beam's party put to good use the building skills they had honed as pioneering settlers.[32] On August 27 they "*Commenced raising our house*" and finished framing it on August 30. On the last day of the month and then on September 2, Beam crossed the river for timber to make siding. He borrowed a saw and froe (a splitting tool) to fashion boards for the siding and floor, just like the Ebey houses on Whidbey Island. He and his companions bunked in on September 9 and started a chimney the next day. The rest of the flue and hearth waited for cooler weather on October 4. When A. Mickie arrived on October 4 "*with no provisions and . . . Strapt*" for cash, Beam and Charles Powell offered temporary accommodation. Mickie soon started building his own house, which was ready for occupation on November 7.

On September 24, Beam noted "*the Miners are building houses on the bar for the winter.*" The *Pioneer and Democrat* printed a letter predicting that "most of the 200 men now on the bar will remain during the winter . . . with comfortable cabins, provisions, etc."[33] By September 30 the number of "*Houses going up on the Bar*" was notable. Enough men were making money to support a small settlement on October 20 called "*Pike Town.*" The earliest establishments, probably in tents, were a "*Recorder's office*" to register and clarify claims, and an "*apothecary Shop.*" November 1 saw "*a grocery going up on the Bar,*" probably a small wooden building that could withstand winter cold.

Travel between Fort Hope and Fort Yale became much easier. The gruelling canoe trip was replaced by a road built by the unemployed. On September 16, Beam saw about "*twenty five mules and ten Men . . . formerly from California*" using the trail on the east bank of the river.

— • —

Beam's diary contains the most detailed day-to-day mining record of any 1858 document so far discovered. It contains a wealth of information about every aspect of placer mining that year, including descriptions of various mining methods, an unwitting account about the

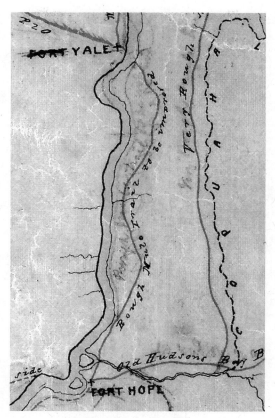

The 1858 road from Fort Hope to Fort Yale
on the east bank of the Fraser

dangers of working with mercury, a meticulous day-by-day schedule of work, a table of employees hired to maximize profits, notes about how weather affected the digging, arguments about water supplies, notes about the establishment and transfer of claims, an account of a drawn-out claim dispute, and an altercation with the government licencer.

Beam, his friends, and their hired hands were on Puget Sound Bar for ninety-seven days between August 11 and November 12.[34] They were able to mine on sixty-three days. On thirty-one days they had up to five hired hands. Mining ceased for thirty-four days. Miners

Table of work done by seven employees of George Beam from October 5 to November 11, 1858

generally followed the government stipulation that "Sundays [were] to be observed properly," which meant thirteen Sabbath breaks. Some miners spent the day away from slogging to separate their gold from mercury amalgam through retort boiling. Rising river levels prevented work on nine days, but Beam was lucky to have a claim that could be worked on high banks when others were flooded out. Heavy rain forced everybody inside for eight complete days. On October 19, *The River raised very fast in the evening So that Some of the Miners on the bar . . . Feared that the water would Come over and damage them.*"

The necessity of building a house (from August 27 to September 10) and digging drainage ditches diverted some of the men from rocking and panning. The commotion caused by the visit of the gold licence commissioner on September 28 meant a few hours lost. Two full days vanished with imperatives: registering claims plus a miners' meeting about disputed claims on August 12 and Charles Powell's trip to Fort Yale in search of news about the Fraser River War on August 18.

September 25 was spent negotiating a separation from Ben Powell and having a lawyer draft "Articles of Agreement between G. Beam & C.E. Powell, Co-partnership," signed on September 25, 1858. This invaluable document outlines the expected equal sharing of assets, expenses, and profits, but also shows the legal formality of some mining associations. Under the contract (Beam and Powell, 1858c):

> Each agree to furnish what amount of provision, mining tools, camp equipments, etc. etc. that each at present own, together with the following [three] described claims on said Puget Sound Bar. . . . Said partnership to continue to an indefinite period and not to be dissolved except by consent of both parties, and the said parties agree and bind themselves to divide equally and fairly all the profits of said partnership and pay equally the expenses of said partnership, and that each will devote his time and talents for the interest of each.

Summer began with almost all miners using rockers. On September 15, there were "more than 800 rockers . . . doing tolerably well—

The end of the partnership agreement between George Beam
and Charles E. Powell, September 25, 1858

some few, first-rate" on the Fraser according to the *Victoria Gazette.*[35]
When mercury became available in June, men seized on it to save the
fine gold that was slipping away. Beam's party's experiments with
quicksilver and their illness caused by poor handling of the material
are detailed in Chapter 3. Production increased dramatically once
water wheels and sluices came into operation, as explained in Chapter 3.

As the number of miners increased, water supply and drainage required more effort and led to disputes. On Puget Sound Bar, *"Some of
the Miners have no water and Some have too Much."* Beam noted the
digging of several ditches, some to bring water to claims, others to
drain it away from the rockers. Constant maintenance was required
as water was diverted by other claims or outflow created erosion.
Beam and his colleagues were lucky to have a *"Spring below"* that

could be relied on. Even so, on September 28 they found themselves *"Scarce of water owing to the Miners on the head of the Bar opening a ditch above."* They had to dig another channel to service their claim. When Beam had up to three cradles operated by seven men, drainage became a grave problem: *"Powell dug a ditch for the water to run from the Rockers in to the main ditch. Graham has got so potgutted that he won't let it run by him."* The runoff created potholes down the slope and washed away Graham's paying dirt before it could be panned. A different exit ditch had to be dug.

Beam used his pan for prospecting expeditions as well as *"panning out."* Most Puget Sound boys brought rockers, using timber along the river for repairs and new cradles. By October 4, Beam and Powell had made enough money to hire a *"strong Man . . . to wash for us"* and clear away the mounds of rocky tailings so that all areas of the claims could be worked efficiently. That hired man proved so helpful that three more hands were engaged from October 11, four from October 13, then five from November 2 until Beam left for the coast on November 11. With that assistance, two or three rockers operated per day, and debris was removed promptly. Another advantage was that each new partner could hold an additional claim, pushing the joint holdings up to five claims.[36]

Beam almost never specifies the wages paid. In his letter of September 1, he comments on the desperate condition of many unsuccessful men: *"hundreds have just enough to get here with, and they can't get away and they have to dig it to get grub at one to two Dollars per day."* He may have had a pang watching *"men passing up and down every day wanting work, but all can't get it."* On the same bar, George Slocumb worked at heavy lifting for a short time for $5 dollars a day, but had to drop back to 50¢ for the less strenuous tasks he could actually perform. Other claim owners paid between $4 and $8 a day. On September 20, Beam hired *"one Chineyman"* for a day, who settled for the racist discount of *"three and a half Dollars."* Probably the repeated fours and fives in a table listing Beam's hired men refers to their daily wages in dollars.[37]

Disputes over mining claims could lead to fisticuffs

On October 30, Beam and his companions *"moved the Rockers back on our upper Claim and brought the water up from the Spring below."* They were taking advantage of both the government regulation that "Mining claims have twenty five feet front" and the local custom that claims extended "back into the hills indefinitely."[38] On Puget Sound Bar, claims were numbered in sequence up stream or down stream from a centre stake.[39] Because there were so few British licence regulators on the river, miners took charge of registering and regulating claims. Shortly after staking their claims, Beam and Ben Powell *"Went and had our Claims Recorded." "The Recorder Charges fifty Cents for Recording."* The official recorder, called an alcaide,[40] was selected by the miners: *"Mr. Todd leaving, we elected another Recorder of Claims and U.E. Hicks of Washington Territory was chosen and Elected."* Hicks won the miners' confidence because a friend pointed out that he had served as auditor of Thurston County on south Puget Sound and as a member of the first Washington Territorial Assembly in 1853.

If a man left a claim temporarily, he could return and find it occupied by somebody else: *"Some Miners jumped another Claim and they had a Miners Meeting and the Claim was given to the first Claimant."* On other occasions, miners found themselves in a tug-of-war.[41] Miners' meetings were then called to present arguments on both sides and to decide through democratic vote. Beam found *"Our Claim in dispute between two Men. The one first Claiming held it had a Claim giving to us in the Middle of the Bar and will Commence work tomorrow."* Though the wording is contorted, the decision favoured Beam and he started mining. However, the original litigant would not let go:

> *My opponent Called another Miners Meeting and after discussing Parliamentary Rules some time we got to business, but I beat him in every point two to one and the last Meeting was Recinded null and void and tried the Case over. . . . The Claim was awarded to Me . . .* [with] *Greate rejoising.*

Unfortunately, even that second vote dissatisfied some:

> *There is a greate deal of hard feelings on the part of the California Miners and the Puget Sound Boys every Since I had trouble with one about a Claim. The Puget Sound Boys decided in My favor.*

Early arrivals may have staked an unreasonable number of claims that got jumped.[42] At an August 26 meeting, the Puget Sound *"Miners passed a law that Miners Could hold one Claim by location and one by purchase or gift."* The opaque wording seems to mean that one claim could be made on previously unoccupied ground, while a second claim could either be purchased from or given by somebody else. This decision led to a scramble on the bar. One transaction sounds like a legal fiction: Charles "*Powell had his Claim transferred from Daniels to him, one by gift.*" Hicks juggled imaginatively to get enough land for wheels and sluices at both ends of the bar: he "*bought a claim at the lower end of the Bar today and sold one and located another one at the up end of the Bar.*" Sometimes claims were sold for ready cash: "*Mr. Prouty gave B.W. Johns a bill of Sale of his Claim on Puget Sound Bar to day as he leaves tomorrow up the River.*" On other occasions, payments were deferred. Charles Powell sold a claim for $125, "*to be paid by . . . Hartsock & Co. out of the first money made by said Company out of any of said Company's Claims.*" Gallatin Hartsock was lucky: as Urban Hicks's father-in-law, he was known to Powell and Beam. When Puget Sound Bar occupants left for the coast, they sold their claims, on one occasion for just $75, "*very Cheap,*" but typically for $100, $125, $150, $200, $300, and as much as $500.[43]

Other factors changed conditions favourably or disastrously for miners. With the river at a level low enough to reconnoiter more of the bar, "*we measured our Claims on the head of the bar and they Came farther down stream than we thought we would.*" That discovery might have pleased Beam, but it could have cut into areas that other miners considered theirs. As a result, a miners' meeting on September 10 appointed "*a Committee . . . to measure the Claims on the head of the Bar. There is a greate deal of dissatisfied with the way the Claims are situated.*"

Even more unsettling news came on September 14, as James Douglas passed through:

> The Governor was on the Bar today to see how the Miners was getting along. It is reported that the Miners Can't hold but one Claim. Some of the Miners are very dissatisfied. It may end in a fuss. I heard that there would be a Magistrate here tomorrow.

Earlier, miners had to relinquish all but two claims. They must have been furious when they learned that they could in future hold only one patch with 25-feet frontage on the river. In the rough and ready gold fields, a "fuss" was an angry dispute that could lead to drawn pistols, not just heated words. When the British gold licencer arrived on September 28 to collect the $5 monthly fee, he was greeted with hostility:

> *The English Commission for this district Came up today but the Miners did not untie to him. He claims to be sent by the home government but it was no go. The Miners did not know him and he Could not Come in. He told us that if we would not pay he would Sell our Claims, but we told him to send men to work them if they wanted to go up the flume, but he won't send them.*

"To go up the flume" means to be killed. One can only imagine several hundred American miners refusing payment, standing their ground under the Stars and Stripes and threatening the commissioner off their property. Perhaps at gunpoint.

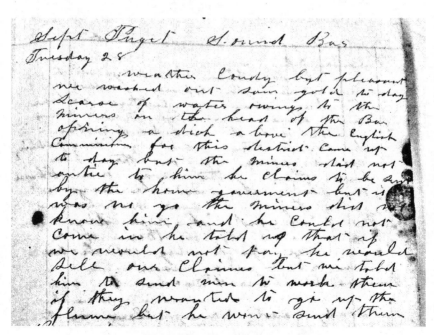

George Beam's diary for September 28, 1858

— • —

On November 11, Beam and his mining partner Charles Powell "*Sold our claims . . . for three hundred each.*" Two days later they "*Sold the most of our things*" so that they could travel light back to the coast. After overnighting on November 14 with a friend at Fort Hope, they pushed off down river by canoe at 8 a.m. Despite hard rain and strong wind, the current drove them to Fort Langley by 10 p.m. on November 15. It took a second day of hard tramping on the 16-mile waterlogged trail to Semiahmoo, where Beam "*Bought a pair of Boots for I was bare footed.*" At least that shortcut avoided a long paddle down the Fraser and over stormy November seas on the Strait of Georgia. With a light load and good tides, they arrived at Whatcom on November 18 at 8 p.m., "*and put up at the What Cheer house.*" At that point, the entries for 1858 end. With a handsome $1,000 profit, he returned to Whidbey Island, having sold his Protection Island claim.[44]

Beam's first cousin and future wife, fifteen-year-old Almira Neff Ebey Wright, had written him a letter on October 16, 1858, while he was mining on Puget Sound Bar.[45] It brims over with teenage melodrama and manipulation: "Excuse these blots caused by my tears." Convinced that he had blamed her for intentionally losing a letter, she prompted him to write an abject apology for berating her, "in a way suitable to my taste," to be signed "Yours affectionately & faithfully until death, George W. Beam." She pleaded with him to return to Puget Sound before meeting a dreadful end: "I bet if I was up there I would bring you down in a hurry."

Despite that outburst of temper, on January 2, 1859, twenty-eight-year-old Beam married Almira, twelve years his junior. He built a new house and cultivated uncle Jacob Ebey's farm with a mixture of crops and livestock. The couple had a son within a year, followed by two more children. Almira was not particularly happy. As the groom wrote on April 1, 1859, "*We are living in our new house. I am satisfied, but Mira is very much dissatisfied. She would to be with her Mother.*"

Beam sat in the Territorial Legislature from 1863 to 1864. He died of tuberculosis on May 5, 1866, aged only thirty-four years. He was buried in the Sunny Side Cemetery at Coupeville, Whidbey Island. Four years later, Almira moved to San Francisco with her children and remarried. Eventually she returned to Coupeville, where she died in 1909, aged sixty-seven years.[46]

Photograph of Otis Parsons

CHAPTER 7

Otis Parsons' Work on
the Harrison-Lillooet Trail

✍

No mules as yet.
We are all heartily sick of laying here.
—*Otis Parsons' diary, September 1, 1858*

OTIS PARSONS' DIARY was a small book known only from a mediocre microfilm at the British Columbia Archives.[1] When pages rubbed together in his pocket, the pencil smudged, making a few passages almost impossible to read. Parsons was one of the five hundred unemployed men who volunteered to build the road from Harrison Lake to Lillooet Lake, then on to Anderson Lake in August and September 1858. His diary is the only known continuous daily record of the few triumphs and many frustrations of the road builders. Constructing the Harrison-Lillooet route was the largest and most challenging that the colonial government tackled in 1858. To contextualize the diary, this chapter also presents the most extensive treatment of that project to date.

A number of contemporary sources provide a wealth of information. Governor Douglas's colonial correspondence was self-flattering

Alexander C. Anderson, explorer, map-maker, and
supervisor of the building of the Harrison-Lillooet route

at first, then impatient as problems compounded. The *Victoria Gazette*'s
on-the-spot accounts grew increasingly grim as time wore on. The
correspondents were William Wells, former city editor of San Francisco's *Daily Alta California*, Henry de Groot, formerly of the San
Francisco *Times*; at least one anonymous road cutter; and eventually
"A.B."[2] Joseph McKay sent such a problematic assessment of the
route on October 2, 1858, that Douglas commissioned three reports
by experienced surveyors in early 1859. Judge Matthew Begbie,
Naval Lieutenant Richard Mayne, and Royal Engineers Lieutenant
Henry Palmer filed three candid, often critical reviews.

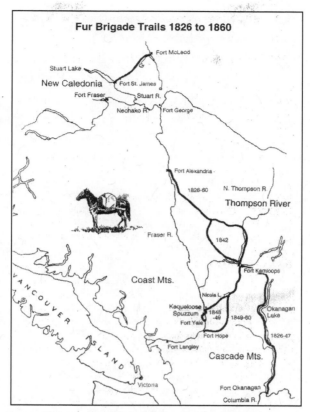

The Hudson's Bay Company brigade trails,
1826-1860

By July 1858, Governor Douglas had become increasingly troubled by reports of miners drowning in the turbulent Fraser Canyon and starving above Lytton. He hit on the clever strategy of developing the Indigenous trails linking the north end of Harrison Lake to Cayoosh on the Fraser River via the Lillooet River and several lakes. Alexander Anderson had surveyed that area and the wilder Fraser Canyon in 1846-1848 during a search for a Hudson's Bay Company supply route that lay entirely within British territory north of the forty-ninth parallel.[3] In 1858, the Harrison Lillooet route looked attractive because it had no life-threatening cliffs, could be completed

quickly, was assumed to be open year round, and ended with conven-
ient access to the Interior north, south and west of Cayoosh.[4] After
1862, the Harrison-Lillooet route fell into disuse because a new road
up the Fraser Canyon avoided seven cumbersome transfers from land
to water and back. All measurements in this chapter are given in
British feet and miles, as recorded in nineteenth-century sources.

- **1858 ROUTE DISTANCES TO CAYOOSH**[5]
  - Steamboat from Victoria to the north
    end of Harrison Lake — 175 miles
  - From Harrison River's mouth to
    Harrison Lake's north end — 35 miles
  - Trail on Lillooet River from Port Douglas
    to Lillooet Lake — 39 miles
  - Lillooet Lake crossing — 16 miles
  - Trail from Lillooet Lake up Gates River to
    Anderson Lake — 26 miles
  - Anderson Lake crossing — 13 miles
  - Trail from Anderson Lake to Seton Lake — 1.5 miles
  - Seton Lake crossing — 13 miles
  - Trail from Seton Lake to Fraser River at Cayoosh — 3.5 miles

- **1858 TOTAL DISTANCES**
  - Water distance across Lillooet, Anderson,
    and Seton Lakes — 42 miles
  - Land trail distance from Port Douglas to Cayoosh — 70 miles
  - Distance on both land and lakes from
    Port Douglas to Cayoosh — 112 miles
  - Undeveloped, dangerous land trail distance
    up the Fraser Canyon from Yale to Cayoosh — 92 miles

TABLE 4: 1858 LANDMARKS FROM PORT DOUGLAS TO CAYOOSH

PLACE NAME IN TEXT	CURRENT NAME OR LOCATION	PLACE NAME IN PARSONS' DIARY	PLACE NAME ON PALMER'S 1859 MAP, PLAN OF ROUTE
Port Douglas	Douglas	Aug. 8-9 "Port Douglas"	"Port Douglas"
Sevastopol	Steep ravine north-west of Douglas*		
Gibraltar Hill	Same ravine down to Lillooet River†		
Lillooet River	Lillooet River	"The river"	"Lillooet River"
4 Mile House	Lelachen Indian Reserve No. 6‡	Aug. 12 "moved to river"	"4 Mile House"
10 Mile House	At current Frank Creek opposite a steep cliff	Aug.16 "about 10 miles from" Port Douglas. There until Aug. 25.	"10 Mile House" opposite "Steep Cliff"
16 Mile House	At current Gowan Creek	Aug. 25-28 Back and forth move to 16 Mile House. There until Sept. 2.	"16 Mile House" on east bank of "Acchuchlah River"
Skookumchuck (Indigenous term meaning "powerful rapids")	About 2 miles north of 16 Mile	Aug. 28 (first version) "rapids . . . called the falls"	"Rapids"
20 Mile House / St. Agnes Well Hot Springs	Tsek		"St. Agnes Well"
29 Mile House	At southeast end of Tenas Lake, also called Little Lillooet Lake	Sept. 2 "Foot of lake about five miles from the Lillooet Lake"	"29 Mile House" southeast end of Tenas Lake
Cayoosh	Lillooet	Cayoosh	Cayoosh

*Reid 1942: 32 / †Syrette 2010: 11 / ‡administered by Xa'xtsa (Douglas First Nation)

On July 19, 1858, Governor Douglas addressed miners in Victoria, recommending the route "by Harrison's River . . . [as] the best, and we are now preparing to get a road opened that way; in fact I expect to see teams and wagons . . . [there] before many months are over."[6] The *Victoria Gazette* also trumpeted the path's virtues. The land route north of Harrison Lake followed Indigenous paths, so that "a good trail can be cut by a dozen men in a week." Between Lillooet Lake and Anderson Lake, "a foot trail already exists which is travelled every week by Indians and others, and horses have been once or twice across." The steamer *Umatilla* left Victoria on July 25 for Harrison Lake with eighty exploratory prospectors determined "to carry their provisions by hand-barrow across the" proposed route.[7] An Indigenous man named Shackles piloted the vessel up the lake.

A *Gazette* reporter noted that "All agreed upon one thing: that nowhere—not even in California—not even in the boasted Yosemite Valley—had they ever seen its equal for wildness and colossal magnitude."[8] The *Daily Alta California* ran an even more rapturous description:

The most splendid natural effects are to be witnessed here, changing and varying as you advance. Snow-capped pinnacles towering into the clouds, bald serrated ranges sharply defined against the blue sky for a background; great sugar-loaf peaks, showing beetling precipices that seem falling over upon you, as you hurry along under their vast shadows: cataracts issuing from the grey crevices of the rock, two thousand feet over your head, and splashing into the calm waters beneath; now preserving the appearance of silver threads glistening in the sunbeams, and anon whisked into variegated spray by some current of wind unfelt below, and wavering in mid air like a rainbow.[9]

Thick underbrush, lack of food, and poor gold prospects disappointed the first party. However, the reports from a second expedition solidified Douglas's resolve. He promised a speedy survey. Private contractors could then bid, "giving security for the faithful performance of their agreements." Douglas felt that "a road, practicable for

View of Harrison Lake

loaded wagons, could in a short time and at a moderate outlay be constructed . . . [for] say six thousand dollars."[10] That educated guess turned into wishful thinking.

At the end of July, unemployed miners, including "British subjects, Americans, French, Germans, Danes, Africans, and Chinese," approached the governor with a different plan "so advantageous for the country, that it would have been unwise of me [Douglas] to decline them."[11] Five hundred men would work "from four to six weeks—or longer if necessary" on an animal "pack-trail . . . sixty miles or less in length" from Harrison Lake to Lillooet Lake. A wider "wagon road . . . thirty miles in length" would connect Lillooet Lake and Anderson Lake. The government would supply all food and equipment, as well as "whip-saws, tools, nails, etc." to build bateaux for lake transport. Those vessels would "remain the property of the miners."[12] The models were Hudson's Bay Company boats that carried 3 tons of freight. Made of hard pine boards, they were 32 feet long and 6 feet wide (10 by 2 metres). They carried up to three tons of cargo and were paddled by eight men led by a "padroon." A Washington Territory

A Hudson's Bay Company bateau

pioneer found that one Hudson's Bay Company bateau could hold "five wagons taken to pieces, then all the baggage piled on them and the families on top."[13]

To join the road-building force, each worker had to deposit $25, which would later be traded for goods delivered to the road at Victoria prices. Everybody would receive free cartage to the upper Fraser River and first access to the opened roads.[14] Working with volunteers seemed perfect for the government's tiny budget. However, costs spiraled out of control and the government failed to meet its commitments while the project dragged on longer than anticipated. As Waddington observed, "Some got dispirited, left and sold out their tickets cheap.... The whole thing was unskillfully managed, and many of the miners who would have remained in the country returned home disheartened and discouraged."[15]

Initially, the bargain appealed to unemployed miners who were prevented from working by the Fraser River runoff. The full complement signed up on one day, August 3. Twenty companies of twenty-five were formed, each overseen by an elected captain who reported to a central administrator. Alexander Anderson, the colonial collector of customs, was chosen to oversee the work because he knew the country.[16] The first 250 volunteers left on August 5, their number limited by the small steamer *Otter*. At Point Roberts they transferred to the *Umatilla*, whose shallow draught could navigate the Harrison River. The remaining volunteers left Victoria on August 10 with the same transfer.

No single source describes the plan in detail. Still, by piecing together details from many sources it is possible to create a probable scenario.[17] A trail for laden mules accompanied by drivers required a path at least six feet wide. Single-file wagons needed ten feet for comfortable passage and sixteen feet for passing or two-way traffic. Bridges ranged from six to ten feet wide, but most were built at nine feet for wagon use. First-growth cedar, hemlock, fir, maple, alder, and birch had to be cut down with axes and whipsaws used by two people. Thousands of fresh trunks, a tangle of old deadfall, and underbrush had to be removed from the right of way. Stumps and large boulders had to be pried away. Unfortunately, only three jacks were sent for twenty companies. Picks and shovels produced crude grading; no machines were available to grind gravel. Log bridges crossed sixty-two gullies from twelve to a hundred feet across. Cut logs were laid down side by side for corduroy roads through wet areas. A wider wagon road up to sixteen feet wide was possible in the more open country between Lillooet Lake and Anderson Lake. Although gruelling, the work could be said to resemble placer mining with its removal of rocks and cutting of trees for sluice rights of way. The rhythms created within groups of twenty-five men lightened the burden, just as rockers and sluices needed congenial teams. Douglas and Anderson knew the terrain and its challenges well enough that their consignment of five hundred men seemed equal to the task.

— • —

Otis Parsons (1831-1875) left Litchfield, Connecticut, for California in 1849 or 1850.[18] By 1856 he was operating a stabling and merchandizing business on Don Pedro Bar, a rich gold town in Tuolumne County. It is a truism that merchants generally earned more money

A page from Otis Parsons' diary

than most miners. With business stagnant in California during 1858, Parsons decided to follow the thousands who needed supplies in Fraser River country. On July 2, he left San Francisco on the steamer *Orizaba*. The ship reached Esquimalt on July 8, overstuffed with an illegal load of 1,500 passengers. At Victoria, he pitched his *"tent and camped in the afternoon"* in a field outside town. (*Italics indicate passages from Parsons' diary.*) Not a word in his diary recounts his month there, but he would have met merchants he later collaborated with.

On August 3, Parsons leapt at the opportunity of joining the first *"250 men to cut a trail to Anderson Lake."* On August 5, the *Victoria Gazette* reported that "a salute was fired from the Fort" as the group *"left Victoria on H.B.Cº Steamer Otter"* at 7:30 p.m. to catch advantageous tides.[19] They arrived at Point Roberts around 2 a.m. Several passengers bought goods at the *"two or three houses"* built there. Twelve hours later they had transferred to the *Umatilla* and reached Fort Langley at 1 a.m. on August 6. Parsons saw the usual congestion of *"a great many miners. . . . Some bound up and others down."* They left the fort at 9 a.m. on August 7 "having two of the H.B.Co.'s barges in tow, taking with them some of the Co.'s Indians and men."[20] Parsons enjoyed the eight-hour passage up the Fraser, *"a most beautiful stream averaging about ½ mile wide with a current of from 3 to 6 miles per hour."* He found the Harrison River *"nothing more than a succession of small Mountain lakes varying from one to 2 miles wide. The scenery around is grand and imposing."*

After a night at Umatilla Cove on Harrison Lake, the steamer arrived at the north end of the lake in time for 9 a.m. breakfast on August 8. The group disembarked on "a narrow skirt of low land" in front of a thirty-foot-high "thickly timbered inclined plane," as described by the *Victoria Gazette*.[21] *"We are encamped on a beautiful grove of Spruce and Cedar which are fast falling before our axes."* The hot summer forests *"strongly reminds me of home, and I look forward with pleasure to the time when I shall be enabled to return to my dear friends to whom I have so long been a Stranger."* Others noted varied flora and fauna: fir, cypress, hemlock, pine, birch, maple, raspberry, blackberry, serviceberry, whortleberry, salal, California grape, bear, deer, squirrels, wild sheep, grouse, pigeons, salmon, and mountain trout.[22] Prospectors to the core, a few took out their pans every day but found only fine gold in quantities too small to work for profit.

Construction began immediately on a log "*Block House for our provisions.*" So many helped that the twenty- by thirty-foot structure was raised, floored, roofed, and filled with provisions the next day. A few tackled a wharf for steamers next.[23] On August 9, "*Most of people* [were] *employed on Road which was cut for four miles*" up a steep-walled valley from mile zero. After months of stultifying idleness, "*Everybody* [was] *in excellent Spirits on account of progress made.*" To celebrate, that "*Evening before Supper* [we] *held a meeting and named our camp Port Douglas in honor of Gov. of Vancouver Island. Three Cheers were given in honor of him and also for Collector Anderson who was present.*"

Two days passed with rain and moving tents "*about 1 mile on trail.*" That distance sounds trifling, but the land rose steeply from Port Douglas, gaining around 600 feet in just one mile, up an 11% grade. The road builders with heavy kits nicknamed it Sevastopol after the bloody Crimean siege of 1854-55.[24] The difficulty of moving camp should have warned the town-trained surveyors to choose less challenging grades. Little distance was added on August 11. Lieutenant Palmer condemned this section, because the trail "descend[ed] very precipitously by a zigzag path" at about 20% to the Lillooet River.[25] It became known as Gibraltar Hill. Concurrently, according to the *Victoria Gazette*, "two companies remained behind to bridge and finish up the trail which we traversed yesterday . . . [so that it more] resembles a wagon road than a trail for mules."[26] After four days' work, the "*road to the river*" had reached the spot where Four Mile House was erected for refreshment and overnighting. Work progressed so quickly that the surveyor amplified his staff with twelve more men.[27]

On the morning of August 12, camp "*moved to river which caused a good deal delay.*" Everyone communicating with the *Victoria Gazette* found the terrain arduous: "we packed . . . up and down some pretty 'tough' places, finding our loads as much as we could well stagger under, with occasional slides down hill."[28] Adding to the burdens, dismaying orders came "to remove the individual tools, cooking utensils, etc., that had been deposited for safety and general convenience in the log house at [Port Douglas] . . . until the Trail should be completed."[29] The space was needed for storing the workers' food. Just as victuals were running dangerously low, good news came in as the "*Umatilla arrived with 250 men, the balance of our party*."

Anderson returned to his customs duties in Victoria on the *Umatilla*. He was accompanied by Charles Bedford Young, the supervising surveyor who owned a wharf on Victoria Harbour, who reported that the road would be "easy to make."[30] G.B. Wright, who later operated a mule train out of Port Douglas, said that "about ten miles of the trail" to Lillooet Lake had been finished in a week. Based on those reports, Wright's estimate of completion in "four or five weeks" sounded reasonable. However, the distance actually finished was only four of thirty-nine miles. Wright warned that the goal of "four to six miles per day" depended on "full arrangements for transporting provisions." As of August 19, there was not "a sufficient number of pack mules."[31] Worse, once found in Victoria, the mules could not be carried on the *Umatilla*. Because the next update did not reach Victoria until two weeks later on August 27, the government blindly assumed the project was running smoothly.

On August 12, the first group "*extended trail about two miles through a level country.*" The next day repeated the same blazing and tiresome relocation: "*made about 3 miles Trail along the river. Moved camp.*" Each removal was increasingly exasperating, as the road cutters told a *Victoria Gazette* correspondent: "Whilst tramping along the tedious side hills of loose rocks the heat has been excessive, and the strongest men complained of the severity of this mulish labor."[32] When he traversed the route in 1859, Lieutenant Palmer found grades up to thirty degrees—"almost impracticable for waggons."[33]

Half of the company worked on road cutting, completing nine miles between August 8 and 13. A few took breaks for prospecting: "*Gold has been found in all the gulches about here.*" The next mile consumed three more days. Work stalled on August 14, because "*very few men at work on trail. Most of them gone to Port Douglas for provisions.*" The rest planned for Sunday, August 15 was broken by "*a good deal excitement in Camp in regard to a difficulty which happened between two*" men. This California ritual played out with an aggrieved party shouting "Defend yourself!" to somebody who had to grab his gun quickly before the shooting began.

On August 16, the full contingent finally "*extended trail to about 10 miles from camp.*" The next day, "*Mountain trout was caught . . . in the small creeks.*" The site was Ten Mile House, south of Frank Creek and another small stream. Petrifying resignation set in: "*We are now so far from our depot that to go farther is impossible until the arrival of mules to pack our provisions. All are regretting the delay but it is unavoidable.*" Day after day, most "*laid in Camp, nothing doing.*" The anticipation of "*expecting mules every day*" ended in continual disappointment. The contingent remained there for nine more days, until August 25.

Fortunately, fifteen days of rations were sent from Victoria on August 14 via *Otter* with a transfer to *Umatilla* at Point Roberts. Because of low water, passengers and cargo had to be dropped at the mouth of the Harrison River, to be taken by canoe to Port Douglas at further expense and delay. The provisions consisted of 7,620 pounds of flour, 7,620 pounds of beans, 5,716 pounds of salt pork, 119 pounds of tea, 238 pounds of coffee, 952.5 pounds of sugar, 952.5 pounds of rice, and 3,810 pounds of onions. The food would have cost at least $2,600, plus over $1,687.50 in shipping charges on thirteen and a half tons, for a total of $4,287.50.[34] Since road building took another four weeks (from August 29 to September 28), two more shipments of food would be needed, not counting the supplies promised after the road was done. Douglas's guess of $6,000 for the entire project was already shattered.

On August 17, an advance party was sent upstream to build Sixteen Mile House at the Acchuchelah River, now Gowan Creek: "*Some few* [built] *a house for provisions about 15 miles from Port D——.*" A few men set to work "bridging two or three small streams . . . and building the half-way house," as recounted in the *Victoria Gazette*. Lacking mules, food suppliers decided to try the river: "We received a canoe-load—about a ton—of provisions a day or two ago, and this morning we learned that a similar cargo . . . was swamped, involving a total loss."[35]

Most remained at Ten Mile looking for distractions to break the tedium. Parsons *"sent letter to Bn. Everett"* on August 18. To their peril, some took to the water on August 20, tired of stones piercing their boots: *"Several boats upset in river and a number drowned."* Others found the land just as dangerous on August 22: *"Several men passed down the trail this morning having lost one of their members and all their provisions etc. in trying to ascend the m[ountain]."*

Suddenly on August 21, there were *"plenty of Indians in Camp."* The next day, the *Umatilla* arrived from Fort Hope with *"no news of mules"* but *"news of a severe fight between the Whites and Indians on Frazer River."* Reports of the Fraser River War spread quickly. Optimism tempered Parsons' unease: *"We do not anticipate any trouble on this route, but there is no trusting them."* As will be seen, Indigenous warriors on the Lillooet River turned to armed resistance at the end of September.

A week crept by as many men slogged provisions from Port Douglas. The planned move of camp on August 23 was halted because rain soaked everything, and *"Mr. Blessing from Wisconsin dropped dead on the trail. He was alone but no marks of violence being found, the conclusion was he died in a fit. This melancholy event has caused a deep feeling throughout the camp. He was buried this afternoon."*[36] So many back-and-forth trips were necessary to lug everything from Ten Mile House to Sixteen Mile from August 25 to 28 that Parsons became confused and decided to rewrite two pages of his account.

Discouragingly, on August 26 *"Part of our Company was sent back to Port D. to erect another House for provisions. . . . Our company not being all here we are obliged to make two trips which makes it very tedious."* On August 28, the corps finally reached the place *"where we shall probably Stay until the balance of our Company comes up."* Two weeks had elapsed with little road work. Supervisors noted the general exhaustion and declining morale. At that point, "half or two-thirds of the way to [Lillooet] Lake, . . . a large portion of us have received orders to remain encamped until we are furnished with mules to transport the grub."[37] That encampment would become Sixteen Mile House. An advance party had already started to build "*Block House no. 2*" there on August 17.

Two miles upstream from the camp was:

> *a Succession of rapids in the river which are called the falls. It is a great resort for Indians, it being one of their Salmon Fisheries. Numbers are here encamped on both sides of the river. These Indians have been visited by R.C. priests and make the Sign of the Cross with as much solemnity as anyone.*

Roman Catholic Oblates of Mary Immaculate had a mission there near the Skatin Indigenous settlement at Skookumchuck ("strong water") Rapids.[38] Supplementary food was now plentiful. On August 29, Parsons:

> *took a loaf of bread and went to Indian Camp and procured for it two fine Salmon. This being their principal food they would not sell them for any money but readily barter them for food or clothing. I do not know which was most gratified, myself to get the Fish or they to get the bread.*

The next day, he wandered over the broad plain and "*spent most of my time in gathering berries and Hazel nuts which are very plenty here. In prospecting the bank of the river, gold was found in Small quantities.*"

For most, lethargy sapped any sense of purpose. On August 31, Parsons:

> *Laid in Camp all day. Amused myself as usual, but time passes Slowly as we are all anxious to get ahead. Sept 1st. No mules as yet. We are all heartily Sick of laying here. Today our rations ran out and we Shall be obliged to go back for more in a day or two.*

Parsons perked up, because surveyors returned from upcountry *"and want me to go. I shall jump at any thing."* On September 2, Parsons left *"with Surveyors. Travelled 14 Miles and camped at the foot of Lake* [Tenas] *about five miles from the Lillooet"* Lake.[39] There Twenty-Nine Mile House was soon built on a rare patch of fertile ground owned by the Samahquam First Nation.

The advance party spent two days *"trying to get provisions to last us across the Lake"* in a sturdy London Patent Life Boat commandeered from miners without compensation.[40] The best news on September 4 concerned *"the arrival of 35 mules at Port D. The trail will now be put through without doubt."* Four days later, it was clear that the mules available could "only transport provisions for about one half of the Brigade" building the road, and that "250 mules will be required to enable the 500 men to reach Frazer river with their necessary provisions," as promised in the original contract. A petition explaining the hardship was sent to Governor Douglas in Victoria.[41]

The petition would have reached officials in Victoria who were just as frustrated. They had been working constantly to secure enough mules, but every initiative was impeded by scarce supply, high prices, and unreliable transport. On September 16-17, Vancouver Island customs paid an outrageous $3,075 for just four mules (at $200 each), ten horses (at $100 each), and seven wagons (from $100 to $275 each) "for Harrison River road."[42] Those payments were competitive with published costs on Puget Sound.[43] At those rates, 250 mules would have cost an impossible $50,000. The small number that had actually been obtained left Victoria on September 16 via the steamer *Otter*, which transferred them to the river steamer *Maria* at Fort Langley on September 18. Its draught was shallow enough that it had been able to navigate the Harrison River during the summer. Unfortunately, water levels there had fallen and *Maria* was grounded on September 21. It was back at Fort Langley on September 24, but it is not known whether the animals reached Port Douglas before or after *Maria* was out of service.

Parsons and company avoided a swampy slog along sheer cliffs by paddling up Tenas Lake and the river with a *"very Strong Current"* leading to Lillooet Lake. *"We came very near losing one of our party, Mr. Conant, by drownding. . . . We managed to get a Pole to him and he was Saved."* Strong convection winds complicate afternoon boating on B.C.'s narrow lakes.[44] The party with Parsons and Superintendent Adams left anyway, arriving at the head of Lillooet Lake in the dark, *"about 10 o-clock at night, and Camped."*

At around 6:30 a.m. on September 7, *"at daylight we were on our way up the river to where the portage commences."* They passed the Lil'wat First Nation on the way to an ancient trail up the Scaalux River, renamed the "Mosquito" by miners, then the Gates.[45] Three men hiked seven miles, but were unable *"to over take a Mr. Young, who had come up from Victoria."* Charles Young arrived at Tenas Lake on September 4, "followed by . . . five mules laden with provisions, and the glad tidings that thirty more pack animals were at Port Douglas."[46] September 8 was spent on *"a long pull against a head wind"* down Lillooet Lake to bring the rest of the road cutters north to *"a Small Island."* On September 9, they *"commenced Cutting logs for House"* that would become Port Pemberton, perched inappropriately on an easily flooded minuscule strip of land underneath high cliffs. A number of men started *"to explore a trail from this point to the portage trail."* After two days, *"blazing"* began, which took from September 12 to 19. From then on, the party *"Camped . . . on portage trail."* Parson's account of the road building ends abruptly. With a secure food supply, the crew easily converted the existing trail to a mule path. Vigorous physical labour replaced Parsons' idle days scribbling notes.

— • —

The *Victoria Gazette* detailed the rest of the year's complications that are found in the next sections. Weeks of frustration erupted into mutiny after Charles Young appeared on September 4 with fresh government directives. A no-nonsense businessman who had built a wharf in Victoria, he expected orders to be executed immediately without question. His officiousness evoked sarcasm as he was seen "flitting from point to point along [the trail], issuing prohibitory orders, making [Indigenous] reservations, surveying towns, and indulging big ideas generally [about] a new El Dorado . . . and that this is the thoroughfare . . . along which a magnificent chain of cities is to be erected."[47] Ineffectual Superintendent Adams had already become "generally and publicly reviled for the *fix* in which we are all placed." Port Lillooet, at the south end of Lillooet Lake, had been nicknamed "Adams' Hole, in honor of that worthy individual, on whom has been heaped [the most] bitter and contemptuous language" imaginable.[48]

Three hundred workers moved across Lillooet Lake to the next trail. Immediately a quarter of them were detailed to packing supplies more than twenty miles. They revolted against being "made pack animals" once again. Concerned about food, "the Chinese Company . . . are continuing to ferry provisions across Lillooet Lake, despite all efforts on the part of our Superintendent to displace them."[49]

Conflicting instructions worsened the nightmare. Adams "inform[ed] us that a *wagon road* was under the circumstances, absolutely impracticable."[50] Commissary General RWD Bryant, highly esteemed by everybody, intervened "to induce them to make the road suitable for wagons . . . with but little extra labor," but the workers ignored his request.[51] Insubordination increased as "the track marked by surveyor Young" was abandoned in favour of "the 'blazes' made by a party under Mr. French on the *opposite* bank of the stream."[52] All agreed that was "the most eligible ground."[53] On September 28, the trail was "completed to Anderson's Lake. The boats will be done in three days more, and then the route may be considered opened."[54] Nobody was in a mood to celebrate.

— • —

The aggression of whites in Washington Territory and north of the border, as well as Captain Snyder's forced treaties, showed Indigenous residents along Lillooet River what would happen to their settlements, mines, fish, and crops as they were pushed aside. The new road promised a flood of white adventurers, and some of the best land along the Lillooet River had been confiscated for road houses. At the end of September, the workers were obviously vulnerable because of poor morale and disorganization. At that point, Indigenous people did everything they could to reverse the invasion. The *Victoria Gazette* reported how some whites were halted "by an armed party of Indians, who were only prevented from firing . . . by the timely display of revolvers." On another occasion, "two bateaux which left [Port Douglas] with supplies for the road-cutters, were stopped by the Indians when about fifteen miles up the Lillooet River, who refused to let them proceed." Elsewhere, "a young man while packing a heavy load over the trail beyond the Lillooet Lake, was attacked by an Indian," who stabbed him five times. The youth responded with three fatal shots. "An old man . . . was robbed of ten dollars [with] a knife to his breast."[55] Once the road cutters dispersed, Indigenous residents understandably attacked travellers on the new road north of Port Douglas so aggressively that residents sent a petition to the governor in November begging for relief.[56] Accounts by whites accepted no responsibility, but saw the increasing confrontations as unmotivated: the "Indians are . . . in a bad mood."[57]

The early packers wondered what to do about the narrow road. On September 7, the *Victoria Gazette* had encouraged "parties having animals, to get them in readiness . . . as their services will no doubt be in demand at highly remunerative prices." By September 23, wagon drivers at Port Douglas were "much perplexed as to their future movements." Some owners decided to send their disassembled "wagons up the Lillooet river by canoes and pack their animals over the trail, and try and induce the men to make the road fit for wagons." Another man had his wagon "fitted with short axletrees, and the mules harnessed *tandum*." Others debated whether to stay or return to Fort Langley or Victoria.[58]

Most of the road workers had determined to explore "the entire country above, even though it involve . . . six months time, and lead them hundreds of miles," as the *Victoria Gazette* noted.[59] The earliest arrivals could choose the most promising claims. Those who came later had to manage with poor prospects or nothing. Every miner knew that timing meant the difference between boom and bust. The government had been fulfilling its promise to supply them with goods at Victoria prices by laying in "fifty or sixty tons, consisting mostly of flour and beans" at Port Douglas.[60] Would the men also have been expecting salt pork and coffee?

Then shocking news arrived. Young made everyone at Anderson Lake "highly indignant" when he announced that the supplies would not be delivered there. Everyone had to return to Port Douglas for them. Young had little choice, because too few mules were available for packing up the trail. Nevertheless, the men were greatly "dissatisfied at being . . . compelled to walk back a distance of seventy-five miles; the same to be retraced after a few weeks, when they are already so near the place of their destination."[61] Even worse, Young announced that the workers would get an allowance of just 4¢ for cartage when packers were charging 20¢ per pound to carry goods from Port Douglas to Cayoosh. Many simply "abandoned the idea of going to the mines" and accepted Young's offer to have their $25 pledge "refunded them, and their passage paid" to Victoria.[62] Because the contract had been violated so many ways, the road builders sent a deputy with a nine-page petition of grievances for Governor Douglas on October 18, complaining about Young's "contradictory and unsatisfactory reports and propositions . . . as well as his haughty and insulting manner of treatment both towards the Officers and Men of this Brigade."[63]

On October 26, Douglas swiftly intervened. Decades of wilderness experience with Hudson's Bay Company privations sensitized him to a genuine grievance. With typical fairness in a crisis, he offered cartage to the miners at 18¢ per pound and contracted with "competent parties to pack at that rate." As colonial administrator, though, he was faced with endless, spiralling costs. At the beginning of November, a cap had to be set. Each miner was offered a final "sum of $36.18 each, in lieu of transporting their provisions to the

Upper Fraser." That was the reported cost, and it released the government from further obligation. Because this sum "was not provided for in the original agreement," the editors of the *Victoria Gazette* commended Douglas's "praiseworthy liberality."[64]

Too few animals were available. Packers started charging 26¢ for private contracts and ignored the road cutters. Rates went even higher when barley and hay for mules had to be brought in at 17¢ a pound for Port Douglas and twice that for Port Pemberton. The fare for boat passage on the lakes was also high—$6 total for all three lakes, plus another 10¢ or so per pound for cargo. Protesting the high costs, the road builders blocked the trail in late November, but the governor censured them on November 30. His resources and patience had run out.[65]

Those who persevered to the Upper Fraser found none of the promised goods there. Near Bridge River, thirty-six miners petitioned the governor on October 21 that seven hundred to eight hundred local miners would "soon be destitute of the necessaries of life, and would most respectfully request . . . measures for our immediate relief." Cold and high prices drove many back to the coast, leaving only "five or six hundred" miners overwintering north of Lytton.[66] Lack of good shelter, scurvy, and starvation led to many deaths.

The first season of the Harrison-Lillooet road cutting was imperfect, but its scale provided an invaluable learning experience for future projects. By August 3, steamers supplied Harrison Lake regularly.[67] At the beginning of September, Joseph McKay, the governor's first reporter, rode a mule from Port Douglas to Lillooet Lake in just two days. Primitive way houses built by the road cutters stood along the Lillooet River at four, ten, sixteen, twenty, and twenty-nine miles, at Port Pemberton, and half way up the trail to the west end of Lake Anderson. Way houses on the shores of Anderson and Seton Lakes were left to private enterprise.

In October, a few men built bateaux, which were paddled across Lillooet, Anderson, and Seton Lakes. The Canadian miner took them on his return to Victoria. Depending on winds, crossings took from four to eight hours, though poor weather or heavy traffic could delay people for days.[68] American entrepreneur W.A. Dozier spent $180 on a mile-and-a-half road from Anderson Lake to Seton Lake. He charged a half-cent per pound toll for freight hauled in his wagon. He also bridged Seton River with a sixty-foot toll span.[69] From nearby Cayoosh on the Fraser River trails fanned out north, east, and south to every part of the Interior.

— • —

Work on the Harrison-Lillooet route continued until 1862. Its impact was so strategic that a brief account is worth providing here. Back in 1858, the challenges pushed Douglas further than he could ever have imagined when he thought that the road along the Lillooet River could be completed quickly for around $6,000. Even with volunteers, the tally for the first season rose to a staggering £14,000 ($70,000) or higher.[70] Worse, news soon arrived about the route's serious deficiencies. In early September 1858, Douglas's envoy Joseph McKay found that "The bridges . . . are in general too low, most of them will be swept away during the next freshets" of spring runoff from melting snow. Toward autumn, water fell so low that steamers could not pass over a shoal on the Harrison River or reach Port Douglas.[71] To his credit, Douglas pressed on.

Decades with the Hudson's Bay Company and his stint as governor of Vancouver Island had taught Douglas strategies of formulating plans for infrastructure, the necessity for on-site reports, the challenges of working on tight budgets, the inconvenience caused by hostile points of view, and the politics of communicating with superiors. Prioritizing work for 1859 required reliable information gathered from reports requested from Judge Begbie, Lieutenant Mayne, and Lieutenant Palmer. They recommended removing the shoals on the Harrison River to ensure year-round access to Harrison Lake. All condemned the site of Port Douglas, which was inaccessible by steamer because of low water for almost half the year and prone to flooding the rest. Begbie noted that paths built on dry creek beds during autumn were inundated in spring: "The whole locality should be carefully surveyed before the floods, and then again when they are at their height."[72] Palmer's assessment was chilling:

The bridges and corduroys are indifferent, and the road stony throughout, and in many places swampy for the want of small culverts and drains. . . . The present trail rises in several places over spurs in the hill at grades impassable for any animals but mules, and barely so for them.[73]

In July 1859, a hundred Royal Engineers started improving the road along the Harrison River. That late beginning was interrupted when the Pig War on San Juan Island took most of the soldiers away to protect British interests against interloping American settlers. The few remaining workers completed only seven miles.[74] A year had been lost.

A plea to the Colonial Office for a gift or loan of £200,000 was refused. Even £30,000 was rebuffed with the insistence that public works had to be paid out of local revenue. Douglas used customs revenues, liquor taxes, and mining licences to pay the first year's bills. Merchants at Port Douglas raised $300 in cash and promised an additional "10 percent on the value of their property." Much larger sums were later raised through additional taxes and bonds.[75]

With a stunning conflict of interest, Judge Begbie had his brother in London propose a toll road for which he would hold the monopoly. The British Colonial minister, the Duke of Newcastle, refused to "sanction . . . a monopoly of a road—a monstrous proposal in such a Country!" In a despatch to the Colonial Office, Douglas debunked the proposition of a toll road. He pointed out that a mule trail was already in use and was being expanded into a wagon road. A monopoly would add an unacceptable additional fee, leading to "a transport charge of Fifty Dollars a ton on all goods carried from Douglas to Cayoosh."[76]

Persistence garnered rewards in 1860. Douglas reported to the

Colonial Office how, in March, Captain John Marshall Grant and eighty Royal Engineers "embank[ed] the shoals near the mouth of the Harrison River, for the purpose of deepening the channel." Then they reconstructed the first sixteen kilometres (ten miles) of road along the Lillooet River north of Port Douglas and the section south of Tenas Lake. At the same time, civilian contractor Joseph William Trutch finished the middle "section of 6 miles . . . [at] £550 [$2,750] per mile."[77]

Douglas spent September 1860 viewing the route first hand.[78] Steamers plied the lakes—on Lillooet the *Martrelle* or *Marzelle* (18 x 4 metres), on Anderson the *Lady of the Lake* (22 x 4.5 metres), and on Seton the *Champion* (22 x 4.5 metres). Getting the parts north on the road from Port Douglas was no mean feat. Douglas wrote in a despatch that "the boilers, being too heavy to carry on mules, were rolled over the tail, as far as the 28-mile house, in five sections."[79] Near Pemberton, settlers' crops of corn, potatoes, tomatoes, cucumbers, oats, and hay proved the agricultural value of the land and eliminated scurvy.

In 1858, the ancient trail up the Gates River had been made into a horse path. In 1860, Indigenous people talked about a better route along Cayoosh Creek to Lillooet Lake. A year earlier, Begbie had recommended exploring that option, "as it would be shorter than the present Lillooet route."[80] Douglas sent Royal Engineer Corporal James Duffy with Indigenous guides to explore. Too much new, expensive land work would be involved. Duffy's name survives for a lake and a road, but Colonel Moody demoted him for obeying Douglas without permission. Duffy died of winter exposure a few months later, an inexplicable end for someone with experience in the area.[81] Was his death self-inflicted because of shame?

Satisfied that no more practical route existed, the governor issued a contract to J.C. Colquhoun of Victoria to complete the road from Port Pemberton to Anderson Lake between autumn 1860 and spring 1861. Final touches were a tramway over Seton Portage in July 1861, reduced grades around Gibraltar Hill in 1861, and Goulding's Dam

Colonel Richard Clement Moody, commander of the Royal Engineers

in 1862, which made Tenas and Lillooet lakes one continuous water-way for steamers.[82]

The governor was vindicated as the route became heavily used. By July 1859, 100 pack mules left Port Douglas every week and carried 3,600 tons of freight to the Upper Fraser. Competition drove cartage costs down from 90¢ a pound in early 1858 to 18¢ at the end of 1858, 11¢ in 1859 and 5¢ in 1860.[83] Food costs fell proportionately. By April 1860, miners could finally "live substantially for 1½ dollars per diem, instead of 3 or 4 dollars," which had previously consumed their entire earnings.[84]

TABLE 5: 1858-1860 FOOD PRICES (PER POUND)
IMPACTED BY THE HARRISON-LILLOOET TRAIL[85]

FOOD	AT FOUNTAIN 10 OCT. 1858	CAYOOSH/ BRIDGE R. DEC. 9, 1858	PORT PEMBERTON MAR. 25, 1859	BRIDGE RIVER APRIL 1860
Flour	80¢	50¢	40¢	16¢
Beans	$1.00	45¢	—	16¢
Bacon/Salt Pork	$1.50	75¢	65¢	28¢

— • —

Otis Parsons was quick to capitalize on the merchandizing opportunities offered by the Harrison-Lillooet route. When road building ended at the end of September 1858, he returned to Victoria and stocked up on supplies to transport to the Interior and sell there.

A context for Otis Parsons' trading business is provided by a short diary and three letters to American friends written by merchant Cyrus Phillips. After being "burned out" in Forest City, California, Phillips sailed to Victoria in July 1858.[86] With G.B. Wright (the Port Douglas mule train operator) and Mr. Land (a Yale sawmill owner), Phillips purchased 3,200 pounds of boots, shoes, and clothing to sell at Fort Yale. Shipping proved expensive. Since individuals were allowed only 400 pounds of freight each, he had to purchase nine mining licences at $5 each, plus seven fares at $20 each before boarding: "So I took the passage tickets & Stood by the clerk's Wicket & Sold five of mine, there being but two of us Going up." The shippers "measured our Goods & called them 5,200 [pounds] at two cents per lb.," that is $104. On the *Surprise*, they "had to pay one Dollar a meal & three Dollars for our State Room." Despite these costs, everything was sold within two weeks for a profit of "Six Hundred Dollars."

Buoyed by success, Phillips partnered with Wright on the Harrison-Lillooet trail. He was stalled at Port Douglas from the first of September until after the road was finished. On November 12, the first of two lots of merchandise realized 47 ounces of gold dust, or $752 at $16 per ounce. He sent other goods to a store on the Bridge River north of Cayoosh. He wrote that he paid $3 per day rent for "a low log Hut without floor or window." Because of miners "leaving very fast on account of Cold Weather . . . We are crowding it in as fast as We can & Selling as cheap as We can afford it. I Gave orders To Sell flour for 50 cents per lb., it has been $1.00." Tragedy struck in January, 1859, when "We Lost a Schooner & cargo on Harrison lake . . . in Which we had to Sustain a Loss of over $3000. So goes business here. Business now is very good. . . . I think that Miners now average better pay per day than in California, but California has the most beautiful climate that you can imagine . . . & all are better off there." Despite the ups and downs, Phillips made money.

Otis Parsons' businesses were even more profitable over a much longer term. By December 27, 1858, he was back on the trails between Port Pemberton and Frenchman's Bar near Cayoosh. There he "*commenced packing for Nelson*," his merchant business partner.[87] Parsons' diary notes on commercial transactions continue until March 25, 1859. Several pages of unannotated figures tally large quantities of goods, income, and expenditure. Enough supplies had reached Port Pemberton by January 9, 1859, that Parsons hired Indigenous packers to haul 2,430 pounds of supplies to Port Anderson. The $5 he paid (just two-tenths of a cent per pound) undercut white transporters' rates that peaked at over 26¢ a pound.[88] He mentions many businessmen: Victoria grocer and provisioner Robinson; mule packer and merchant G.B. Wright, of Port Douglas and Lillooet; W.A. Dozier, who owned the road between Anderson and Seton Lakes; packer Hutchinson at Lillooet; and Robbins & Waldron.[89] The number of merchants in several distant places and the quantities of goods he sold suggest that Parsons was a wholesaler as well as a retailer.

The usual miners' staples included flour, rice, beans, bacon, coffee, sugar, boots, a purse (to carry gold in), rope, blocks, and spikes. Parsons also carried less common goods such as yeast, meal, and vinegar. Shrewdly, he imported expensive barley and hay to feed pack animals. He sold a horse for $75, and apparently bought a mule at $12 that was later sold for $110. Profits were legendary on liquor and tobacco. Brandy was sold at 87-1/2¢ for four ounces, quite a stiff drink. He needed to charge enough to make a profit, but he was not mercenary. Miners made most purchases with gold, since coin was very scarce in 1858. Parsons gave $16 per ounce for unassayed gold. His diary records $1,040.20 paid to miners for 49.4 ounces of gold. Greedier merchants shortchanged desperate miners by paying them $1.50 less per ounce.[90]

From 1859 on, Parsons continued packing and merchandizing between Pemberton and Lillooet. He ran a ferry across the Fraser River and eventually founded Parsonville on the east bank.[91] Parsonville connected with the new road into central B.C.'s Cariboo country in 1862.

In 1871, Parsons took over the business of retiring ship Captain John R. Fleming, then ran the steamers *Hope* and *Lillooet* from the mouth of the Fraser as far as Yale. The gold strikes in the Cassiar region during 1873 emboldened him to sail the *Hope* in order to carry prospectors to the Stikine River for three seasons. To replace the ageing *Lillooet*, Parsons had the luxurious steamer *Royal City* built at Victoria in 1875. Because traffic on the Fraser was very light that year, he decided to sell out to his competitor and retire to California at the age of forty-five, which was close to the average age of death in America. He left with his wife Jenny and infant child. They all drowned when the steamer *Pacific* struck another ship and sank on November 4, 1875.[92]

Photograph of the anonymous Canadian miner

CHAPTER 8

A Canadian Miner's Success

∽

The gold here is certain.
—*The Canadian's Diary, October 3, 1858*

AN ANONYMOUS MINER wrote in faint pencil about his search for gold in a *Pocket Diary for 1858* with printed dates for a full week on each opening. He and later owners carefully preserved the leather-bound book from damage.[1] He most likely came from Canada West (now Ontario). After he drowned in B.C., his diary reached Nelson Landon of Gananoque (near Kingston). Landon must have been a close friend or relative for the book to have made that expensive and otherwise inexplicable sea journey by mail or carried by someone from Victoria, across Panama, then on to Canada.

This diarist was an "invisible Canadian." His spelling of only one word is Canadian or British rather than American—"licence."[2] With British formality, he referred to Gold Commissioner Travaillot as "*Captain*" or "*Mr.*," to Hudson's Bay Company clerk Manson as "*Mr.*," and to miner Daly as "*Mr.*" (*Italics indicate passages from the anonymous miner's diary*). Americans preferred unadorned surnames

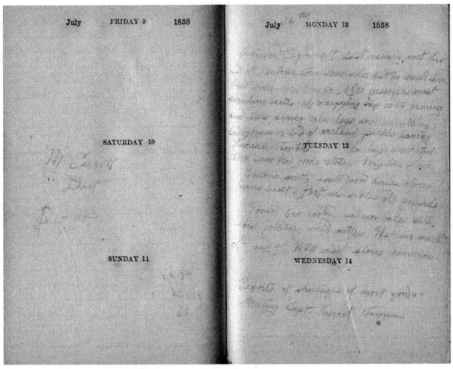

The first two pages of the anonymous Canadian miner's diary

or given names.[3] The Canadian never referred patriotically to the Stars and Stripes or hoped that the Fraser River fell in American territory. He used his gun only to hunt food. Unlike Americans who called for the extermination of Indigenous people, he expressed genuine admiration for the Indigenous guides who helped him over the dangerous trails up the Fraser Canyon.

The unnamed man's demeanour was classically British North American, providing a lively contrast to the Americans who wrote the other diaries. The loyal colonist paid for his mining licence in Victoria without complaint. Comfortable with the Canadian's demeanour, Captain Travaillot told him about the best available mining opportunities, which resulted in a trek to Fountain, farther north than any of the other diarists. Because so many thousands were milling around Victoria, Travaillot may have helped the Canadian to jump the queue waiting for the next available sailing up the Fraser River, by the Hudson's Bay Company requisitioned steamer, the *Surprise*. Travaillot gave him a letter of introduction to the fee collectors up-river and likely asked him to write a report about his trek up the Fraser Canyon. William Manson, the Hudson's Bay Company trader at Lytton, was his first mining partner, an extraordinary extension of comradeship that could not be offered to every passerby.

Accompanying the diary is an albumen print photograph of the miner taken after 1855, probably in California, since the studio furniture matches no photographer's in Canada or Victoria. The picture shows a well-dressed young man in excellent physical condition. He looks twenty-something, the typical mining age. The relaxed pose does not resemble the classic American frontier sharpshooter with ramrod spine, tight lips, and piercing eyes, like George Beam's. Gary Kurtz, former director of the California State Library at Sacramento, knows thousands of nineteenth-century photographs. Kurtz instantly pegged the sitter as Canadian.

Could the anonymous miner have left Canada West in 1858? News about the Fraser gold strike reached the Toronto *Globe* newspaper too late—on May 24. To reach Victoria forty-nine days later on July 12 would have been virtually impossible even by the quickest means. Preparations to leave were necessary, he would have to travel to New York and wait for a steamer, and most steamers took more than forty days from New York to Panama, then on to San Francisco and Victoria. Furthermore, his brother had preceded him to Victoria to work out of a shop. The only place that brother could have come from in July was San Francisco, following many other business people from California who opened branches in Victoria. As for the miner, his diary shows that he was no greenhorn. Independently, he used all the techniques of placer mining with great skill, earning over a thousand dollars in just two months when most discovered nothing. He also knew what supplies were required. Such expertise could only have been learned first-hand in the 1850s gold fields of California.

After Nelson Landon received the diary, he used it for his financial accounts between 1861 and 1863.[4] Those notes show why so many Upper Canadians were forced from home. Nelson's younger brother John took over their father's farm. Because the land was too small to support more than one family, the five other siblings had to leave. Nelson moved into Gananoque as a woolens merchant. The widespread economic depression and competition from two large established cloth businesses led to his financial failure. His brother Edgar settled in Gananoque and prospered as a saddle maker. His sisters, Caroline and Sarah, married Canada West farmers' sons and departed for greener pastures in Michigan. On February 28, 1862, Nelson gave his brother "Ephraim $300 to take him to British Columbia." That entry is tantalizing, because the Canadian diarist called his brother "E.," and Ephraim cannot be traced in Canada West records from mid-1857 until 1861, when Nelson started writing in the diary. Even more suggestive, on February 7, 1862, debt-ridden Nelson suddenly had $600 to purchase land, which is best explained as a windfall from the anonymous miner's earnings. Discouragingly, several months of intensive research at the Archives of Ontario and in Leeds County record repositories uncovered no unambiguous family connection between the anonymous miner and the Landons.

— • —

On July 12, 1858, the anonymous miner arrived at Esquimalt Harbour on the Pacific Mail steamer *Oregon* from San Francisco.[5] In most of his diary, telegraphic notes in the present tense focus on immediate concerns of prospecting and survival. His initial comments, however, use the past tense, summarizing highlights of the steamer passage. Unfortunately, he omits details about his original point of departure and why he decided to venture north. The diary may well have been acquired in Victoria, with the first entry as a catch-up scribble.

The 1,600 kilometre *"calm"* voyage from California took *"6 days— very little sleep,"* with *"1500 passagers most standing berths only."* Does the word *"most"* mean that the Canadian was one of the few who had purchased cabin passage? *"Gaming and tales . . . and drinking"* passed the time, while *"some had goods stolen."* On the voyage, *"Californians told of overland parties having Indian trouble."* The Canadian transferred from Esquimalt to Victoria the safest way, *"by small steamer."* On July 14, the *Victoria Gazette* recorded the arrival of 15,000 passengers from California by that date. News was spreading that Fraser River levels were too high for successful mining, but the flood of adventurers still seemed unstoppable. During the week while the anonymous miner was in Victoria, at least eighteen more ships carrying thousands of men added to the confused congestion as he *"saw many miners arriving—from California and Wash. Territory."* His practiced eye noted that *"Some are come with hope and not much else."*

The Canadian spent over $600 getting from San Francisco to the Fraser gold fields—up to $70 for the passage from California, $5 for the steamer to Victoria, $279.53 for mining and food supplies in Victoria, over $60 for passage up the Fraser with his overweight cargo, and at least $244 in wages at $16 or more daily to four Indigenous guides who carried his gear. These figures were much higher than anyone associated with the Landons in Canada West had access to.

B.C. Governor Frederick Seymour *(far left)* and companions
drinking and gambling on the steamer *Oregon* in 1864

The Canadian's earnings in the Golden State had to have been very good. He did splurge on a fine suit for his California photograph. Usually, though, his behaviour resembled the temperate Methodist and Presbyterian lives of the Landons and their relatives. His diary shows a man focused on work, who never mentioned gambling and never included alcohol in his lists of provisions.

Victoria looked primitive to the miner after San Francisco—"*mostly small board houses* [and] *stores being built. Fort resembles old palisade.*" Some improvements were being made, but hordes of strangers meant that "*rooms are scarce to be had for any price.*" San Francisco entrepreneurs imported doors, windows, and other supplies for slapdash wood structures as early as May. However, extensive construction did not begin until mid-July, when lumber from nearby Puget Sound settled down to affordable prices.[6] Tents in outlying fields accommodated "Near Six thousand People there waiting for they Hardly Knew What," as Cyrus Phillips wrote in his diary.[7]

The shortage of coins meant that "*Cash* [was] *hard to come bye,*" and credit was almost never extended. Supplies were inadequate: "*Reports of shortages of most goods.*" Even so, the Hudson's Bay Company store was "*busy at all hours. Cries of merchants and men haggling in English French* [and] *German*" filled the air with tumult. "*Talk of gold or highjinks*" preoccupied the newly arrived "*rough sort,*" with "*liquor in much demand.*"

The Canadian was lucky to have a brother in Victoria, called only "*E.,*" who sent "*letters back home*" with no hint where that was. The pair sat down to home-cooked "*salmon baked with local potatoes* [and] *wild nettles,*" which lose their sting when boiled like spinach.[8] A few days later they feasted on "*two ducks*" shot during a walk to Esquimalt for a look at Navy vessels. E. tended a wood frame store. On July 18, the brothers "*Returned to find lock had been broken but shop not entered.*" Break-ins and thefts were often reported by the *Victoria Gazette* and *Daily Evening Bulletin*. There were numerous "thieves, Indian and white, in Victoria." Professionals from San Francisco made off with "a chest of apparel and $1,167" from an upper room at James Yates's

Ship Inn on the waterfront, while a storehouse down the street was robbed of "nearly $1,000."[9] E. could have been an employee of a San Francisco outpost, or else operating his own business. No obvious advertisement in the *Victoria Gazette* of 1858 helps to identify any "E."[10]

The Canadian noted an *"auction at Fitch's,"* on July 15. Henry S. Fitch, a San Francisco auctioneer, was selling Victoria building lots.[11] The anonymous miner jotted down the names of merchants he patronized. J.D. Carroll sold groceries and liquor, while P.C. Dart carried provisions and miners' equipment.[12] Were *"L—and F,"* who invited him to their shops, employees in those stores? At those outlets the miner spent $279.53 in preparation for his trip, likely including tools, boots, and months' worth of flour, coffee, salt, sugar, and salt pork.

Crucial for the miner's adventures was the *"meeting"* with Captain O.T. Travaillot (called *"Capt. Treviot,"* *"Capt.,"* *"Mr. Travillot,"* and *"T."* in the diary). He was a Francophone trader and miner working near Forks, where the Thompson River meets the Fraser. In June 1858, Governor Douglas appointed him Assistant Commissioner of Crown Lands and Revenue Officer for the District of Fort Dallas, the unfinished Hudson's Bay Company post at the Forks. He and others collected gold licence fees. Because the miner met him instead of a lower officer so quickly after his arrival with thousands of others, his brother may have arranged the interview. The men's Canadian behaviour singled them out from hundreds of others waiting in line.

Captain Travaillot submitted an extensive report on the mines to Governor Douglas on June 24, 1858.[13] It provided the basis for his conversation with the Canadian. Travaillot repeated the despondent talk of the town: between Fort Hope and Fort Yale, the *"River is too high for working and rising."* However, *"coarse gold"* nuggets, unlike the fine dust of the Lower Fraser, had been found *"near Forks, where I am gone."* On Mormon Bar, rockers yielded between $50 and $100 a day; at Fountain, the daily range was between $37 and $55. There were *"better prospects and some dry digging in Canyons above Forks."*

The miner's ability to understand the Captain shows he was no novice. Even more helpful, the "*Capt. left route tho I am assured guides will be certain.*" Whether that itinerary was verbal or a glimpse of the map of *Reconnaissance of Fraser's River from Fort Hope to the Forks* that had been sent to London, the miner had accurate notes of mileage and geographical names that soon peppered his journal. In San Francisco or Victoria, the Canadian might have purchased a copy of Alexander Anderson's *Hand-Book* with its excellent *Map Showing the Different Routes*, or Alfred Waddington's *Correct Map of the Northern Coal & Gold Regions Comprehending Frazer River*. This last map showed the Douglas Portage from Fort Yale to Spuzzum, the trail on the east bank of the Fraser to Forks, and the chain of Seton, Anderson, Lillooet, and Harrison Lakes that the miner returned on. The miner used the spellings of place names on Waddington's map. When the Canadian arrived upriver, he hired Indigenous guides who knew the land better than any current map.

Travaillot's reports were corroborated in the July 14, 1858, issue of the *Victoria Gazette*.[14] On the negative side, at Fort Yale the river had "risen six or eight inches within the last ten days, and the miners are mostly idle in consequence." A white man working near Cayoosh had 200 pounds of flour stolen by Indigenous people who were starving because their dried salmon from the previous year had run out. The implication is that the current year's salmon run was failing. With little food available, that white man's weight dropped from 165 to 121 pounds. On the positive side, one Aaron Post had "prospected all along the river from the Big Canyon to one hundred and sixty miles above the Forks . . . and found gold on every bar. . . . In one day . . . he and his partner made $197 with a rocker." The *Gazette* reported that Post's gold was on view at the California Hotel near the Johnson Street ravine. The Canadian may also have met Alfred Waddington, who was in Victoria collecting information about northerly findings.[15] Armed with positive news, on July 19 the Canadian miner "*Determined to leave for Frazer's R. though water reported high still at all points.*"

— • —

On July 20, the miner left Victoria's harbour, "*loading at H.B.Co. wharf for steamer . . . filled with passagers and loaded with Co. goods.*" After a "*pleasant voyage of 12 hours*," everybody disembarked from the steamer *Surprise* at unnamed Fort Langley, while the boat took on wood for its boilers. "*Mountain rises to south still covered peaks in snow.*" Mount Baker, towering 2,385 metres (10,778 feet), dominated the southeast. Before tenting overnight, everyone ate the frontier staple of imperishable "*boiled bacon and molasses.*" The 500 miners camping there provided a constant stream of news. The Canadian heard that "*all here are waiting for water to fall but a few are pulling up stakes' and returning.*" He "*visited workings,*" but reported no local success. More promisingly, "*some men from Texas and Emery's still managing a few hours when R. is lower—$2.00*" earned per day.

While waiting at Fort Langley, the miner took scrupulous stock. There was "*not much here for a town. . . . Although food rather scarce, the Company are well supplied for now.*" On July 22, the Canadian jotted "*Goods arrive here from Whatcum trails even tho HBCo controls trade.*" While "*Co. policy is blamed for many losses. . . . I think the majority come ill equipt and no capital.*"

The steamer to Fort Hope "*commenced journey after delay from some trouble between whites and Indians*" during which one man was "*slightly injured with knife.*" Relations with Indigenous locals were deteriorating, according to an account in the *Victoria Gazette*. On July 26, an Indigenous woman "arrived at Fort Langley from an Indian Rancheria about twelve miles below the fort, reporting that a white woman was detained prisoner by the Indians, and that she had been wounded in a fight." The next day, "forty-five volunteers were armed with muskets from the Fort" and departed to rescue her.[16]

At Fort Hope on July 25, the miner hired four Indigenous guides, as Travaillot had advised: "*Stin-oop and Kam-uck and their boys, speak some English.*" The Canadian had hundreds of pounds of mining tools and food for weeks upriver—much more than most brought. It

Mount Baker seen from Fort Langley with surveying steamer
HMS *Plumper*, an Indigenous canoe, and a river steamer

filled "*2 open canoes. Several newcomers tried to buy passage, but too loaded.*" The party began the 24 kilometre journey at "*5 AM, passing small camps of miners mostly idle and waiting for water. Arrived Yale at noon.*" The miner found "*Few supplies here and most have erected tents or lean-tos on ground below Fort*" on the bank of the river. The *Daily Alta California* amplified details. There were around "2,000 men within a mile," most of them "idle—eating up their stores. I never, in my life, saw so many poor men—so little money among so large a number of able-bodied men."[17] The fort could become the head of navigation where "*Steamers may come regular when water falls.*" It would be a major commercial storehouse "*if HBCo allows open trade.*" As recently as July 21, the sternwheeler *Umatilla* had been the first ship to land there, struggling five hours upstream from Hope. That experiment was repeated on September 5, when the steamer *Enterprise* made the same trip.

The Canadian crossed the river to explore legendary Hill's Bar on July 26 or 27. While he was still in Victoria, he could have heard about that location and even read in the *Gazette* how one miner's claim there "has thus far yielded him about $1,000."[18] But instead of

El Dorado, the Canadian found *"only a few mining gold while waiting for conditions to improve."*

Like other sensible miners, the Canadian avoided the turbulent river through the Fraser Canyon and set out on the Douglas Portage toward Spuzzum. On July 28, he packed north *"about 8 miles"* (13 kilometres) on the unimproved path. He watched in awe as *"Stin-op carries twice as much as seems possible, 100 lbs. or more."* He found the trail *"very loose and rocky"* with *"Feet very agervated."* That injury haunted him for the rest of the season. A year later, Navy Lieutenant Richard Mayne found the trail from Yale to Lytton "the roughest on which I have ever travelled, the greater part of it being over sharp pointed rocks or granite boulders."[19] Novices in B.C.'s mountains soon discover the need for good, snugly tied boots to prevent blisters, lost toe nails, sprained ankles, and twisted knees.

The party camped by the creek now called Sawmill, the most reliable source of water north of Fort Yale. As elsewhere, the Canadian's mileage is dead accurate. His group dined on *"flour with berries*

Nicaragua Bluff in the Fraser Canyon was impassable before the Cariboo Road

gathered by Indians," a bonus given the scurvy-inducing diet of most miners. Thursday brought a shorter trek to "*Spuzzum,*" followed by a descent to the Fraser's banks: "*4 miles—very steep. Impossible for pack animals.*" That trail has long disappeared under voracious forest growth, but several contemporary maps show a landing just north of Spuzzum Creek. Eagerly, the miner took out his pan, but found "*only colors.*" He left "*some 20 or 30 miners*" to their lacklustre claims.

In his typical laconic style, the Canadian does not describe the river crossing. Canoes ferried miners over, ending in disaster for one group when a boat "capsized, and . . . six men, including the ferryman, were drowned," according to the *Victoria Gazette.*[20] The wide east bank offered an easy path to a long-lost Indigenous settlement, the "*Indian Rancheria Kekloos,*" spelled Kequeloose in most nineteenth-century sources.[21] It lay just north of the Alexandra Bridge. Arriving there on July 30, the party found "*Indians here have some gold to trade, mostly small flakes.*" The miner's "*Guides roasted horseflesh for meal— welcome and usual fare.*" The miner would have had only his own salt pork if Stin-oop had not been there to negotiate.

Between Boston Bar/Quayome and Kequeloose, the Fraser River falls about 66 metres (217 feet) in a succession of violent rapids as it slices through the mountains. Hell's Gate is the most turbulent obstacle. Mayne's 1859 *Sketch Map* is filled with warnings: "The Big Canon, High Cliffs, Dangerous Reach." The Canadian wrote that the "*Trail ascended high cliffs and defile to fork of Anderson R.*" From the ridges, the Fraser could be seen, with the water "*very rapid, mostly gravel ground. Large rapids below here where many have lost their lives in attempting ascent in canoes.*" He continues more expansively than usual, perhaps having read Alexander Anderson's recently published *Hand-Book and Map*: "*Saw-aah-nees . . . gather below to catch the salmon in summer and are disposed to be suspicious of other* [Indigenous people] *as well as some miners who would take them.*"

At the beginning of August, the party reached the plain at "*Kwak-a-hum*" (Quayome), where the Anderson River flows into the Fraser.[22] The Canadian claims to have seen the grave of a Hudson's Bay "*serv-*

ant said to have killed self*" there. The Indigenous cedar memorial statue under a shelter was actually at Kequeloose. The verb tenses imply that the note was written at least a day afterward, explaining the confusion. Here, as elsewhere, frustrated men waited for lower water so that they could earn their *"$5-10 per man."* An *"easier trail"* lay ahead.

The guides broke the journey at the Indigenous *"Skoose village."*[23] It stood south of Siska Creek, where an 1860 survey shows an "Indian Reserve" beside a commercial garden that expropriated part of the fertile plateau. The decline of rainfall north of Boston Bar is so dramatic that the miner noted the change from the huge conifers of the coast: *"Country here is timbered with popler, pine and little grass. Much drier than lower on the R."* Exhausted by heavy loads, the packers rested four days, from August 3. A walk up the creek in search of game brought the Canadian close to *"a small bear, but it fled before they could procure it."* The Indigenous residents *"traded some tobacco and flour for fish smoked and dried—and a few small birds (grouse)."* Such smart trades meant that *"we have no fear of want at present."* In a few weeks, the guides would be missed.

The Canadian found the inhabitants of Skoose *"handsome and friendly disposed,"* though inquiries about gold were met with vague gestures toward the river and hills. His guides prevented theft. The locals simply *"inspected packs"* instead of stealing from them as miners so often complained. A few items may have been presented as gifts. Once again the miner took out his pan. On August 5, he *"washed some nuggets from a small creek coming from the mtns. in the East. They are my first."* On August 7, all reached the Hudson's Bay post at Forks, where the Thompson's clear waters flow into the muddy Fraser. It was renamed Lytton in mid-August.

— • —

Forks was the northern post of 1858 gold licencers, where the anonymous miner was *"Entertained by 4 of Capt. Travillot party. There was some could play a tune and singing, nor to spare the rum!"* This kind of reception could not possibly have been offered to all the thousands of miners parading along the river. The Canadian had probably brought communications from Travaillot, so the fee collectors extended a hearty welcome. On August 8, the miner sent "*letters to E. and T.*," his brother and most likely Travaillot. The implication is that the commissioner had asked for a report on what was happening on the river. Any up-to-the-minute news would be welcome about Indigenous unrest in those days before Snyder began his march up the Canyon. The Canadian might even see things from a fresh perspective not captured by regular employees. The Canadian's mail was carried free to Victoria by the captain's officials on that occasion and also on September 19. The thousands of other miners north of Forks had to pay Ballou's Express $2 for a letter from there to reach Victoria.[24] On August 9, "*Two of my Indians go down river.*" Were they leaving to join the hundreds of Indigenous warriors who were mobilizing against American aggression?

Travaillot's introduction opened the door to William Manson, the Hudson's Bay Company clerk at Forks.[25] Manson had seen many come and go, but this Canadian newcomer was well equipped and shared stories about previous experiences. Soon the trader was confiding that nearby he had "*taken some gold this past Winter.*" The two joined forces and worked together for seven days without interruption, then on and off until August 29.

On August 10, the pair "*camped about 12 mi* [19 kilometres] *from Forks in a very pictures valley,*" Izman Creek, called "Cowman" in the diary.[26] It is the one large, ever flowing rivulet with lush trees on the east bank between Lytton and Lillooet. On August 10, Manson and the miner "*each washed several good coarse pieces. He estimated 12–14 dollars.*" Two days later the Canadian found "*One large nugget which M. reckons $20.00.*" He despaired that most of the gold was as fine as flour: "*The leavings may be a third too small to sift. No quicksilver to be had.*" Even so, with Manson's effective help over five days, the miner earned $109. Other miners sold Manson a tender piece of bear "*hump . . . which was most delicious.*" Game was very scarce, but the

Hudson's Bay Company clerk had to be humoured since his stock was limited.

Manson filled the Canadian in on earlier history. The Company had long kept the Indigenous discovery of gold "*hidden.*" Women and small children "*use stout sticks to pry the rocks and dirt and use their baskets to winnow the larger nuggets from the stones.*" During seven years of service, Manson had developed good rapport with the Indigenous residents of the region. The miner watched as he "*treated one old man with liniment for foul bruse on back.*" No wonder some Indigenous people took special trouble on August 13 and "*crossed river (Thom.) to visit Mr. M they know from before. They seemed most willing and helpful.*" They brought a present of "*small fish and pounded berries dried in cakes.*" Four days later, they traded "*for tobacco and 20 lb flour.*" They would also have passed on distressing news about Americans driving Indigenous people out of the canyon. Manson spoke to the visitors in their own tongue, or Chinook, or even French and may have kept the news from the Canadian to keep him from worry.

The return to Forks on August 18 oppressed the miner with typical "*very hot,*" dry summer temperatures. Food prices were high. Tensions would have risen the next day when "*about 20 miners from U.S. of A. arrived. . . . Report many more on trail from Columbia R. All were supplied with pack horses.*" The Canadian noted even more arrivals on September 6. From the Columbia, "*miners [were] now packing with horses thru to Great Falls*" just north of Bridge River.

The journey to Izman Creek and back allowed the miner to check out other locations mentioned by Travaillot in Victoria. On August 21 he visited "*Mormon Bar,*" around ten kilometres (six miles) north of Lytton.[27] There he found "*about 100 miners working the ground with 100 more on small bars. I have seen lumps of gold like pigon eggs— coarse most.*" He himself "*rocked $15.00, corse flakes.*" He returned briefly "*to Lytton for flour and broken ax handle*" on August 24. Manson was there, dealing with the fallout from Snyder's treaty with Cexpe'ntlEm on August 22. The miner recorded another "*Indian visit*" on August 26. Finally the water level of the river was falling.

The banks witnessed constant motion, *"miners moving upriver each day"* without impediment. On August 29, the Canadian *"bought from Mr. M. $31.80"* of Company supplies and headed north.

Moving upriver on a *"very good trail,"* the Canadian noticed that *"Miners work the whole R. from below to dry diggings at benches 400–500 ft above."* Sluices were serviced by *"some small ditchs to reach the deposit from the old River bed."* A *"left foot very bruised"* forced him to rest in camp during the first five days of September. He reflected on the striking difference between the hard rock faces of the canyon below Lytton and the sediments deposited by the post glacial stream: *"The ground is sandy or reddish packed earth not too hard for a pick and shovel. Some timber pine and grass. The creeks are small."* The miner's physical well-being under the protection of his Indigenous guides and Manson gave way to the painful recognition that *"The Frazer is not to be depended on for supplies."* Alexander Anderson's book had warned that *"every miner . . . [should] supply himself well beforehand, as he can depend upon little in that region, save what is imported by himself or others."*[28] Fortunately, Indigenous locals who knew about the recent Fraser Canyon War could distinguish King George men from Bostons. The Canadian found *"Indians not troublesome."*

On September 6, he was well enough rested for the thirteen-kilometre (eight-mile) hike to Fosters Bar, half way between Lytton and Lillooet.[29] Because the area was busy with *"75 miners at work on Bar with claims on all,"* he moved *"3–4 miles"* north: *"Mr. Daly works a claim on south end"* of *"a small bar or point."* On September 8, Daly earned $15 to $20, the Canadian $12; the next day fortunes reversed, with Daly $12 to $14 and the Canadian $20. They celebrated with *"slapjacks."*

— • —

At Victoria and Lytton, the miner had heard that abundant gold had been found on Cayoosh Creek, Bridge River, Pavilion River, Pavilion Lake, and even the Chilcotin River.[30] He headed north, but the record of that journey on the leaf for September 10 to 15 has been torn out of the diary. The narrative resumes with him near "*Frenchman's*" Bar (just north of Lillooet) and sluicing works on the nearby "S" curve of the Fraser. On a plateau over two hundred metres above that stretch of the river lie fields lush enough for summer gardens watered by a spring and a mountain lake. The settlement at "*Fountain*" with "*2 new houses or <u>shacks</u>*" provided a haven for desperate "*miners arriving every day with <u>Nothing</u>.*"

In 1859, Lieutenant Palmer lamented, "as long as bacon and beans are the sole articles of diet, few, if any, will be found with the heart or strength to do more than support themselves by mining for a few

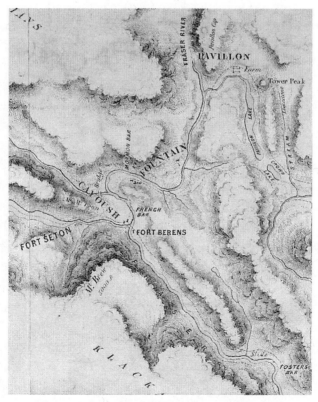

The area from Fosters Bar to Pavillon/Pavilion
worked by the Canadian miner

hours each day" there.[31] For the first time, the miner spent as much time scrounging for food as he did mining. The *"fresh meat, $4.00"* he bought at Fountain on September 19 must have tasted particularly delicious. On September 22, he *"saw few ducks this AM, but too far for shot. Surprised a large lynx or wild cat. . . . Gave us both a fright."* Four days later, he *"fished below falls but nothing."* Salmon should have been plentiful near the Great Falls by mid-September, but Indigenous fishermen were complaining because mining debris downriver was killing the fish.

By mid-July the Fraser around Fountain was fully "claimed and occupied by some 50 American miners, and a large number of French half-breeds and Indians. . . . Those in possession declared they would rather starve or suffer martyrdom before they would abandon" their rich claims, so the *Daily Alta California* reported.[32] Extensive tailings still line the river there. The Canadian miner may have had to fork out several hundred dollars to purchase his claim. It was worth $400 a month later.

The journal notes dwindle to a trickle, mainly recording daily takings and the pain in the miner's foot. Even though September 17 had been a *"very good day, $50.00,"* September 27 proved a *"poor day though hard work since sunrise."* For the rest of the time, he usually made more than $10 per day, and excellent returns between $20 and $30 on six days. The higher amounts came from working a *"sluice-box,"* which needed repairs on October 5. During autumn 1858, "a company composed of Germans, French and Italians . . . dug a ditch to bring water from a small lake a few miles east of the Fountain . . . [which] cost about $5,000. . . . [They] are now running three sluices, and working fifteen men, with an average yield of $12 a day to the hand."[33]

Life in the field ran its course. The anonymous miner listened from a distance when *"Mr. Bell brought segars and whisky up and some miners are with him now and such a howeling."* According to California custom, *"F. has called a meeting of miners on this bar"* to resolve conflicts or establish local practices. The gold officials remained good friends.

On September 19, *"Two of Capt. T. men arrived from Forks with some news from Victoria and to collect licence fees.* [Sent] *letter to E. per Capt. men."*

On September 21 the Canadian *"set out for Trout Lake about 18 mi. by river route from Pavillon and Frenchmans. Steep from junction with river."* He was checking Waddington's report of rich claims in the July 21st *Victoria Gazette*, either sent by brother E. or bought from Ballou's Express. The destination was Pavilion Lake, up a steep ravine from the Fraser and approximately eighteen miles (twenty-nine kilometres) from Fountain.[34] His weak foot forced a return the next day without having reached that destination. On September 30, *"20 miners mostly from US passed, bound for Chapeau R. where new diggings are reported in the papers."* They would have followed the valley east of Pavilion where Highway 99 now passes, on their way to the Chapeau River, renamed Hat Creek by the English.

The push north had begun in earnest. On October 3, *"about 10 men left for upper R.,"* *"two more left"* the next morning, *"Several large partys bound upr*[iver]*"* on October 7, and forty-eight hours later he saw the *"trail to Pavillon with many groups of 2–3 miners."* On October 1, Oregonian entrepreneurs passed *"Frenchmans . . . upper Pavillon R. and North to winter. Two timber saws for fluming and houses."* The lure must have been strong, but the Canadian stayed put because his foot ached, *"and the gold here is certain."* He benefitted when another miner left: *"I am working his ground too."*

One day he found *"Laroux with good $180.00"* at Frenchman's Bar. Another miner *"took out two thousand mostly coarse, and some large, and two sacks fine."* The Canadian's adventure ended with *"First snow on mountains"* on October 8. Rising prices at Fountain did not augur well for a winter stay. On October 12, he *"sold paying ground for $400.00 to M. Samuelson Co."* Unfortunately, the licence for this transaction, which might have identified the miner, has not survived. The Canadian's two months of earnings since August 10 were not among the highest of the year, but his $1,115 was far, far beyond what most men dreamed of.[35]

— • —

"*Heavy snow on mountains*" forced a judicious departure on October 13. The Canadian followed the advice of Travaillot's crew by taking the newly built "*lake route*" from Cayoosh to Harrison Lake. A day's hike on the "*high plateau*" above the Fraser where Lillooet now sits brought him to a camp "*on a broad ridge with the Lake a fine view.*" Seton Lake offers a breathtaking vista, with bare ochre-coloured hillsides. He "*saw miners going to Great Falls and beyond, but I think the season is too far advanced.*" Most would have been road builders with many complaints. Victoria offered a safer haven with his brother.

On October 16, he was "*troubled once again by this foot.*" Persistent rain made the trails "*very muddy.*" He had to wait his turn for ferry passage and did not cross Seaton Lake until October 18, after a "*fine trout for dinner*" the night before. A private boat was now servicing the lake route: "*M. R—? has small house on lake and a bateau for a ferry here.*"

On October 19, he crossed the "*good portage from the foot of Seton Lake to Anderson Lake about 1 mi. at the small creek joining the two.*" There "*a small party of Indians camp . . . from Liloot,*" not the current town on the Fraser, but the Lil'wat Indigenous settlement near Port Pemberton. The note about "*camp at mouth of fine stream*" on October 20 indicated that he paid the $2 fare for the five-hour boat crossing of Anderson Lake. Once again, Canadian mannerisms saved him: "*3 Indians passed but did not trouble me.*" American road cutters who had recently been working on the Harrison-Lillooet route were not always as lucky. The workers told him about "*the new trail to the lower Frazer open from the Indian trail.*" Because of the constant "*rain which renders the trail very muddy*" he slipped and hurt his bad foot on the forty-eight-kilometre (twenty-six-mile) path to Lillooet Lake. It took five days to reach the next bateau.

On October 25, the miner paid another $2 to cross Lillooet Lake: "*Am taking the ferry below to upper Harrison.*" Fortunately, the sixty-three kilometres (thirty-nine miles) to Port Douglas had less elevation

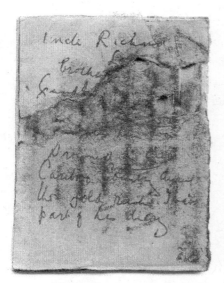 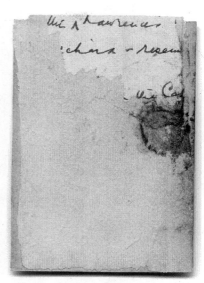

Two ball-point pen inscriptions, ca. 1950, about the drowning
of the Canadian miner

drop. Still, four days of trekking were involved: *"Trail very muddy.
My boots are done."* Finally, on October 29, the miner could rely on
marine transportation down Harrison Lake, the Fraser River, and
Strait of Georgia to Victoria: *"Start for* [Fraser] *R. tomorrow."* The
passage to Victoria was so straightforward that it was not mentioned.
Nor was the reunion with his brother. That meeting would have been
a cause for celebration, if not howling. In the safety of Victoria, a
doctor could at last examine his foot and a store supply new boots.

— • —

Like everyone in Victoria, the Canadian heard reports about prospecting as far north as the Chilcotin River. Gold was discovered further north in the Cariboo district during early 1859. The next few
years saw a massive rush to that area. The Canadian knew how to
mine effectively, so he returned to the gold fields. After 1950, an
untraced descendant wrote a partially destroyed note about the diary
with a ball point pen: "Uncle Richard | L . . . | brothe . . . | Grand[fa?]

. . . | [at least one line lost] | . . . sembles him too. | Drowned in the | Cariboo Country during | the gold rush. I own | part of his diary." The Canadian could have died in any number of treacherous waterways during 1859, 1860, or even early 1861. His 1858 diary reached Gananoque by July 15, 1861, when Nelson Landon started writing in it, not just to save paper, but probably to keep the miner's memory alive.

PART C

Looking Forward

Judge Begbie (*left*) proclaims the Colony of British Columbia and swears in James Douglas (*centre foreground*) as governor

CHAPTER 9

Perspectives beyond the End of 1858

❧

O brave new world that has such people in it!
William Shakespeare, The Tempest[1]

ON NOVEMBER 19, 1858, Matthew Baillie Begbie, an English judge
sent by the Colonial Office to administer justice, officially inaugu-
rated the Colony of British Columbia at Fort Langley and installed
James Douglas as its first governor.[2] This uncompromising assertion
of British sovereignty was seen as so important that the official party
left Victoria almost immediately after Begbie's arrival on November
16. Witnesses included Rear Admiral Robert Lambert Baynes, Captain John Marshall Grant with other Royal Engineers, and Captain
Chartres Brew, the new Commissioner of Police for British Columbia. There was so little infrastructure on the Fraser River that all but
the Royal Engineers quickly returned to Victoria, where Douglas
administered both the new colony and the Colony of Vancouver Island until he was replaced in 1864.

The British Colonial Office wanted British Columbia to have a
more representative House of Assembly than Vancouver Island's.

However, Douglas remained temperamentally unable to move beyond his autocratic Company style. He delayed setting up the assembly on the mainland, as he had on Vancouver Island. He also stalled cutting his ties with the Hudson's Bay Company, which was a condition of his accepting the governorship of British Columbia.

On December 25, 1858, another official sent from London arrived at Victoria. Colonel Richard Clement Moody had twenty-eight years of distinguished colonial and War Office experience. The Colonial Office had appointed him Chief Commissioner of Lands and Works for the Colony of British Columbia, commander of the British Columbia Detachment of Royal Engineers sent to British Columbia, and Lieutenant Governor of British Columbia when Governor Douglas was absent from Vancouver Island. Moody's duties for British Columbia included selecting a capital city, surveying town sites and harbours, planning roads, and reporting on resources.

Governor Douglas had wanted British Columbia's capital to be on the south bank of the Fraser near Fort Langley. Moody protested that the location was less than a day's march from the American border over flat land. In January 1859, he chose an easily defendable bluff across the Fraser, which was named New Westminster by Queen Victoria. January also saw Moody and Judge Begbie end a complicated disturbance between miners at Fort Yale and Hill's Bar, which became known as Ned McGowan's so-called bloodless war.[3]

Soon Moody was effectively engrossed in the most important challenges of the year: upgrading the Harrison-Lillooet route and surveying future roads. Since Douglas stayed put in Victoria, it was fortunate that British Columbia had an active administrator on-site. Because Moody and Douglas had such differing administrative experience and incompatible senses of authority, their small disagreements soon grew into mutual rancour.

— • —

Vancouver Island and the mainland were no longer the exclusive preserves of the Hudson's Bay Company trading with Indigenous people. Victoria's commerce was now handled by many entrepreneurs, while British Columbia provided a vast frontier open for mining exploration and white settlement. During the summer of 1858, Victoria enjoyed the boom of a new mining town serving tens of thousands of transient miners. The bust came by November, when 13,000 Californians had decamped back to the Golden State. Vancouver Island was suddenly much quieter: "The storekeepers of Victoria felt as if annihilated. . . . The exodus of miners . . . was followed by that of traders, restaurant and hotel keepers, and all those who could conveniently leave, or had never intended to remain," wrote Alfred Waddington. However, by the end of 1858 the town boasted:

> eight substantial wharves carried out into the harbour, two brick hotels and other brick buildings, numerous frame houses and stores, . . . twenty or thirty restaurants and coffee houses, [and] steamboats built and launched. . . . Where in the United States a city without taxes, lawyers, or public debt? Where in the United States the town or city, where there is more money to be made, even now, by the industrious trader or craftsman?[4]

Indeed, a thousand people stayed to pursue their livelihood in Victoria, as Charles Coulson Gardiner wrote in a letter.[5] The seat of

Government Street in Victoria as it was built in 1858

government guaranteed the town's continued existence. Until the first Canadian Pacific Railway train arrived at Port Moody on July 4, 1886, Victoria remained the port of entry for British Columbia. Its businesses supplied the slowly growing mainland. Up the east coast of Vancouver Island, Nanaimo's coal supplied countless steamers with fuel for voyages up the Fraser River or to San Francisco.

By late 1858, the Fraser River was also less populated. Thousands, like George Slocumb, returned to California penniless. But not everybody was poor. The *Victoria Gazette* of December 9, 1858, reported that at least $756,000 worth of gold had been mined that year.[6] George Beam, for example, returned home to Whidbey Island with $1,000. And not everybody left. Over 10,000 men remained on the river at the start of November: 6,300 between Hope and Yale, 900 at Lytton, 600 at Port Douglas, and 3,000 between Lytton and Fountain.[7] As cold weather took hold, many retreated south to avoid freezing and starvation. In the dead of winter 1858, Otis Parsons started his lucrative career as merchant and wholesaler between Pemberton and Lillooet, ensuring that supplies would never be short upriver again.

The anonymous Canadian miner overwintered in Victoria with his brother, then Cariboo gold beckoned him back to the British Columbia Interior. Prospectors like these made B.C.'s Cariboo region the epicentre of gold discovery in the 1860s. Others headed east to an expanding number of mining opportunities.

Thousands who had made good strikes overwintered on the Fraser, hoping for further success in the springtime when they were searching for richer strikes upriver. By mid-September 1858, Fort Hope had grown to 300 permanent residents with wooden stores and cabins. Other small settlements dotted the Fraser River. George Beam described Pike Town on Puget Sound Bar with its cabins and stores. Ned McGowan and his companions stayed on Hill's Bar into 1859 with almost a hundred others in wood cabins and tent houses. Emory City perched on the edge of Emory's Bar, and Boston Bar was populated further north. Fort Yale had the largest population, because its

Watercolour of Nanaimo on May 20, 1858, by Alexander Grant Dallas

2,000 hopefuls wanted to be as far north as possible to start trekking north in the spring of 1859. Many of those sites were abandoned by whites within a few years, though Indigenous residents and prudent Chinese miners continued to pan and rock for gold on the Fraser below Lillooet.

Enough people wanted to settle that at the end of 1858 building lots were surveyed and auctioned at Fort Langley, Fort Hope, and Fort Yale, with Port Douglas following in 1859.[8] Generous provisions were offered to naturalize aliens. Colonial Minister Lytton encouraged this development. The offer of British citizenship lessened the push for American annexation, and the sale of land raised badly needed revenue for the new colony.

Opportunities seemed endless for everyone poised to seize them, and transportation was readily available. The termination of the Hudson's Bay Company's monopoly on September 2, 1858, meant that "every American citizen would have as good a right to trade with our Indians as he has . . . at Toronto and Montreal," as Victoria promoter Henry de Groot observed.[9] Anyone, British or foreign, could mine, trade freely, and set up any type of business. The old Company catering mainly to Indigenous peoples was simply left behind.

Yale around 1862

Shipping access to the river had already moved decisively away from the Hudson's Bay vessels *Beaver, Otter,* and *Recovery,* as detailed in Chapter 2 and Appendix 1. The biggest money-making American steamers left the river by mid-October, but sternwheelers *Enterprise* and *Maria* remained into 1859. A flotilla of small Puget Sound and Victoria-based sloops and schooners also sailed in to fill the void. Late in 1858, a bold venture was started by Vancouver Island customs chief, Alexander C. Anderson, Captain William Irving, and others. Their Victoria Steam Navigation Company built two ships at Victoria, and soon moved them to mainland headquarters under the British Columbia and Victoria Steam Navigation Company name. The sternwheel steamer *Governor Douglas,* completed early in 1859, brought passengers and cargo across the dangerous Strait of Georgia to New Westminster. There transfers were made to upriver boats, including the company's sternwheel steamer *Colonel Moody,* launched May 14, 1859. Shipping companies resorted to cutthroat strategies to stifle competition. The British Columbia and Victoria Steam Navigation Company bought *Maria* in November 1859. *Enterprise* retreated to the Chehalis River, Washington, a financially disastrous decision. Much later, diarist Otis Parsons found himself in the Fraser River shipping business, replacing Captain John R. Fleming in 1871, and running sternwheelers *Hope*, *Lillooet*, and *Royal City* until retiring in 1876.

— • —

Accurate maps and charts were needed to record settlement, build roads, aid travel, assist navigation, develop resources, pinpoint arable land, and provide government oversight.[10]

The first task was to catch up with developments on Vancouver Island. The colonial surveyors were equal to the task. Throughout 1858, the Hudson's Bay Company had sold hundreds of new building lots in and around Victoria, making earlier official maps obsolete. The colony's surveyor, Joseph Despard Pemberton, and a newly hired assistant, Hermann Otto Tiedemann, produced three new maps that documented growth: "Esquimalt District—Official Map," "Official Map of the Town of Victoria," and "Victoria District—Official Map" north to Cadboro Bay. By September 16, anyone could view these plans at the Land Office. In November, surveyors Lammot, Freeman, and Green offered copies for sale. Alfred Waddington, who had been first off the mark with a map of the Fraser gold fields in April 1858, copied the survey for his *Map of the City of Victoria*, lithographed at San Francisco in December.

By mid-1858, the influx of foreign vessels seemed unstoppable, with ninety-nine ships arriving at Victoria and Esquimalt in August, and over fifty more every month afterward. The mercantile success of the British Empire was founded on reliable nautical charts. The British government also used charts and maps to reinforce its ownership of lands around the world. The creation of the Colony of British Columbia solved one issue of sovereignty, but a dispute with Americans over ownership of the San Juan Islands continued. New charts of the Pacific Northwest were necessary to solve those and other challenges. Marine surveys were paid for by the Imperial government. They began promptly, but took two years to complete.

Captain George Henry Richards, U.K. Navy surveyor

Naval Captain George Henry Richards had arrived in 1857 on HMS *Plumper* to help survey the forty-ninth parallel with American counterparts.[11] That task was soon forgotten. The events of 1858 diverted the *Plumper* to place buoys marking the passage through treacherous sand banks at the entrance to the Fraser River and to enforce licensing until August. The British navy and an increasing stream of Victoria-based vessels and arrivals from Puget Sound and San Francisco needed accurate soundings for *Esquimalt Harbour*. Richards made them in 1858, but they were not published until 1861. Ships had much more trouble negotiating the shallower waters and

Fisgard Lighthouse, built at the entrance to Esquimalt Harbour in 1860

rocks of Victoria Harbour—most notoriously the steamer *Constitution*, which ran aground on July 19, 1858, and steamers *Pacific* and *Sea Bird*, which foundered on September 5. In 1859, Richards took extensive new soundings for *Victoria Harbour* on a chart also published in 1861. Safer passage around the tip of Vancouver Island was proposed with lighthouses charted in 1859 at the *Entrance of Esquimalt Harbour*, the hazardous rocks at *Race Islands*, and *South East Part of Vancouver Island*. Britain paid half the cost of £7,000.[12] Earlier completion of that project might have saved steamer *Pacific* from damage on October 23, 1858.

Richards' surveys during 1858 to 1859 for *Haro and Rosario Straits* provided expert navigational aids for the Strait of Juan de Fuca, north Puget Sound, the San Juan Islands, the Gulf Islands, the Strait of Georgia, and the Fraser River entrance. The 1859 and 1860 survey of *Fraser River and Burrard Inlet* explored the stream up to Harrison River and was promptly published to ensure safer navigation. Concurrently, Naval Lieutenant Richard Charles Mayne continued that survey with a *Sketch of the Upper Part of the Fraser River from Langley to Yale*, including five landscape views.[13] That chart was rushed into print in May 1859. Those accurate charts encouraged the development of commercial shipping up to Yale.

The thousands flowing into mainland B.C. required accurate land maps for building roads and developing natural resources. Alexander Anderson's earlier surveys provided an excellent starting point. Naval surveyors were already on site. Colonial Minister Lytton sent 150 Royal Engineers from England under Colonel Richard Moody to survey routes for new roads and record mineral deposits. They arrived in stages between October 29, 1858, and June 27, 1859.

One of the earliest productions was a War Office overview of southern B.C.: *North America. Map of Part of the British Possessions to the West of the Rocky Mountains.* A reference key indicated flora and fauna as well as areas for growing crops. It may have been intended as a stimulus for immigration, since a large British influx was necessary to counterbalance the numerous foreigners, especially Americans. Others embarked on surveys of British Columbia's rich mineral resources. Doctor Charles Forbes' report on the geology of Harrison Lake and the Lillooet River was published with a coloured map in a British Parliamentary blue book of 1862.

Three extensive surveys of the Interior from the mouth of the Fraser up to Fountain were completed in early 1859. Naval Lieutenant Richard Charles Mayne produced one of the most spectacular maps ever made of B.C.—a *Sketch of Part of British Columbia*. It showed the banks of the Fraser River from Harrison River north to Fountain, the new roads from Harrison Lake to Seton Lake, the Thompson

Lieutenant Richard Charles
Mayne, U.K. Navy surveyor

Lieutenant Henry Spencer Palmer,
Royal Engineers surveyor

River past Fort Kamloops, Nicola River, and Nicola Lake. It boasted the most complete contemporary collection of place names and river mining bars. The map accompanied Mayne's report about the area, based on his journey there from April 10 to June 19, 1859.

Royal Engineers Lieutenant Henry Spencer Palmer produced a more detailed survey and report of just the trails from Harrison Lake to Fountain during May and June 1859—*Plan of Route from New Westminster to Fountain in British Columbia.*[14] Royal Engineer Lieutenant Arthur Reid Lemprière's manuscript "Sketch of Trail from Hope to Boston Bar" showed the "Old Mountain Trail" followed by many 1858 miners, up the Douglas Portage from Fort Yale, and across the Fraser to Boston Bar. Gentler slopes up the "Coquahalla River" from Fort Hope promised easier passage. Private citizens started building a road there in 1858. Intolerable winter conditions killed that project.

By 1860, so many trails had been completed along the lower Fraser River that Colonel Moody had the Royal Engineers plot them on a map presented to Governor Douglas: "Sketch Map of Part of British Columbia Shewing Trails and Routes of Communication." Royal

Engineers surveys for the Cariboo Road from Yale up the Fraser Canyon waited until 1860 under Sapper James Turnbull for the east side of the river and 1862 under Sergeant William McColl for the west side.

In June 1859, eminent London map-maker John Arrowsmith was commissioned to produce a map based on recent government surveys for a Parliamentary blue book. His map of *The Provinces of British Columbia, & Vancouver Island . . . Compiled from Original Documents* was also sold to the general public with a stern warning, "This Map is Copyright, Having Been Constructed from a Great Variety of Original Materials & at Great Labour. The Copyright Will Be Protected." In 1861, the *Journal of the Royal Geographical Society* reprinted it to illustrate the reports by Begbie, Mayne, and Palmer that have been referred to several times.

Sea voyages to Vancouver Island took so many months that private citizens proposed a transcontinental railway that would speed from Halifax, Montreal, and Toronto to British Columbia in just a week.[15] The London *Times* estimated that voyages to Victoria that took eight months sailing around South America, or around forty days by steamer via Panama, would be cut to seventeen days: ten days steaming from Liverpool to Halifax, then seven more by rail to the mouth of the Fraser River. The benefits for trade between England and Asia would be enormous. The centuries-old dream of a northwest shipping passage through the Arctic Ocean now had a viable solution. The year 1858 saw the revival of proposals for a cross continent railway that had foundered in 1851 and 1852. Given the problematic terrains of what is now northern Ontario and British Columbia, these proposals were audacious. After all, Americans did not complete their first railroad to the Pacific Ocean over a less difficult route until 1869. Nevertheless, commercial benefits and new technologies made British Columbia seem within reasonable reach to Canada's economic establishment in Montreal and Toronto. Politicians agreed. A railway across the continent was a condition of British Columbia becoming the fifth province of the Dominion of Canada in 1871.

— • —

A practical outcome of the mapping of British Columbia was the continuing development of roads into the Interior of British Columbia. Road building had already been Douglas's most impressive achievement as governor in 1858. Henry de Groot praised him for his initiatives, since he was "prompt and liberal [with] improvements . . . not less than $150,000 having already been expended . . . in opening new routes . . . into the mines."[16] The governor bragged to London that the terrain is "the most rugged and impracticable in the world, and the cost of the work commensurably great. However . . . we have succeeded . . . in opening Pack trails through the Cascade range of mountains, both from Yale and Douglas."[17] The Harrison-Lillooet route has been described in detail in Chapter 7. The governor's hard-won experience there meant that future projects would have better long-range planning, brilliant engineering, and more informed costing.

The rough Douglas Portage north of Yale to Spuzzum and the more problematic trail on the east bank to Lytton served the immediate purposes of 1858. In 1862, an expensive, eighteen-foot wide wagon road was completed up the Fraser Canyon from Yale to Lytton. The Alexandra Bridge provided the final link in 1863. Highway 1 follows that route. The Cariboo wagon road was extended from Lytton as far as Barkerville by 1865. A reasonable road (now abandoned) had been blazed on the east side of the Fraser from Fort Hope to a ferry that crossed the river to Fort Yale. Tentative 1858 forays up the Similkameen River (where Highway 3 now travels) and the Coquihalla River (the location of Highway 5) commanded fuller attention in 1859 and later.[18] The gold rush of 1858 set the government on increasingly ambitious road projects that left permanent footprints in British Columbia.

— • —

Indigenous people continued to command Douglas's attention. During 1858, he had been increasingly frustrated as they were displaced by miners. Even though Colonial Minister Lytton urged considering "the best and most humane means of dealing with the Native Indians," he more emphatically insisted on "exercising due care in laying out and defining the several reserves, so as to avoid checking at a future day the progress of the white colonists."[19] What could be done to help First Nations?

In previous years, Douglas and his Métis wife had cultivated amicable relations with the Indigenous peoples. He championed the British colonial policy of extinguishing Indigenous title to land through treaties and financial settlement. Between 1850 and 1854, he had made fourteen treaties on Vancouver Island to prevent conflict between the original occupants and new settlers.[20] Indigenous people agreed to leave lands that would become white settlements in exchange for as much land as they asked for elsewhere. Old settlements, burial places, and enclosed fields would remain their property forever, and the Indigenous would be allowed to hunt and fish on all unoccupied lands in the colony. Every family also received two pounds and ten shillings cash payment ($12.50).

During the tumult of 1858, Douglas was able to save only one unidentified fishing spot on the Fraser:

> one small party of those natives laid claim to a particular part of the river, which they wished to be reserved for their own purposes, a request which was immediately granted, the space staked off, and the miners who had taken claims there, were immediately removed, and public notice given that the place was reserved for the Indians, and that no one could be allowed to occupy it without their consent.[21]

Miners took little note of that precedent. Douglas's instructions to create reserves along the Harrison-Lillooet trails in September 1858 were met with derision from the frustrated road cutters.

In March 1859, Douglas pondered several solutions for Indigenous people.[22] He did not want to repeat American-style wars that confined them to costly reservations and left them "rapidly degenerating." Equally unsatisfactory was the conversion by Spanish missions in Mexico. They left Indigenous people "in a state of pupilage, and not allowed to acquire property of their own, nor taught to think and act for themselves." Douglas strove to find ways to ensure that Indigenous peoples could thrive despite the influx of white settlers. To make large reserves financially self-sustaining, Douglas proposed leasing unoccupied portions, with the proceeds "applied to the exclusive benefit of the Indians," including the building of schools that would prepare them for lives integrated with white settlers. This plan differed profoundly from later residential schools because it left Indigenous children with their families on protected lands where they could continue their traditional lives. The educational programme promised to give Indigenous people agency to cultivate useful skills on their own terms.

Douglas prioritized setting aside large areas of land before white settlement impinged on them. He established 39,900 acres of reserves on the Fraser River below Fort Hope, numerous smaller reserves on the Fraser between Fort Hope and Lytton, more reserves on the Lillooet River, and several square miles of reserves on the Thompson River. As was the case on Vancouver Island, surveyors were instructed to give the Indigenous residents all the lands they requested.

A document from 1860 shows how thoughtful and wide-ranging Douglas's provisions were for that time. When visiting Port Pemberton (present Mount Currie, which is at the centre of large Indigenous reserves), he told the thirty families living on a reserve of several hundred acres that:

> the Magistrates had instructions to stake out, and reserve for their use and benefit, all their occupied village sites and cultivated fields, and as much land in the vicinity of each as they could till, or was required for their support; and that they might freely exercise and enjoy the rights of fishing the Lakes and Rivers, and of hunting over all unoccupied Crown Lands in the Colony; and that on their becoming registered Free Miners, they might dig and search for Gold, and hold mining claims on the same terms precisely as other miners: in short, I strove to make them conscious that they were recognized members of the Common-wealth, and that by good conduct they would acquire a

certain status, and become respectable members of society. They were delighted with the idea.[23]

As Douglas knew from his Hudson's Bay Company experience, hunters and fishers needed large tracts of land, all handsomely provided by this agreement. He also wanted Indigenous people to have farming acreage for their own produce and possibly for sale. Even more significant, he gave them agency equal to white people for pursuing livelihoods outside reserved lands if they wanted. They could even purchase and hold non-reserve property on the same terms as whites.

A full treatment of how quickly Douglas's successors revoked those policies can be found elsewhere.[24] However, the forces of white settlement are a problematic legacy of the gold rush of 1858 that need to be acknowledged here. In 1864, during the final days of Douglas's tenure as governor, Joseph William Trutch was appointed Chief Commissioner of Lands and Works for B.C. An Englishman, he amassed lucrative real estate holdings in B.C. Like many English and Americans, he thought that Indigenous people were "the ugliest & Laziest creatures I ever saw, & we should as soon think of being afraid of our dogs as of them."[25]

Trutch is the punching bag of everybody who believes in common law legal precedent, inalienable property rights, and equal opportunity. Shortly after Douglas resigned, he swept aside treaty agreements made with Indigenous people as mere "verbal instructions."[26] That falsehood was given to justify his reduction of Douglas's reserves by 92%, thus freeing 40,000 acres for white possession. Indigenous people were left with no more than 10 acres per family and forbidden to own property off reserves. In stark contrast, every adult white settler was allowed to pre-empt 160 acres and purchase a further 480 acres.[27]

It took over a century for those policies to be revisited. In a gesture of reconciliation, on July 8, 2021, the Vancouver City Council voted unanimously to change the name of Trutch Street to a name to be proposed by the local Musqueam people.

Even more substantially, on June 26, 2014, the Supreme Court of Canada ruled in favour of the Tsilhqo'tin First Nation against the Province of British Columbia. The judgement held that "the nature of Aboriginal title is that it confers on the group that holds it the exclusive right to decide how the land is used and the right to benefit from those uses," though the province's rights to regulate forests were also upheld.[28] That decision returned to Governor Douglas's conviction that Indigenous people deserve as much autonomy and economic opportunity as other British Columbians. Nowadays, many Indigenous voices with a variety of perspectives are contributing to decisions on many issues.

A century and a half on from British Columbia's first gold rush, the provincial government attempts to balance the interests of Indigenous peoples with environmental concerns, resource development, and expanding urbanization. Indigenous concerns do not have single answers for unsettled land claims, the fostering of ancient traditions, the protection of natural resources, and the desire for gainful employment. Nor is there a single Indigenous proposal for any given issue. The challenges that British Columbia now faces continue to be as complex as they were in 1858.

APPENDIX 1

Ships

∽

DURING 1858, the sea and rivers provided highways for long-distance travel from San Francisco to Victoria, short hops to adjacent Puget Sound in neighbouring Washington Territory, and access to the Fraser River gold mines. Ships carried passengers and their baggage, as well as food, materials used by miners, a wealth of other goods needed for domestic and commercial life in town, and construction supplies for the building booms. They were also the irreplaceable conveyers of local as well as international news, personal mail, business communications, government communiqués, and naval plus army personnel. Everything now transported by cars, trucks, trains, planes, ships, the post office, couriers and even email went by ship in 1858.

Forty-seven ships are mentioned in this book and the diaries it is based on. Some of them appear more than once, and little is known about a number of them. Rather than bury information in one reference that would be difficult to rediscover, this appendix collects the information in a form that can be consulted whenever needed. Because of space limitations, this appendix consists of just four topics: a brief overview of the sources, a description of all the types of vessels, a week-by-week record of the number of passengers that travelled from San Francisco to Victoria, and details of the forty-seven vessels as they pertain just to this book.

— • —

Books about early B.C. history frequently mention the steamers *Beaver*, *Enterprise*, *Maria*, *Otter*, *Surprise*, and *Umatilla*. However, contradictions in secondary sources and the lack of extensive shipping information led to almost a year of research combing through two weekly San Francisco maritime newspapers for 1858 (the *Mercantile Gazette and Shipping Register* and *Prices Current and Shipping List*), as well as short maritime notices in the *Victoria Gazette*, Olympia's *Pioneer and Democrat*, Steilacoom's *Puget Sound Herald*, and Whatcom's short-lived *Northern Light*. Twenty volumes of 1858 customs house records from Port Townsend, San Francisco, and Victoria were consulted: see the abbreviations PTBC, PTBU, PTE, PTI, PTRC, PTRD, PTRF, SFA-1 through 7, SFC-1 through 3, VICB, VICL, and VICR in the Abbreviations. A wealth of information was found in the log book of the Hudson's Bay Company steamer *Otter* (OtterL), now preserved in the Hudson's Bay Company Archives in Winnipeg. Mid-nineteenth-century ship registers contain useful statistics for many of the vessels. A few other sources were enlisted when they contained reliable information.

That original survey provides the first comprehensive overview of shipping around Vancouver Island, in Puget Sound, on the Fraser River, and from San Francisco during 1858. The activity irreversibly changed the development of the Pacific Northwest. It amplifies and corrects *Lewis and Dryden's Marine History of the Pacific Northwest*, ed. E.W. Wright (Portland: Lewis and Dryden, 1895).

American-owned vessels cleared for July 1858 sailing from
San Francisco to Victoria and other foreign places

Many surprises emerged from the information. For example, at least 276 vessels made over 1,600 sailings in the areas of concern during 1858. One hundred and forty-two vessels carried passengers from San Francisco to the Pacific Northwest. Most were sailing ships, not steamers. Most of the vessels were seaworthy ships and not tubs in poor repair, as is often repeated. The first pool of ships to sail from San Francisco to Victoria at the height of demand were locally employed California vessels, while the second group were large vessels that interrupted international schedules for one or two lucrative trips to Victoria. Cargo lists for dozens of sailings indicate what items were shipped north and when certain badly needed items started to be transported. At least fifty-two known ships transported passengers and freight up the Fraser River. Dozens of small craft from Victoria and Puget Sound provided local services as the year ended with the cancellation of the Hudson's Bay Company monopoly on trade.

— • —

Thirteen main types of vessel voyaged to Victoria in 1858.

Ocean steamers had deep draughts for stability in rough water. They were powered by sidewheels or screw propellers, and most had supplementary masts for sails. They ranged from 187 to 2,187 tons with sixteen to seventy-six crew. Although much faster than sailing ships, they needed frequent and expensive refuelling. Their deep draughts made river travel impractical.

River steamers had flat bottoms, shallow draughts, and rear paddlewheels that could run them across some shoals and up river banks for easy loading. They ranged from 66 to 439 tons. Crew numbers have not been found. They were unsuited for rough open waters such as the Strait of Georgia.

Steam tugs (30 to 132 tons) towed ships and barges, sometimes long distances.

The word "ship" usually means any large vessel, but also refers to a specific type. Ships were the large queens of sail, usually with three masts, rarely more. Their square sails, rigged across the ships, caught the east-west trade winds that facilitated voyages around the world. They ranged from 273 to 3,594 tons with twelve to thirty-five crew. Clippers had concave prows that cut through water at twice the speed of regular vessels but sacrificed much cargo space.

Barks (barques) had three masts, the front two rigged with square sails,

236 / *Gold, Grit, Guns*

the last one rigged fore and aft with moveable triangular or trapezoidal sails that facilitated north-south tacking. They ranged from 109 to 700 tons with six to twenty-five crew.

Barkentines (barquentines) had the front mast square rigged, and the other two fore and aft rigged.

Brigs had just two square-rigged masts. They ranged from 124 to 254 tons with six to eighteen crew.

Brigantines had the foremast square rigged and the rear mast fore and aft rigged.

Schooners had two masts (occasionally more), all fore and aft rigged. A scow schooner had a flat bottom and very shallow draught suitable for the shallow shores of Puget Sound. Schooners ranged from 4 to 218 tons with two to thirteen crew. Because their rigging facilitated tacking on north-south travel, they were the most popular ships on the Pacific coast, the waters around Vancouver Island, and on Puget Sound.

Sloops had just one mast, fore and aft rigged. They were usually small, at two to thirty-seven tons and two to seven crew.

Canoes of Indigenous peoples were dugouts carved from cedar logs. Around six metres long (twenty feet), they needed several paddlers. They could carry several passengers and hundreds of pounds of cargo. The make-shift small canoes made by prospectors could easily come to grief.

Rowboats (skiffs). Several kinds of small rowed craft were used to cross the Strait of Georgia and ascend the Fraser River. Some unsafe craft were improvised by prospectors. Professionally built Hudson's Bay Company bateaux made of hard pine boards were 10 x 2 metres (32 x 6 feet). Eight men rowed or paddled them under the direction of a "padroon." They carried up to three tons of freight. Smaller whale boats held several passengers and cargo.

— • —

The San Francisco maritime weeklies the *Mercantile Gazette and Shipping Register* and *Prices Current and Shipping List* regularly listed the number of passengers who travelled to and from Victoria. Their conservative numbers were based on ship manifests and San Francisco Customs House records. Both of those newspapers comment that ships often carried more passengers than they were allowed by law. In those cases, shipping agents and captains lied and reported numbers that were below the legal limits. Indeed, the numbers of arriving passengers published in Pacific Northwest newspapers are often higher than the numbers found in San Francisco records for the same sailing. For example, diarist Otis Parsons left San Francisco on the July 1 sailing of the steamer *Orizaba*, which had just 786 passengers according to San Francisco's *Daily Alta California* newspaper. By contrast, the *Victoria Gazette* of July 10 reported that it landed with 1,300 people. The implication is that the figures published in San Francisco sources are too low. However, the 24,509 people said to have travelled by ship from San Francisco plus the additional 5,000 to 7,000 said to have come overland do bring the total close to the 33,000 so often referred to in history books.

The numbers of people in the following chart come from the San Francisco maritime newspapers, *Prices Current and Shipping List* and the *Mercantile Gazette and Shipping Register*. They usually have the same day number for the last day of one group and the first day of another. The last day number has been reduced by one, since it would take a day or two for figures to reach the newspaper office. Sailings are given rather than vessels, because some vessels made more than one sailing in a month. The number of sailings for April 20 to June 24 come from *PCSL*, since other records list many fewer sailings. After June 25, the numbers of sailings come from San Francisco Customs House clearance records, *MGSR*, and *PCSL*.

TABLE 6: IMMIGRATION TO FRASER RIVER FROM SAN FRANCISCO IN 1858

DATES/VESSELS	MEN	WOMEN	CHILDREN	TOTAL	SOURCE
April 20-30 8 sailings	640	10	—	650	*PCSL* June 19
May 4-29 8 sailings	1,841	28	6	1,875	*PCSL* June 19
June 4-17 16 sailings	6,546	118	27	6,691	*PCSL* June 19
June 18-24 14 sailings	5,075	80	8	5,168	*PCSL* June 26
June 25-29 9 sailings	1,450	50	28	1,523	*PCSL* Oct. 4
June 30-July 9 25 sailings	5,901	136	22	6,059	*PCSL* July 19

DATES/VESSELS	MEN	WOMEN	CHILDREN	TOTAL	SOURCE
July 10-17 22 sailings	746	35	6	887	*PCSL* July 19
July 18-25 15 sailings	340	11	3	354	*PCSL* July 27
July 26-Aug. 2 12 sailings	270	24	7	301	*PCSL* Oct. 4
Aug. 3-10 9 sailings	262	13	20	295	*PCSL* Oct. 4
Aug. 11-17 4 sailings	30	6	—	36	*PCSL* Oct. 4
Aug. 18-25 3 sailings	109	11	5	125	*PCSL* Oct. 4
Aug. 26-30 1 sailing	30	5	—	35	*PCSL* Oct. 4
Aug. 31-Sept. 10 3 sailings	37	4	1	42	*PCSL* Oct. 4
Sept. 11-18 3 sailings	62	5	—	67	*PCSL* Oct. 4
Sept. 19-24 0 sailings	—	—	—	—	*PCSL* Oct. 4
Sept. 25-30 1 sailing	50	—	—	50	*PCSL* Oct. 4
Oct. 1-Dec. 31 21 sailings	431	—	—	431	*MGSR* Jan 4, 1859
TOTALS: APRIL 20-DEC. 31	23,838	536	138	24,509	*MGSR* Jan. 4, 1859

OVERLAND FROM WASHINGTON AND OREGON IN 1858: 5,000-7,000 (*PCSL* July 3)

RETURNS TO SAN FRANCISCO FROM THE FRASER RIVER IN 1858:
   May 1-October 31: 8,290 (*PCSL* Nov. 4, 1858)
   May 1-December 31: 12,976 (*MGSR* Jan 4, 1959)

VICTORIA RESIDENTS AT END OF 1858: 1,000 (Gardiner 1858: 252)

FRASER RIVER RESIDENTS AT END OF 1858: 10,000 (*PRBC* 2.29)

— • —

Each of the following forty-seven descriptions of vessels at work in 1858 includes, where known, all of the following information: the name and registry of the vessel, type, tonnage, length and breadth, year and place of building, when it arrived on the Pacific coast, its captain in 1858, crew numbers, movements in 1858 only as they relate to this book, and selected references.

A.Y. Trask, a Puget Sound schooner, 22 tons, 14 x 3.7 metres (46 x 12.25 feet), built 1854 and based at Port Discovery on the Strait of Juan de Fuca, Captain Philip Bynum, three crew. In 1858, it was the first recorded vessel to take prospectors up the Fraser River, not only from Puget Sound, but also from Victoria. (PTRF 1857.05.07). April 13, left Port Townsend for Victoria (PTE); April 15, left Port Townsend for Fraser River with merchandise and passengers (*PCSL*, May 4). April 18, arrived at Port Townsend from Fraser River (*PCSL*, May 4); April 20, left Port Townsend for Victoria with passengers (*PCSL*, May 4). April 25, arrived at Port Townsend from Victoria, loaded passengers from San Francisco off the steamer *Columbia*, then left for Fraser River (*MGSR*, May 13).

Active, a U.S. Pacific Coast Survey sternwheel ocean steamer, 510 tons, 52.4 x 8.2 metres (172 x 27 feet), built 1849 at New York as commercial *Goldhunter*. Bought for U.S. Pacific Coast Survey, 1852-61. It spent August 2 to October 11, 1858, on Puget Sound and the Fraser River helping to establish the forty-ninth parallel under Captain Lieutenant James Alden and thirty crew. "Active (1852)," *Wikipedia*, photo; Heyl 1965: 4.121-4; Lytle 1975: 2, 86, 264; *VG* Aug. 3: 3.2.

Beaver, a Hudson's Bay Company sidewheel ocean steamer based at Victoria, 187 tons, 31 x 6 metres (101.7 x 20 feet), four six-pound guns, built 1835 at Blackwell, England, for Pacific Ocean trade. In 1858, Captain John Swanson with thirty crew (twelve sailors, eighteen traders) served Vancouver Island, Puget Sound, the Pacific coast up to Fort Simpson at the Russian America border (now Alaska), and the Fraser River in November and December. Delgado 1993: 13; PTE; *VG*; Wright 1895: 14-8, 218, 361.

Bellingham Bay Scow—see *H.C. Page*, schooner

Caledonia (*Caledonian, New Caledonia*), a Vancouver Island sidewheel steam ferry, 30.5 x 5.6 metres (100 x 18.6 feet), named after New Caledonia (now mainland British Columbia). The first ship built at Victoria, it was launched under Captain Frain on September 8, 1858. It was built by James W. Trahey (from Nova Scotia), for San Francisco merchants Faulkner, Bell & Co. It began ferry service between Esquimalt and Victoria on October 26, 1858. Affleck 2000: 48; Hacking 1944: 278; Hacking 1946: 2-4; Victoria *Colonist*, Dec. 28, 1868 (Trahey's obituary); *VG*, Sept. 9, 1858: 3.1 and 17: 2.4; *VG*, Oct. 28, 1858; Wright 1895, 74-5, 87-90.

Carnatic, a U.K. ship, 732 tons, twenty-five crew, announced from London to Vancouver Island October 30 and reached Victoria April 13, 1959. *MGSR* Dec. 18; *VG*, Dec. 28, 1858: 4.1 and April; VICR 2.

Champion, a B.C. lake steamer, 30.5 x 6.7 metres (100 x 22 feet), built 1860 at Victoria, assembled on Seton Lake for Taylor and Co. Governor Douglas saw it in 1860, noting: "The boilers . . . were cut into five sections and then rolled over the trail" from Port Douglas. *British Colonist*, June 12, 1860: 1.2; *CD* 1860.10.9; Edwards 1978: 133; Hacking 1946: 12, 38; Macdonald 2004; Wright 1895: 98.

Cleopatra, a California sidewheel river steamer, 80 tons, built 1853 at San Francisco for the Sacramento and Feather rivers. Fare to San Francisco cost $11. On April 14, 1858, diarist George Slocumb used it to get from Marys-ville to Sacramento (diary, p. S2). Chamberlain & Wells 1879: 107-10, Lytle 1975: 39, Trimble 2011.

Colonel Moody, a B.C. sternwheel river steamer, 44.2 x 8.2 metres (145 x 27 feet), being built at the Songhees First Nations village opposite Fort Victoria August 6, 1858, by James W. Trahey (from Nova Scotia). Launched May 14, 1859. It ran from New Westminster to Fort Hope and Fort Yale, connecting at Harrison River with steamer *Maria* for Port Douglas. Affleck 2000: 50; Hacking 1944: 278; Hacking 1946: 6, 18, 21, 25, 38-9; *VG* Aug. 6: 2.2. Wright 1895: 81-82.

Columbia, a California sidewheel ocean steamer, 777 tons, 59 x 8.8 metres (193.5 x 29 feet), built 1850 at New York for the Pacific Mail Steamship Company, Captain C.C. Dall. On April 27, it arrived at Port Townsend with 250 passengers and mail from San Francisco. Some hopeful miners trans-ferred to the schooner *A.Y. Trask* for passage to the Fraser River. Heyl 1953: 1.97; Lytle 1975: 42; *MGSL*; *PCSL*; SFA-1, *VG*, July 14, 1858: 3 and July 17, 1858: 3.3; Wright 1895, 35 (picture), 70.

Commodore (*Brother Jonathan*), a California sidewheel ocean steamer with 350 berths, 1,359 tons, 67 by 12 metres (221 x 36 feet), built 1851 at New York as *Brother Jonathan* (an early personification of the U.S.). John T. Wright (Merchants Accommodation Line) bought it in 1857 and brought it to San Francisco under the name *Commodore*. Under Captain George W. Staples and thirty-six crew, it was the first large vessel to bring 420 passengers from San Francisco to Victoria, including diarist George Slocumb and a hundred African-Americans escaping racism in California. They left San Francisco on April 20 and reached Victoria on April 25. It completed three more voyages north in 1858 before storm damage crippled her early in July. Bowers 1999; Heyl 1953: 1.63-4; Heyl 1969: 6.25-6; Lytle 1975: 25, 247; *MGSR* April 27, cargo list; George Slocumb's diary; Wright 1895: 69-71.

Constitution, a Puget Sound propeller ocean steamer, 530 tons, 51 x 7.9 metres (167 x 26 feet), built 1850 at Philadelphia and purchased by the Pacific Mail Steam Ship Company for short trips from San Francisco, 1851-7. In March 1858, Captain A.B. Gove bought it and from May 10 it made weekly mail circuits around Puget Sound. George Beam saw it at Whatcom on July 19. Hacking 1944: 256-7, 263 ($25 fare); Lytle 1975: 45; *MGSR*; *PCSL*; PTE; PRTD 1858.05.17 (A.B. Gove master); *VG*; Wright 1895: 63, 71.

Cortes (*Cortez*), a California sidewheel ocean steamer, 1,117 tons, 68.6 x 9.8 metres (225 x 32 feet), built 1852 as *Saratoga* at New York. It was sent as *Cortes* to San Francisco for the Nicaragua Steamship Company. In 1858, it sailed from San Francisco to Victoria and Puget Sound six times. Returning from Bellingham Bay to San Francisco on July 12 under Captain R.H. Horner and seventy-five crew, it carried 150-250 disappointed miners and refused passage to those who could not pay the exorbitant $30 fare (*SDU*, July 19, 1858: 3.2). Heyl 1969: 6.79-81; Lytle 1975: 46, 253; *MGSR*; *PCSL*; PTE; SFA-1; SFA-4; SFC-2; *VG*; Wright 1895: 69.

Ellenita, a New Granada (now Panama) clipper brig, 182 tons register, Captain Augustin F. Gerard, eight to nine crew. In 1858, it made three trips from San Francisco to Victoria. On its May 31 sailing from San Francisco it carried construction materials, arriving at Victoria on June 26. SFC-1; SFC-3; *MGSR*, June 4, list of cargo; *VG*, June 30: 3.4.

Enterprise, an Oregon, then B.C. sternwheel river steamer, 194 tons, 35 x 6.7 metres (115 x 22 feet), draught 16 inches light or 31 inches loaded, built 1855 at Canemah, Oregon for the upper Willamette River, Oregon. Captain Thomas Wright bought it in July 1858 and had the ocean steamer *Pacific* tow it to Esquimalt on Aug. 20. Comfort made *Enterprise* the most popular boat on the Fraser. Contrary to most sources, the *Victoria Gazette* records that Wright ran it from Victoria as far as Fort Hope and back eleven times. On September 5, it became the second steamer to reach Fort Yale, after *Umatilla*. After November 21, the government restricted it to the Fraser River due to winter storms on the Strait of Georgia. It remained on the Fraser River until autumn 1859. Affleck 1992: 16, Affleck 2000: 12, Hacking 1944: 272-5 and 279, Lytle 1975: 65, *VG* (especially Aug. 21: 2.1 and Dec. 18: 2.2-3), *Wikipedia* "Enterprise (1855)" (photo), Wright 1895: 56-7, 72-3, 87.

Euphrates, a U.K. bark, 413 tons, fifteen crew, announced October 30 from London for Vancouver Island, left London on Jan. 3, 1859, arrived at Victoria June 25, 1859. *Lloyd's* 1859; *MGSR* Dec. 18; *VG*, Dec. 28, 1858: 4.1; VICR: 4; Woodward 1975: 12.

Fauntleroy, brig—see *R.H. Fauntleroy*.

Ganges, HMS ship of the line (U.K. navy), 3,594 tons, eighty-four guns, 59.9 x 15.8 metres (196.5 x 52 feet), built 1821 at Bombay; forty-six officers, 444 seamen, 150 Marines, sixty boys, fifteen bandsmen—total 715. On October 17, it arrived at Esquimalt from Valparaiso, Chile, under Rear Admiral Robert Lambert Baynes to enforce British sovereignty against the influx of Americans. On December 22 it left for Valparaiso. Colledge 1969: 227; *VG* Oct. 19: 2.2, 28: 3.1-2, Dec. 23: 2.3; Wright 1895: 88.

Georgiana, a New Granada (now Panama) clipper ship, 460 or 800 tons, Captain G.S. Porter, thirteen to thirty crew. An international trader, on June 12 it made one trip from San Francisco, arriving at Victoria around July 4 and sailing through Port Townsend on July 8 to load Puget Sound lumber. It advertised that "her between-decks [were] upwards of eight feet in height, with side ports and thorough ventilation" (*PCSL*, May 27). PTE; SFC-3; VICR: 8; *VG*, July 7: 3.4.

Goodman Castle, a California sternwheel river steamer, 71 tons, built 1857 at San Francisco. George Slocumb boarded it in Sacramento and reached San Francisco in over five hours (diary p. S2). Lytle 1975: 87, *Map and Record* 1988: 15.

Governor Douglas, a B.C. sternwheel river steamer, 44 x 8 metres (144 x 26 feet) floated at Victoria October 30, 1858, for Victoria Steam Navigation Company, completed in January 1859. It brought passengers and freight from Victoria to New Westminster then transferred them to the *Colonel Moody* to proceed upriver. Hacking 1944: 278; Hacking 1946: 4-5, 18, 21, 25, 38-9; *VG* Dec. 30: 2.2; Wright 1895: 81-2.

H.C. Page (*Bellingham Bay Scow*), a Puget Sound scow schooner based at Whatcom, 42 tons, 21 x 5 metres (68.5 x 17.5 feet), built 1854 at Whatcom, Captain H. Roeder, three or four crew. On July 26, diarist George Beam saw the steamer *Surprise* towing schooner *H.C. Page* up the Fraser River, likely with cargo to replenish Hudson's Bay Company supplies at Fort Langley. Its relatively shallow draft of just 1.2 metres (4 feet) when fully loaded made river travel and unloading easy. Beam diary, July 26, p. B5; *PSH*, Sept. 10: 2.5; PTRD 1858.11.30; Wright 1895: 53.

Hope, a B.C. sternwheel river steamer, 29 x 5.5 metres (95 x 18 feet), built 1860 at Victoria by James W. Trahey for Fraser River service under Captain Charles Thomas Millard. Bought in 1867 by Captain John R. Fleming. In 1871, ailing Fleming took Captain Otis Parsons as his partner, then retired to Oakland, California. Parsons ran the *Hope* and *Lillooet* on the Fraser. In 1874, Parsons sent prospectors on the *Hope* to Fort Wrangell, Alaska, and up the dangerous Stikine River for the Cassiar gold rush. By August 1875, the worn-out *Hope* was moored at Fort Wrangell, and broken up in 1882. Affleck 1992: 20-1, 35; Akrigg 1977: 153; *British Colonist*, September 25, 1860: 2.2; Downs 1992: 36-7; Hacking 1946: 14, 30-36, 39; Hacking 1947: 70-83; Wright 1895: 120, 223-8.

Lady of the Lake, a B.C. sternwheel lake steamer, 22 x 4.6 metres (72 x 15 feet), built at Victoria and assembled at Anderson Lake 1860 for Chapman and Company. *British Colonist*, June 12, 1860: 1.2; *CD* 1860.10.9; Edwards 1978: 133; Hacking 1946: 12; Wright 1895: 98.

Lillooet, a B.C. sternwheel river steamer, 39.6 x 8.5 metres (130 x 28 feet), built 1863 at Victoria by James W. Trahey for Captain John R. Fleming's Port Douglas Steam Navigation Company. In 1871, ailing Fleming took Captain Otis Parsons as his partner and soon retired to Oakland, California. In 1874, Parsons ordered the *Royal City* to replace the *Lillooet*. Even so, the

Lillooet was refurbished and used in reserve for several years. Affleck 1992: 25; Downs 1992: 33, 35-6; Hacking 1946: 25; Hacking 1947: 70, 81; Wright 1895: 120.

Maria, a California then B.C. sternwheel river steamer, 69 tons, 39 x 7.3 metres (128 x 24 feet), built 1857 at San Francisco for the California Steam Navigation Company for Sacramento River service. Bought in 1858 by Captain William M. Lubbock on the stipulation that he would never use it on the Sacramento River. (Lubbock sneakily had the steamer *Umatilla* shipped south in October to replace *Maria* on the Sacramento River.) On July 29, *Maria* was placed on the barge *Sacramento* and towed from San Francisco by the steam tug *Martin White*, arriving at Esquimalt August 9. It then ferried thousands up and down the river. On September 18 at Fort Langley, it received cargo for the Harrison-Lillooet road builders, including ten animals, five wagons, and ten men with baggage that had left Victoria via the HBC steamer *Otter* (OtterL) on September 16. On September 21, it was seen aground in Harrison River with the passengers who had left Victoria on September 16 via the *Otter* (*VG*, Sept. 22: 2.2). It remained on the Fraser River in 1859. Affleck 1992: 26; Hacking 1944: 270-1, 278-9; Lytle 1975: 136; *VG*, Aug. 3, 1858: 2.2; *VG*, Aug. 10, 1858: 2.3; *VG*, Aug. 31, 1858: 2.1; *VG*, Dec. 9, 1858: 2.2; *VG*, Dec. 30, 1858: 2.2; Wright 1895: 72-3.

Marzelle (*Martrelle*), a B.C. sternwheel lake steamer, 18.3 x 4 metres (60 x 13 feet), built 1860 at Victoria and assembled at Lillooet Lake for Goulding and Company. Affleck 2000: 56; *British Colonist*, June 12, 1860: 1.2; *CD* 1860.10.9; Edwards 1978: 133; Hacking 1946: 12; Wright 1895: 98.

Oregon, a California sidewheel ocean steamer, 1,503 tons, 63.4 x 10 metres (208 x 33 feet), built 1848 at New York. Brought to San Francisco in 1849 to serve Panama for Pacific Mail Steam Ship Company. In 1858, it made four trips to Victoria and Puget Sound under Captain C.P. Patterson and sixty crew. The anonymous Canadian miner left San Francisco on July 7, arriving at Victoria with 1,500 other passengers on July 12. Anonymous Canadian's diary, p. M2; Lytle 1975: 164; *MGSR* July 12 with cargo list; SFC-1; *VG*, July 14: 3.4; Wright 1895: 59-60 (picture).

Orestes, a ship, arrived Port Townsend November 16 with fifty passengers from Melbourne. It was the first ship with gold rush prospectors from Australia to reach the Pacific Northwest. It finally reached Victoria on January 18, 1859, with passengers and merchandise. *VG* Nov. 18, 1858: 2.1 and Jan. 29, 1859: 3.2.

Orizaba, a California sidewheel ocean steamer, 1,355 tons, 75 x 10.7 metres (246 x 35 feet), built 1854 at New York. In July 1858, it made three trips to Victoria and Puget Sound under Captain William C. Pease and sixty crew. Otis Parsons took it from San Francisco, leaving on July 2 and arriving at Victoria with 1,500 other passengers on July 8. Heyl 1953: 1.327-8; Lytle 1975: 165; *MGSR*; PTE; *VG*, July 10: 3.3; Wright 1895: 69, 137-8 (with picture), 254, 283.

Otter, an HBC propeller ocean steamer based at Victoria, 239 tons, 38.1 by 6.7 metres (125 x 22 feet), built 1852 at Blackwell, England, for the Hudson's Bay Company on the Pacific coast, Captain William Alexander Mouatt, sixteen crew. It was the most important vessel in 1858 for the transport of passengers and freight, as well as government business, making eighty-four single trips—forty-four to the Fraser River, twenty-nine north up the Pacific coast as far as Fort Simpson, nine to Puget Sound, and two to Fort Vancouver on the Columbia River. Its deep draft made river travel problematic, so it often transferred passengers and cargo to river steamers at Point Roberts. Its 1858 log book has survived at the Hudson's Bay Company Archives in Winnipeg, providing a wealth of information unavailable for most other vessels. *EBC* 519-20; Heyl 1975: 5.219-21; *MGSR*; OtterL; *PCSL*; PTE; *VG*; Wright 1895: 46.

Pacific, a California sidewheel ocean steamer, 1,003 tons, 68.7 x 9.2 (225.5 x 30.3 feet), built 1850 at New York. It arrived at San Francisco in 1851 then ran to Panama and Nicaragua. In 1858, it was sold to John T. Wright (Merchants Accommodation Line) and made twelve round trips from San Francisco to Puget Sound and Victoria under Captain Robert Haley and forty-one crew. On July 4, notorious California exile Ned McGowan annoyed Governor Douglas by having its cannon fired in Victoria Harbour. On December 4, diarist George Slocumb boarded it at Victoria, reaching San Francisco on December 8. It was lost at sea near Cape Flattery, Washington, on November 4, 1875, taking diarist Otis Parsons, his wife, infant child, and 240 passengers to their watery graves. Hauka 2003: 46, Heyl 1953: 1.331-2, Lytle 1975: 167; *PCSL*, Dec. 13; Wright 1985: 69 and 223-8 (picture).

Panama, a California sidewheel ocean steamer, 1,087 tons, 61 x 10.3 metres (200.3 x 33.8 feet), built 1848 at New York. Brought to San Francisco in 1849 by the Pacific Mail Steam Ship Company to run the Panama route. In 1858, it made eleven trips from San Francisco to Victoria and Puget Sound, mostly under Captain William L. Dall and fifty-two to sixty-five crew. On May 12, diarist George Slocumb wrote that it left Port Townsend for San Francisco with fifty disgruntled prospectors. Heyl 1953: 1.339-40; Lytle 1975: 167; PTE (William L. Dall); Slocumb diary, pp. S43-S44; Wright 1895: 69-70.

Plumper, HMS screw driven ocean steamer, U.K. navy, bark rigged, 490 tons, twelve guns, 42.7 x 8.4 metres (140 x 27.5 feet), built at Portsmouth, England, 1848. Sent under Captain George Henry Richards to survey the waters around Vancouver Island from 1857 to 1861. From May to July 1858, it enforced licencing on the north arm of the Fraser River and laid buoys through the sand banks at the mouth of the Fraser River that helped ships avoid grounding. On July 24, 1858, George Beam reported at Semiahmoo Bay that the "Schooner *Rob Roy* left this place for Port Townsend with a man that runn away from the British Man of War *Plumpit*" (diary p. B4). Richards' charts made an impressive contribution for navigation in the area by including *Esquimalt Harbour* (1858 survey published 1861); lighthouse locations at the entrance to Esquimalt Harbour (1858 surveys published 1859); *Fraser River and Burrard Inlet* (1859-60 survey published 1860); *Haro and Rosario Straits* (1858-59 survey published 1859); and *Victoria Harbour* (1859 survey published 1861). In the B.C. interior, Lieutenant Richard Charles Mayne of the *Plumper* oversaw *Sketch of Part of British Columbia* showing the rivers and lakes up to Fountain and *Sketch of the Upper Part of the Fraser River from Langley to Yale* (both surveyed and published in 1859). It returned to England in 1861. Akrigg 1977: 98-103; CEG 1858: 16; Colledge 1969: 1.227; "HMS *Plumper* (1848)," *Wikipedia*; Wright 1895: 88.

R.H. Fauntleroy (*Fauntleroy*), a U.S. Coast Survey brig, 25.3 x 6.8 metres (83 x 22.2 feet), Captain Lawson. In 1858, it was surveying Puget Sound and assisting the U.S. Coast Survey steamer *Active* on the forty-ninth parallel border commission. On July 23 at Semiahmoo Bay, George Beam and his party "passed the Brig Fontleroy" (diary, p. B4). http://www.history.noaa.gov/ships/fauntleroy.html, with a watercolour by James Alden, the hydrographer of the U.S. Pacific Coast Survey steamer *Active*.

Recovery, an HBC brigantine based at Victoria, 154 tons, 27.4 x 6.7 metres (90 x 22 feet), built 1846 at Baltimore, Maryland as the *Orbit*, purchased by the Hudson's Bay Company in 1852. From August 1, 1858, it replaced the U.K. navy vessels *Plumper* and *Satellite*, checking mining licences and sailing documents on the Fraser River near future New Westminster. In November, it sailed to Fort Langley to billet Royal Engineers while they built barracks there. Brigantine Recovery 2010.

Resolute, a Puget Sound sidewheel steam tug registered at Port Madison, 132 tons 27.1 x 5.3 (89 x 17.5 feet), built 1850 at Philadelphia. In 1858, it ran circuits around Puget Sound, often touching at Victoria. On August 22 under Captain A.W. Pray and six crew, diarist George Slocumb took it from Whatcom to Semiahmoo near the American border. Lytle 1975: 184; *PSH*, Aug. 27: 2.5; PTRD 1859.05.17; Slocumb's diary, p. S56; Wright 1895: 71, 169.

Rob Roy, a Puget Sound schooner registered at Port Townsend, 43 tons, metres (45 x 17.5 feet), built 1854 at Steilacoom, Washington, Captain Alexander McLean, two crew. In 1858, it served Puget Sound and occasionally Victoria. On July 24 at Semiahmoo Bay, George Beam wrote that the "Schooner Rob Roy left . . . for Port Townsend with a man that runn away from the Brittish Man of War Plumpit," that is, HMS *Plumper*. Beam diary, p. B4; PTRF 1859.05.14

Robert Passenger, a U.K. clipper bark, 439 tons displacement and 700 tons burthen, Edward Sayer, nineteen to twenty-five crew. On July 9, 1858, it made one visit to Victoria boasting that "for steerage, she is unsurpassed, having great height between decks, and being thoroughly ventilated." *PCSL*, June 19.

Royal City, a B.C. sternwheel river steamer, 322 or 439 tons, 39 x 8 metres (128 x 26 feet), built 1875 at Victoria for Otis Parsons. Replacing the ageing *Lillooet*, it was called the "finest specimen of steamboat work yet turned out in the province. . . . The ladies *boudoir* and staterooms are beautifully furnished." Captain Asbury Insley was in charge. Affleck 1992: 35; Akrigg 1977: 153; Downs 1992: 36-7; Hacking 1947: 70-83, 108; Victoria *Colonist*, June 20, 1875; Wright 1895: 223-8, 237.

Satellite, HMS, screw corvette ocean steamer, U.K. navy, 2,187 tons, twenty-one guns, 61 x 12.3 metres (200 x 40.5 feet), built 1855 at Devonport,

England. Under Captain James Charles Prevost, it reached Esquimalt in 1857 to work on the joint British and U.S. commission to establish the forty-ninth parallel. From May through July 1858, it anchored near Westham Island, with its launch (the largest boat carried on a naval vessel) and gig (a small boat) enforcing mining and transport licences on both channels of the south arm of the Fraser River's mouth. Government business occasionally took it elsewhere. Akrigg 1977: 98-103; Brigantine Recovery 2010. *CD* 1858.08.16; *CEG* 1858: 16; Colledge 1969: 491; *PRBC* 1859: 1.13; Smyth 1867: 339 and 434; Wright 1895: 64, 88.

Sea Bird, a Puget Sound sidewheel ocean steamer registered in June 1858 at Port Townsend, 325 tons, 46.5 x 7.2 metres (152.7 x 23.5 feet), built 1850 at New York. It was brought to San Francisco by Captain John Wright and ran to San Diego. From March 1858, it served Puget Sound and Victoria under Captain Francis Connor and fifteen crew. On April 16, 18, 24, 26, and 30, it dropped prospectors near the Fraser River at Semiahmoo Bay and Point Roberts. Its first voyage up the river to Fort Hope on June 8 was successful. On the second ascent, it grounded south of Fort Hope from June 24 to September 2, returned to Victoria on September 4, and burned on September 7 near Discovery Island, 29 kilometres (18 miles) from Victoria. Affleck 1992: 36; Hacking 1944: 262-3; Lytle 1975: 196; *PCSL*, June 12, 1858; PTE; PTRF 1858.06.01; Wright 1895: 63-4, 71-2; *VG*, June 25: 2.4. Sept. 7: 2.1, Sept. 8: 2.2; Wright 1895: 69.

Sierra Nevada, a California sidewheel ocean steamer, 1,246 tons, built 1851 at New York. It was brought to San Francisco in 1853 to sail to Nicaragua under the U.S. Mail Steamship Company. In 1858, it made two trips to Victoria and Puget Sound under Captain J.H. Blethen and seventy-six crew. On July 18, diarist George Beam saw it at Whatcom. Heyl 1953: 1.391-2; Lytle 1975: 199, 297; *MGSR* (July 3 and 19 lists of cargo for Victoria); *PCSL*; *VG*; Wright 1895: 69.

Surprise, a California sidewheel ocean steamer, 457 tons, 55.1 x 8.5 metres (181 x 28 feet), built 1853 at Williamsburgh, New York. In 1856 it reached San Francisco for the California Steam Navigation Company and ran to San Diego. In May 1858, it was retained for Fraser River service through the Hudson's Bay Company's San Francisco agents, Forbes and Babcock. On June 2, 1858, Captain Thomas Huntington with eighteen to twenty-nine crew, brought it to Victoria. On June 3, Governor Douglas finally started issuing sufferances with fees for American ships wishing to enter the Fraser River. The *Surprise* was the first American steamer to ascend the river to Fort Hope, making at least ten round trips with up to 500 passengers per sailing. Charging $25 per customer, it "cleared $50,000 for her owners" in the nine weeks from June 4 to August 20. It then returned to California and was replaced by the smaller steamer *Wilson G. Hunt*. Affleck 1992: 38; Affleck 2000: 61; *DAC* (June 20, June 26, June 27, 1858); Hacking 1944: 259-64 ($25 passage); Lytle 1975: 206, 299; *MGSR*; *PCSL*; PTE; *PRBC* 1.18-19 (Fraser River sufferances for American ships); *PSH* (July 9, 1858: 2.1 on HBC purchase of agents Forbes and Babcock in San Francisco); *SDU* (Aug. 20: 1.4 on $50,000 profit); *VG*; VICL; VICB 1; Wright 1895: 72.

Umatilla, an Oregon sternwheel river steamer, 91 tons, 33.5 x 6.7 metres (110 x 22 feet), built 1858 as *Venture* at Five Mile Creek near the Cascades, Washington, on the upper Columbia River. Damaged in rapids during its trial run, Captain John Ainsworth bought and repaired it, then renamed it *Umatilla*. Ainsworth had it towed by the mail steamer *Columbia* for Fraser River service, reaching Esquimalt July 13, 1858. It was the first sternwheel riverboat on the Fraser, reaching Fort Yale on July 21 on its maiden voyage. Its next sailing reached the head of Harrison Lake on July 26. It often met larger vessels at Point Roberts for the ascent up the river. It had a shallow enough draught to take personnel and supplies for the Harrison-Lillooet road building, leaving Point Roberts for Port Douglas on August 6, 11, 15, 18, and 23. On August 31, it left Point Roberts for Fort Hope, carrying Governor Douglas and thirty-three naval and military personnel to deal with the aftermath of the Fraser River War. Details of thirteen trips have been found. Because of falling demand on the river, around October 18, its owners had it sent on the barge *Sacramento* towed by tug *Martin White* to the Sacramento River in California to replace the steamer *Maria*, which was not allowed to return there. Affleck 1992: 40, Begg 1894: 282 (eyewitness in Yale July 21), *DAC* (Sept. 8, 1858: 1.5), Hacking 1944: 264-72, Lytle 1975: 216, Macdonald 2004, *MGSR*, *PCSL*, *VG*, Wright 1859: 72-3.

Wild Duck, a Puget Sound schooner, 4 tons, Captain Ross, two crew. It was one of the earliest vessels to take prospectors to Fort Langley, returning to Puget Sound from there on May 9, 1858. *PSH*, May 14: 2.5.

Willimantic, a Puget Sound brig registered at Port Ludlow, Washington in 1855, 171 tons, 32 x 8 (105 x 26.75 feet), built 1848 at New London, Connecticut, Captain Thomas Coupe, 6 to 8 crew. In 1858, it freighted lumber around Puget Sound. On July 25, diarist George Beam saw it at Semiahmoo (now Blaine WA) after unloading lumber for new buildings there. *American Lloyds* 1862: 353, *PCSL*, PTE, PTRD 1854.04.28, PTRD 1858.Feb. 22, Wright 40 and 230.

Wilson G. Hunt, a California sidewheel ocean steamer, 350 tons, 56.5 x 7.8 metres (185.5 x 25.5 feet), built 1849 at New York for Coney Island excursions. Brought to San Francisco in 1850 and put on the Sacramento River by the California Steam Navigation Company. On August 18, it arrived at Victoria under Captain A.M. Burns with twenty-three crew to replace the steamer *Surprise* on the Fraser River, which had left for San Francisco around August 20. *Wilson G. Hunt* made eight return trips from Victoria and Bellingham Bay up Fraser River as far as Fort Hope. On October 17, declining business forced its departure for San Francisco. Affleck 1992: 42, Hacking 1944: 264 and 273-4, Hacking 1947: 109, Lytle 1975: 233, *MGSR*, *PCSL*, PTE, *VG*, VICL, Wright 1895: 73, 98, 171.

ACKNOWLEDGEMENTS

My deepest gratitude goes to Duncan McLaren, proprietor of Lord Durham Rare Books in St. Catharines, Ontario, who introduced me to the anonymous Canadian miner's diary. Katherine Kalsbeek of Rare Books and Special Collections at the University of British Columbia in Vancouver offered extraordinary assistance. Other invaluable assistance came from the Hope Historical Museum (Inge Wilson), the Tl'kemtsin First Nations at Lytton (librarian and historian John Haugen), the Hudson's Bay Company Archive in Winnipeg, the California State Library (Gary Kurtz), the National Maritime Museum Library in San Francisco (Gina Bardi and Theodore Miles), the Thomas Fisher Rare Books Library at the University of Toronto (Richard Landon and Anne Dondertman), the National Archives at Kew in England (the curator of maps), and the United Kingdom Admiralty Hydrographic Office at Taunton (Adrian Webb). Further contributions were made by the Vancouver City Archives, the Vancouver Maritime Museum, the Vancouver Public Library, the British Columbia Archives in Victoria, Special Collections at the University of Washington in Seattle, the National Archives of the United States (Seattle and San Francisco branches), the Bancroft Library at the University of California in Berkeley, the San Francisco Public Library, the Society of California Pioneers at San Francisco, the California Historical Society at San Francisco, the Archives of Ontario, the Toronto Reference Library, the Land Registry at Brockville in Ontario, Ottawa's Library and Archives Canada, and London England's British Library. This book would not have been possible without the resources of those institutions.

My profound debt to British Columbia historians and geographers is testified in the bibliography. For detailed information about gold and mercury, I am indebted to Professors Dipankar Sen and Vance Williams of the Department of Chemistry at Simon Fraser University, and to Professors John Meech and Marcello Veiga of the Mining Engineering Department at the University of British Columbia. Early on, Professor Michael Church of the Geography Department at the University of British Columbia had an anecdote that conclusively identified the "Great Falls" just above Bridge River, the most dangerous stretch of the Fraser, where even modern rafting is prohibited. He introduced Michael Kennedy, a self-described "Hudson's Bay brat," who knows the river between Lytton and Pavilion intimately from life-long residence and painstaking study of relics of its gold mining past. A long conversation with Kennedy and scrutiny of his publications helped me better understand the landscapes that the Fraser River miners worked in.[1] Lastly, local historian Angus McIntyre helped to establish the itineraries of the miners' diaries during a painstaking road and hiking trip up the Fraser River. The challenge was to correlate miners' descriptions and nineteenth-century maps with recent topographical maps and the landscape of the river.

Finally, a profound thanks to the late Dr. Ronald Hatch, proprietor of Ronsdale Press. Knowledgeable, fastidious, and a problem solver, he was an exemplary editor.

ABBREVIATIONS

BCA. British Columbia Archives, at the Royal British Columbia Museum, Victoria.

BCPC. British Columbia. Papers Connected with the Indian Land Question, 1850-1875. Victoria: Richard Wolfenden, 1875.

CD. *The Colonial Despatches of Vancouver Island and British Columbia, 1846–1871*. Online at bcgenesis.uvic.ca. Some, but not all, were published in *CEG*, *FPBC*, and *PRBC*.

CDNC. *California Digital Newspaper Collection*. Online at cdnc.ucr.edu.

CEG. 1858. *British Columbia. Copies or Extracts of Correspondence Relative to the Discovery of Gold in the Fraser's River District, in British North America. Presented to Both Houses of Parliament by Command of Her Majesty, July 2, 1858*. London: Eyre and Spottiswoode.

CIHM. Canadian Institute for Historical Microreproductions, Ottawa. Microfiches by number. Some items are online at www.canadiana.org.

DAC. *Daily Alta California*. San Francisco, California, newspaper. Online at *CDNC*.

DCBO. *Dictionary of Canadian Biography Online*.

DEB. *Daily Evening Bulletin*. San Francisco, California, newspaper. Microfilm at UBC.

DSJR. *Daily San Joaquin Republican*. Stockton, California, newspaper. Microfilm at University of California, Berkeley.

EBC. Encyclopedia of British Columbia. Ed. Daniel Francis. Madeira Park, B.C.: Harbour Publishing, 2000.

FPBC 3. 1860. *Further Papers Relative to the Affairs of British Columbia*. Part III. *Presented to both Houses of Parliament . . . 1860*. London: Eyre and Spottiswoode. With map. CIHM 29850.

FPBC 4. 1862. *Further Papers Relative to the Affairs of British Columbia*. Part IV. *Presented to both Houses of Parliament . . . March 1862*. London: Eyre. and Spottiswoode. With 4 maps. CIHM 29851.

HBCA. Hudson's Bay Company Archives, Winnipeg.

JRGS. Journal of the Royal Geographical Society.

LAC. Library and Archives Canada, Ottawa.

LTSBC. Land Title and Survey Authority of British Columbia, 1321 Blanshard Street, Victoria, B.C.

MGSR. The Mercantile Gazette and Shipping Register. San Francisco newspaper.

NA. National Archives, Kew, England.

NASEA. National Archives of the United States, Seattle Branch. RG 36. Records of Collector of Customs, Puget Sound District, Washington.

NASF. National Archives of the United States, San Francisco Branch (at San Bruno). RG 36. Records of the United States Customs Service, Collection District of San Francisco, California.

NL. The Northern Light. Whatcom, Washington Territory, newspaper. July 3-September 11, 1858. Copies at BCA E/8/N81; Center for Pacific Northwest Studies, Western Washington University, Bellingham.

ODQ2. The Oxford Dictionary of Quotations. 2nd ed. Oxford UP, 1955.

OED. The Compact Oxford English Dictionary, Complete Text Reproduced Micrographically. 2nd ed. Oxford: Clarendon Press, 1991.

OtterL. Hudson's Bay Company steamship *Otter*. Log Book, December 30, 1852-August 19, 1861. HBCA C. 1/625.

PCSL. Prices Current and Shipping List. San Francisco newspaper.

P&D. Pioneer and Democrat. Olympia, Washington Territory, newspaper. Microfilm at UW (A233), with about a quarter of the printed text lost in shadows.

PRBC 1. 1859. *Papers Relative to the Affairs of British Columbia.* Part I. *Presented to Both Houses of Parliament . . . 18 February 1859.* London: Eyre and Spottiswoode. CIHM 29849.

PRBC 2. 1859. *Papers Relative to the Affairs of British Columbia.* Part II. *Presented to Both Houses of Parliament . . . 12th August 1859.* London: Eyre and Spottiswoode. CIHM 29849.

PSH. Puget Sound Herald. Steilacoom, Washington Territory, newspaper. Vol. 1, no. 1 on March 12, 1858. Microfilm at UW (A7040).

PTBC. 1854-64. Port Townsend Customs House, Bonds Listing Crews to be Presented at Customs on Return to the US. NASEA, RG 36, series NE 34, OE 33, vol. 1.

PTBU. 1852-61. Port Townsend Customs House, Bonds Specifying Use of Vessels. NASEA, RG 36, series 23, vol. 20.

PTE. 1851-61. Port Townsend Customs House Registers of Entrances and Clearances of Vessels. NASEA, RG 36, series 17, vol. 1. Listed chronologically, including captains' names, tonnage, and crew numbers. The most useful Port Townsend document.

PTI. 1853-61. Port Townsend Customs House Registers of Import of Merchandise. NASEA, RG 36, series 11, vol. 1.

PTRC. 1854-61. Port Townsend Customs House Licences for Coasting Trade of Vessels under 20 Tons. NASEA, RG 36, series 22, vol. 14.

PTRD. 1853-61. Port Townsend Customs House Enrollment Certificates for Domestic Trade. NASEA, RG 36, series 21, vol. 1.

PTRF. 1853-61. Port Townsend Customs House Registry Certificates for Foreign Trade. NASEA, RG 36, series 20, vol. 1.

SDU. Sacramento Daily Union. Sacramento, California, newspaper. Online at *CDNC.*

SFA-1. San Francisco ship arrivals. Boarding Officer's Registers of Vessel Arrivals, November 1, 1855-October 30, 1868. NASF, RG 36, ARC ID 4658174, box 2. Contains the most information.

SFA-2. San Francisco ship arrivals. Boarding Officer's Registers of Vessel Arrivals, January 1, 1852-August 30, 1858. NASF, RG 36, ARC ID 4658174, box 1.

SFA-3. San Francisco ship arrivals. Indexes of Vessels Arrivals, January 1857-December 1860. NASF, RG 36, ARC ID 4667378, box 4.

SFA-4. San Francisco ship arrivals. Naval Officer's Index of Vessel Arrivals, January 1856-July 1858 and July 1858-December 1859. NASF, RG 36, ARC ID 4656368, boxes 3 and 4.

SFA-5. San Francisco ship arrivals. Auditor's Report of Vessel Arrivals, 1852-1863. NASF, RG 36, ARC ID 4662597, box 2.

SFA-6. San Francisco ship arrivals. Registers of American Vessels Entered at San Francisco from Foreign Countries, 1853-1874. NASF, RG 36, ARC ID 4662585, box 1.

SFA-7. San Francisco ship arrivals. Registers of Foreign Vessels Entered at San Francisco from Foreign Countries, 1853-1875. NASF, RG 36, ARC ID 4662587, box 1.

SFC-1. San Francisco ship clearances (outbound). Naval Officer's Index of Vessel Clearances, January 1856-January 1858, and February 1858-December 1859. NASF, RG 36, ARC ID 4662495, boxes 3 and 4.

SFC-2. San Francisco ship clearances (outbound). Registers of American Vessels Cleared for Foreign Countries, July 1853-January 31, 1902. NASF, RG 36, ARC ID 4662595, box 1.

SFC-3. San Francisco ship clearances (outbound), Registers of Foreign Vessels Cleared for Foreign Countries, 1853-1875. NASF, RG 36, ARC ID 4662596, box 1.

UBCR. University of British Columbia Library, Vancouver, Rare Books and Special Collections.

UKHO. United Kingdom Hydrographic Office of the Admiralty, Taunton, England.

UW. University of Washington Library, Seattle.

UWSC. University of Washington Library, Seattle. Special Collections.

VG. The *Victoria Gazette*. Victoria, Vancouver Island, newspaper. First issue June 25, 1858.

VICB 1 and 2. 1858. Colony of Vancouver Island. Custom House Blotter (Accounts Book). BC Archives C/AA/30.22A/1 and 2.

VICL. 1858-76. Colony of Vancouver Island. Custom House Letter Book. BC Archives GR-1733.

VICR. 1858-69. Colony of Vancouver Island. Custom House Returns, including goods imported from October to December, and Port of Victoria shipping records from June 14, 1859. BC Archives MS 1073.

VPL. Vancouver Public Library.

Webster. Webster's Third New International Dictionary of the English Language, Unabridged. Springfield, MA: Merriam-Webster, 1993.

WSE. Winfield Scott Ebey papers. University of Washington Library, Seattle. Special Collections, accession 0127-001, with finding list (not online).

INTRODUCTION

1 *PSH*, March 26, 1858: 2.3. Reprinted to stimulate interest in California by *DAC*, April 4, 1858: 1.5.

2 Meldahl 2011: 38. California gold rush: Holliday 1999.

3 Editorial, "All Cannot Make Fortunes," *SDU*, June 11, 1858: 2.3.

4 Bridge 2015: 21-2.

5 Daniel Marshall quotes jingoistic sentences from George Beam's diary in his studies and the video *Canyon War*. I found only four Fraser River diaries from 1858 after consulting many bibliographies and websites, as well as visiting several libraries in B.C., Washington, Oregon, and California. A few dozen letters surfaced, but most contained only fragments of information. When I visited the libraries where longer documents were held, most assigned to 1858 turned out to be reminiscences written at a later date. Some have only a few lines devoted to 1858. Many memoirs were dictated around 1878 for Hubert Howe Bancroft, whose *History of British Columbia 1792-1887* forms volume 32 of his *Works*.

6 George Beam diary, August 13, 1858.

7 Douglas in *CD*, June 15, 1858 = *PRBC* 1.16-7.

CHAPTER 1: Victoria and International Tensions

1 *SDU*, May 25, 1858: 2.2.

2 Douglas: Barman 2007, Adams 2001. Hudson's Bay Company: Galbraith 1957.

3 Economy: Mackie 1992-3. Cost of blankets in San Francisco: *SDU*, July 19, 1858: 1.5 (an American was offered an Indigenous woman "for ten

blankets—equal to about $50"). In London a blanket cost two shillings and nine pence, approximately sixty-five cents (Dower 1858: 41). Coal and cranberry costs: *PCSL*, July 12, 1858, and *MGSR*, July 3, 1858.

4   Lamb 1940.

5   Waddington 1858: 15.

6   Gold in B.C. before 1858: Akrigg 1977: 44-53; Bancroft 1887: 341-54; *CEG* 5-9.

7   Moore 1914/1939: 217. Since Hill's Bar was where gold was first discovered on the lower Fraser River in 1858, the origin is important to determine. Moore's account is as close as we can get, because he was a participant. However, his memoir was written fifty-six years later. Second-hand accounts sometimes contain accurate details. For example, Howay 1914: 2.14 and Milliken 1963/2010: 92 both state that 800 ounces of gold were shipped from Victoria to the San Francisco mint. That exact amount is corroborated by a despatch of April 6, 1858, where Douglas described the discovery of gold on the Thompson River, "about eight hundred ounces, which has been hitherto exported from the country" (*CEG* 10). Douglas provided no details about when, how, or where the gold was shipped, though it was likely through the Hudson's Bay Company.

Many details in these accounts cannot be verified. Moore and Howay state that the gold was shipped in February, 1858, in care of the purser on the Hudson's Bay Company steamer *Otter*. Howay gives his name as Mr. Holt. Watson 2010 lists no Holt among the hundreds of Hudson's Bay Company employees at work at that time in the area, and the term "purser" is never used for Hudson's Bay Company ship personnel. The log book of the *Otter* records no sailing to San Francisco in 1858: every day is accounted for elsewhere. *Beaver*, the other Hudson's Bay steamer stationed at Fort Victoria, did not sail to San Francisco in 1858. However, *Otter* did leave Fort Victoria for San Francisco on November 18, 1857, attended by HMS *Plumper* and HMS *Satellite* (OtterL). That extraordinary send-off during a stormy time of year suggests an important occasion, such as the shipment of gold. *Otter* reached San Francisco on November 22 in just six days with three passengers (SFA-3, SFA-5), then left on December 2 (SFC-3). It returned to Victoria on December 14, after eleven days (OtterL).

Participant Moore writes that he and fourteen companions took a steamer from San Francisco to Port Townsend and Victoria in March (Moore 1914/1939, also Howay 1914: 2.14). The only possible vessel from San Francisco northbound in time for the March 23 discovery of gold on Hill's Bar was the mail steamer *Columbia*, which reached Port Townsend on March 2, in time to connect with the Hudson's Bay Company steamer *Beaver*, which left for Victoria the same day (*PCSL* March 12). *Columbia* then continued its mail run south to Olympia before leaving for San Francisco on March 7. Eyewitness Moore states that he and his companions paddled up the Fraser in "our boats" from Victoria, which would have been large Indigenous canoes. It would have taken over a week to ascend the Fraser.

8   Hill's Bar: *CD* June 10, 1858 = *PRBC* 1.13; Hazlitt 1858: 137-8; Paterson 1985: 30-51; *VG*, July 14, 1858: 4.3. Gold-bearing clay lay two or three metres below the surface. Hill's Bar is pictured approximately thirteen minutes into the video *Canyon War* 2009.

9   *CD*, May 8, 1858 = *CEG* 1858: 13.

10 Emigration numbers appear in Appendix 1: Ships.

11 Nationalities: Moody 1859/1951: 97, Waddington 1858: 17. Trades and merchants: ads in *VG*. African-Americans: Slocumb's diary, April 23 and 30; Cartwright 1985; Gibbs 1902; Kilian 1978; and Pilton 1951. A March 30, 1858, editorial in *DSJR* supported "the bill now before the Legislature to prevent immigration to this State of free colored persons" because "there is a distinction between the white and colored population of this country, that forever forbids an equality in business and social relations." Chinese: Bridge 2015. *MGSR*, May 4, 1858, reported that a law "to prevent the further immigration of Chinese or Mongolians to this State" was approved by the California legislature on April 26, 1858. *VG*, July 14, 1858: 3.3 noted that seven building lots 30 x 100 were sold to Chinese men after being purchased by "Ah Sou, a well known Chinese merchant of San Francisco, who . . . is making arrangements to facilitate a heavy immigration of his countrymen to the new El Dorado of the north." Multicultural mix in early Victoria: Forsythe and Dickson 2007: 70-91, Bridge 2015.

12 Hazlitt 1858: 147.

13 Lord Napier, quoted in Marshall 2000: 296.

14 Albemarle 1858: 499.

15 *DEB*, July 8, 1858: 1.2; Hazlitt 1858: 224; Waddington 1858: 28.

16 Waddington 1858: 17.

17 On May 11, the *Commodore* took nine cases of window sashes north; on May 31, the *Ellenita* packed thirty-two pairs of windows, forty-six doors, and two kegs of nails; and on June 12, the *Georgiana* carried ten pairs of windows, 160 doors, and forty-three bundles of sashes (*MGSR*, May 19, 1858; June 4, 1858; June 19, 1858). Buchanan 1936: 25 notes that in 1855, sixteen sawmills on Puget Sound produced 85,000 board feet per day, which would equal 26,605,000 board feet per year during a six-day work week. Sawed lumber was selling for just $19 per thousand board feet at Olympia, Washington Territory, on July 23 according to *P&D*. (A thousand board feet equals 200 modern 2 inch by 4 inch by 8 foot pieces.) On July 8, rough lumber was selling in Victoria at the exorbitant rate of $100 per thousand board feet, and planed lumber up to $130 (*DEB*, July 15, 1858: 2.2). The building boom began around July 17, when the price fell to around $50. It remained at that cost for the rest of the year. See "Imports for the Quarter ending 31st December 1858" in VICR, pages 2-3, where rough lumber was priced at $3,379 for 163,124 feet, or $48.28 per thousand board feet. On July 13 in Victoria, "Carpenters are those best paid . . . from $6 to $8 a day, but that is not steady work, and only off and on as a building is put up or lumber declines in price" (*DEB*, July 19, 1858: 2.2).

18 Waddington 1858: 18. *VG*, Aug. 18, 1858: 2.2, reported that from June 12 to August 18, 250 wooden and brick buildings were erected, two-thirds of them stores. An additional "one hundred canvas structures [were] used for stores, restaurants, etc." *DEB*, July 6, 1858: 2.2, noted that on June 29, newcomers were "compelled to sleep on the floors of houses, in tents, and in the open air" because speculators refused to build on lots.

19 "New Gold-Diggings, 1," Sept. 18, 1858: 185; Waddington 1858: 19.

20 *NL*, July 3, 1858: 1.4.

21 The circulating currency was American, which by custom, then Act of the House of Assembly of Victoria Island on April 6, 1859, traded at $5 to £1 (*Journals of the Colonial Legislatures of the Colonies of Vancouver Island and British Columbia, 1851-1871*, ed. J.E. Hendrickson. Victoria, 1980, vol. 2, p. 85). Payment could be made in gold, which was always

termed "dust," or in USA coins, up to $20 gold pieces. The California state constitution forbade the use of paper money.

22 *Satellite* and *Plumper*: *CD* June 10, 1858 = *PRBC* 1.13 1859; *CD* July 26, 1858 = *PRBC* 1. 22-7. *CD* August 16, 1858, no. 2 (online only). *Recovery*: Brigantine Recovery 2010. VICB 1 and 2; VICL.

23 *CD* May 19, 1858 = *PRBC* 1.12. *VG*, Sept. 11, 1858: 2.1, reported "the opening of the river to traders." The head tax remained in September: Nugent 1859: 8.

24 VICB 1, Sept. 4, 1858. Nugent 1859: 8 reports the same fees.

25 *DAC*, Sept. 3, 1858: 2.1.

26 *Report Hudson's Bay* 1857: iv. A highly critical "Canadian view of the Hudson's Bay Company and the Fraser River Mines" was published in the Toronto *Globe* of July 27 and reprinted in *DAC*, Sept. 4, 1858: 1.5.

27 *CD* July 16, 1858 = *PRBC* 1.42-3.

28 Ibid.

29 *CD*, July 1, 1858, no. 2.

30 *CD*, July 31, 1858 = *PRBC* 1.46.

31 *CD*, Sept. 29, 1858 = *PRBC* 1.36.

32 *SDU*, July 8, 1858: 1.4.

33 "'Fifty-Four Forty' and Fraser River": *SDU*, June 11, 1858: 5.1-7. See also "Fifty-Four Forty or Fight": *SDU*, June 12, 1858: 3.2.

34 Dr. A.A. Riddel, *CD*, June 9, 1858.

35 Hauka 2003: 46.

36 *VG*, Sept. 14, 1858: 2.2; cf. Waddington 1858: 20.

37 Reid 1944: 57-9.

38 *CD*, Jan. 5, 1859, no, 64.

39 McGowan, June 8, 1878: 10. George Slocumb saw McGowan arrive at Fort Langley on Sept. 1, 1858. On the bloodless events called McGowan's War, see Hauka 2003 (p. 46 on the July 4 guns). See also McGowan 1857.

40 *CD* May 19, 1858 = *PRBC* 1.11.

41 *CD* Sept. 2, 1858, enclosure dated Aug. 16, 1858 = *PRBC* 1.52.

42 Arrival of *Ganges*: *VG*, Oct. 19, 1858: 2.2. Description: *VG*, Oct. 28, 1858: 3.1.

43 Returns to California from Victoria are listed in Appendix 1: Ships. 150,000 ounces of gold in California: *CD*, Feb. 18, 1858 = *CEG* 17.

44 *DAC*, July 23: 1.7.

45 *CD*, May 19, 1858 = *PRBC* 1.11.

46 Secretary of State Cass's full instructions appear in Reid 1944: 72-4.

47 Reid 1944: 73.

48 *DAC*, Aug. 29, 1858: 1.3 wrote that the American naval force to Paraguay "shall be sufficiently formidable to meet all possible contingencies." See "Paraguay Expedition," *Wikipedia*.

49 *DAC*, July 30, 1858: 1.3, reported that Britain had just apologized formally for its recent seizure of American ships off the Nicaraguan coast.

50 *DCBO*; Reid 1944: 59-60; Waddington 1858: 20, note 1.

51 *New York Times*, Aug. 2, 1858, quoted in Reid 1944: 60.

52 Nugent 1859: 10-18.

53 Cass 1858.

54 *VG*, Nov. 16, 1858: 2.3.

55 *VG*, Nov. 16, 1858: 2.1-2.

56 *British Colonist*, Jan. 22, 1859: 2.4.

CHAPTER 2: Travellers to the Fraser River and Their Expenses

1 Letter from James D. White at Whatcom to George W. Woods in Nevada, June 25, 1858, in Swindle 2001: 137.

2 *VG*, Oct. 21, 1858: 1.2.

3 McNeil 1850: 3, 20-1.

4 Thoreau 1995: 6, 4, 3, 50, from the section titled "Economy" in his 1854 book, *Walden*.

5 "Rates of Labor in San Francisco," *MGSR*, Sept. 20 and Nov. 27, 1858.

6 *Report of the Royal Commission* 1889: 146-7.

7 Dolnick 2014: 11, 110; Jameson 2002: 204-8; Kennedy 2008-9: 64-5; and Mouat 2002: 267-82.

8 Dec. 17, 1848 letter of Franklin A. Buck in Buck 1930: 27.

9 Lotchin 1974: 48-52.

10 Evans 1859: 112, 126-7.

11 1856, 1860, and 1861 Tax Collector Rolls for Gananoque, Township of Front of Leeds and Lansdowne, Leeds County, at Archives of Ontario, F 1668-4.

12 Dr. A.A. Riddell, *CD*, June 9, 1858.

13 Hittell 1861: 21.

14 *DAC*, April 4, 1858: 1.5, and many other reports.

15 J.A. La Nauze, "The Gold Rushes and Australian Politics," *Australian Journal of Politics and History*, 13.1 (1967): 94, quoted in Mouat 2002: 281.

16 Akrigg 1977: 91-2; Bancroft 1887: 258, n. 18; 314-27, 400; Duffus, n.d.; *VG*, July 7: 3.1-2 and Sept. 4: 2.2 (unsigned letter from merchants); Watson 2010: 3.991-2.

17 Goodman 1994: 25.

18 *SDU*, May 20, 1858: 2.4 ($300); *San Francisco Herald*, Nov. 20, 1858 ($350 with passage), quoted in *PRBC* 2. 41; letter from Fort Yale, July 2, 1858, in *DSJR*, July 15, 1858: 2.4 ($500).

19 One of many warnings: *DSJR*, Aug. 5, 1858: 2.3. De Groot 1859: 16 wrote, "Let no one who has a living business . . . think for a moment of abandoning the same and resorting to Fraser River."

20 Passenger numbers and ships: Appendix 1: Ships.

21 Imports to Victoria in June were $90,419 (*PCSL* June 26), in July were $699,463 (*PCSL* Aug. 4), in August were $257,776 (*PCSL* Sept. 4), and from October to December were $389,657.97 (VICR: 2-3).

22 California population: *PCSL* Dec. 27, 1858. San Francisco: city directory of 1858, https://archive.org/details/sanfranciscodire1858lang.

23 *MGSR* and *PCSL* often note voyage times. Bennett 1985: 315 for sail.

24 *P&D*, Sept. 3, 1858: 2.6.

25 Edson 1968: 77.

26 George Slocumb's diary for April 23, 1858; *VG*, July 24, 1858: 4.2; *SDU*, June 28, 1858: 1.5.

27 *San Francisco Herald*, July 1, 1858, reprinted in Swindle 2001: 145.

28 Canadian miner's diary, July 12.

29 *SDU*, June 18: 1.5-7; *San Francisco Herald*, July 1, 1858, printed in Swindle 2001: 145.

30 Advertisements for *Georgiana* in *PCSL*, May 27, 1858, and for *Robert Passenger* in *PCSL*, June 19, 1858.

31 *VG*, Oct. 13, 1858: 2.2.

32 Ballantyne 1858: 45-6.

33 *VG*, Nov. 18, 1858: 2.1.

34 *P&D*, Nov. 19: 2.4. At "Hong Kong . . . vessels are up for Frazer, and a heavy immigration is expected."

35 *VG*, Oct. 8, 1858: 2.3.

36 *Carnatic* (announced from England Oct. 30, in *MGSR* Dec. 18, and arrived Victoria June 15, 1859, according to VICR: 2) and *Euphrates* (announced from England Oct. 30 in *MGSR* Dec. 18, arrived Victoria June 25, 1859 according to VICR: 4).

37 *British Columbia and Vancouver's Island* 1858: 66-7, Dower 1858: 41, and Hazlitt 1858: 228.

38 *SDU*, July 12, 1858: 1.4.

39 Advertisement for overland trail in *VG*, July 17: 2.5.

40 De Groot 1859: 16; Helmcken 1975: 155. *VG*, July 14, 1858: 1.5, for example, tells of a canoe capsizing near Birch Bay, Washington Territory, with the loss of three men.

41 *VG*, July 10, 1858: 2.5.

42 George Slocumb's diary, May 1, 1858. Douglas reported in the Colonial Office that transporting prospectors would require "light steamers . . . connecting this port (Victoria) with the Falls of Fraser's River" (*CD* May 8, 1858 = *CEG* 13). Details about *Otter* and other vessels can be accessed in Appendix 1: Ships.

43 Urban Hicks 1893: 296.

44 *MGSR* June 4, 1858; Hacking 1944: 263-4. Hudson's Bay Company purchase of Forbes and Babcock: *PSH* July 9, 1858, p. 2.1.

45 August 13, 1858, letter from Victoria published in *SDU*, reprinted in Swindle 2001: 231.

46 *VG*, Sept. 11: 2.1. Douglas wrote that the shipping arrangements disapproved by the colonial secretary's disapproved shipping arrangements had "fallen into disuse." See *CD* Sept. 30, 1858 = *PRBC* 1.37.

47 *VG*, Oct. 7, 1858: 2.1.

48 Letter of July 10, 1858, in Swindle 2001: 167. See also Hacking 1944: 263.

49 Nugent 1859: 4; *VG*, Sept. 1, 1858: 2.2.

50 Urban Hicks 1893: 295-6.

51 *DAC*, July 23, 1858: 1.6.

52 *SDU*, July 19, 1858: 3.2.

53 *P&D*, Aug. 13, 1858: 2.3.

54 *P&D*, Aug. 20, 1858: 2.3

55 *SDU*, July 19, 1858: 3.2.

56 Urban Hicks 1893: 294.
57 *DAC*, July 23, 1858: 1.7 ($2 up, $1 down); *VG*, Sept. 1, 1858: 2.2 ($3).
58 *DEB*, Aug. 2, 1858: 1.3.
59 *SDU*, Aug. 4, 1858: 1.4.
60 *VG*, Sept. 1, 1858: 2.2.
61 Begg 1894: 283.
62 *SDU*, May 20, 1858: 2.4; cf. *PRBC* 1.59 ($1). *DAC*, July 23, 1858: 1.4 ($2). Douglas 1858: 58 ($3-4). *DAC*, July 23, 1858: 1.3-4 ($3.50). "Charge four dollars . . . 130 pounds": July 17 letter above Boston Bar, in Swindle 2001: 184 ($4). *PRBC* 1.59 ($5-8).
63 Urban Hicks 1893: 292-3; *VG*, July 14, 1858: 4.2.
64 Waddington 1858: 21.
65 *DAC*, Aug. 9, 1858: 1.2.
66 Hou 2009: 7, 9, 17.
67 Sept. 1 letter published by *DAC* in Swindle 2001: 250.
68 *VG*, Aug. 24, 1858: 2.2.
69 *CD* Oct. 12, 1858, paragraph 24 = *PRBC* 2.6.
70 *VG*, Sept. 7, 1858: 2.2; *VG*, Sept. 16, 1858: 1.2.
71 *VG*, Aug. 24, 1858: 2.3; *VG*, Aug. 27, 1858: 2.3; *VG*, Sept. 1, 1858: 2.2.
72 Letter of Sept. 20 from Fort Yale, in *VG*, Sept. 28, 1858: 1.2. On Sept. 16, George Beam wrote in his diary that he saw "twenty five mules and ten Men" on the east side of the Fraser.
73 Many maps are illustrated in Hayes 1999: 151-5 and Hayes 2012: 62-8.
74 Douglas 1858: 62.
75 Reproduced in D. McGowan 1859.
76 Pilot bread was a thin, hard, saltless biscuit that did not spoil in ships or army stores.
77 Secondary sources often give the figure of $5 a day without providing any sources from 1858. On April 23, 1860, Douglas commented that at Cayoosh a miner "can live substantially for 1-1/2 dollars per diem, instead of 3 or 4 dollars . . . last year" (*CD* April 23, 1860, no. 42, paragraph 6 = *FPBC* 4.4). In 1858, daily earnings were probably closely related to daily costs. George Slocum earned $5 a day: diary, Sept. 30, 1858. George Beam's $4 and $5 amounts on diary pages B99-B100 are probably related to daily wages and cost of living.
78 *VG Extra*, July 24, 1858: 1.1.

79 *DAC*, July 23, 1858: 1.4-5.

80 Steilacoom prices from *PSH*, July 9, 1985: 2.5. July 17 prices at Hope from *DAC*, July 23, 1858: 1.5. Aug. 20 at Lytton and Oct. 10 at Fountain from Canadian's diary. Dec. 9 at Bridge River from *VG*, Dec. 21, 1858: 1.2.

81 Deaville 1928: 43.

82 Ballou 1878; "Ballou's Express," n.d.; Bancroft 1887: 351-2; Deaville 1928: 52-3, 80-3; Urban Hicks 1893: 293. "Ballou . . . gave me the [express] agency for the bar . . . [which] enabled me to make enough to keep up expenses"; Wellburn 1970; Wellburn 1987: 28-9, examples of his express. Ballou advertised regularly in *VG*, starting in the third issue (July 3, 1858: 3.2), where he promised "Connecting with Freeman's & Co.'s Express," which shipped mail to San Francisco.

83 Deaville 1928: 45; Walske 2006; Wellburn 1970: 293; Wellburn 1987: 17. VICB 2 has costs for August 21, 1858, "Paid Freeman & Co. postage on a letter to San Francisco, 25 cents" and September 8, "Paid Wells Fargo & Co postage of a letter, 25." Freeman's: Deaville 1928: 51; *VG*, July 21, 1858: 2.4; Wellburn 1987: 19. Wells Fargo: Deaville 1928: 51; Wellburn 1987: 24-79 (Wells Fargo envelopes). Wells Fargo first advertised in *VG* issue 7 (July 17: 2.5). Freeman's Express countered in issue 8 (July 21: 2.4).

84 Canadian miner's diary for August 8 and September 19.

85 Beam's letter of Oct. 8, 1858, p. [2]. For later C.O.D. mail, Wellburn 1987: 76-9.

86 *DAC*, July 23, 1858: 1.6; *DAC*, Aug. 9. 1858: 1.3; *DAC*, Aug. 19, 1858: 1.5.

87 July 1 letter from Victoria published in *DEB*, July 6, 1858: 2.2.

88 *VG*, July 17, 1858 (2nd ed.): 2.5.

89 Mayne 1862: 71.

90 Kent and Smith first advertised in *VG*, Aug. 6, 1858: 2.4.

91 *VG*, Nov. 30, 1858: 2.3.

CHAPTER 3: Gold Mining Techniques and Regulations

1 Eisler 2004: 163-6; "Demand and Supply" at www.gold.org, revised Jan. 28, 2022.

2 Meldahl 2011: 3-18.

3 Canadian miner's diary, August 14, 1858.

4 *DAC*, Aug. 9, 1858: 1.3.
5 Urban Hicks 1893: 293.
6 Placer mining techniques: Basque 1991; Borthwick 1857: 121-4; Dawson 1889; Hittell 1861: 115-6, 129-38; Kennedy 2008-9; Macfie 1865: 266-70; *Miners' Own Book* 1858: 7-11; Nelson and Church 2012; Nelson and Kennedy 2011-2; Paul 1954; Wilson 1918: 1-9, 62-97. Photos of tailings and locations: Kennedy 2008-9: 40-3, 47-59; Nelson and Church 2012: 1214, 1218, and 1224.
7 "Prying": Buffum 1850: 132. "Getting dressed": Dolnick 2014: 225.
8 Long Tom: Lighter 1997: 2.462-3.
9 Eight thousand litres is the metric equivalent of "300 cubic feet of water," a recommended amount that could be varied: Wilson 1918: 76-7.
10 *VG*, July 14, 1858: 4.3.
11 Douglas 1858: 66.
12 *VG*, June 30, 1858: 2.5.
13 Urban Hicks 1893: 293-4; Beam's diary, September 21, October 6-8 and 27, 1858.
14 Richard Hicks, BCA, GR 252, vol. 1, pp. 1-24.
15 Sluices at American, Santa Clara, and Hills Bars: Howay 1926: 6.
16 *P&D*, Nov. 19, 1858: 2.4.
17 Douglas in *CD*, Nov. 9, 1858 = *PRBC* 2.27-8.
18 Waddington 1858: 26; cf. *CD* March 10, 1859 = *PRBC* 2.67.
19 Howay 1926: 21; *VG*, June 16, 1859: 3.1. Two men selling "a sluice head of water . . . are held for the nice little sum of $840: they pay $7 for recording; $10 per month license; $600 per annum license for selling the sluice head of water, and . . . [must pay] the mining licenses of the parties to whom they sell the water."
20 Eisler 2004: 251-305; Stopford 1979; Veiga and Baker 2004; Veiga and Meech 1995.
21 Eisler 2004: 252. "It is alleged that the unit of measure for mercury (the flask) is equivalent to the Phoenician talent, which is indicative of the long association of mercury with gold recovery"; Goldwater 1972: 41.
22 "Specific Gravity," *Wikipedia*.
23 Douglas 1858: 62.
24 Shipments and San Francisco cost: *MGSR*, June 12 and July 3; *PCSL*, Oct. 4. *VG*, June 30, 1858: 3.4, advertised "quicksilver" from the June 27 arrival of the steamer *Republic*. On August 11, the Canadian miner wrote

at Lytton, "No quicksilver to be had." Cost on the Fraser: Hazlitt 1858: 142 ($10 to $15 per pound); Urban Hicks 1893: 295.

25 Macfie 1865: 269. "In an ordinary sluice 40 or 50 lbs. of quicksilver is employed daily, and in a rocker from 8 to 10 lbs." Cf. Wilson 1918: 230-2, on longer sluices than were common on the Fraser in 1858. "An 1800-foot sluice was charged with 900 pounds of mercury, while 150 pounds or two flasks are considered sufficient for a 240-foot sluice." Those figures work out to around half a pound per foot of length, or around 200 grams per 30 centimetres.

26 *DEB*, July 27, 1858: 3.2; *NL*, Aug. 14, 1858: 4.2; Beard 1987, "Mechanisms."

27 Basque 1991: 67-72; Eisler 2004: 253; Veiga and Baker 2004: 19.

28 *VG*, Oct. 28, 1858: 2.3.

29 *DAC*, Aug. 9, 1958: 1.3.

30 Beam's diary, Oct. 17, p. B34.

31 John Meech, Professor of Mining Engineering at UBC, informs by email that "the current rate of [mercury] used to [gold] recovered is about 1.0. I suspect that 155 years ago it would have been double to triple this number" due to poor retorting and recycling; cf. Veiga and Baker 2004: 25, 29.

32 See www.atsdr.cdc.gov/toxfaqs/tf.asp?id=113&trd=24, accessed on March 3, 2020. Cf. Eisler 2004: 287-90.

33 Beam's diary, Oct. 17-27, pp. B34-B38.

34 Clarkson and Marsh 1982: 552-4; Stopford 1979: 375-83; Veiga and Baker 2004: 139-147.

35 "Scene of lawless misrule", ten-shilling fee, and twenty-one-shilling fee: *CEG* 1858: 8-10 (Dec. 29, 1857, and Jan. 22, 1858). On B.C. gold finds before 1858: Akrigg 1977: 44-53; Bancroft 1887: 341-57, *CEG*.

36 *CEG* 5 (April 16, 1856).

37 *CD* July 1, 1858 = *PRBC* 1.19.

38 *CD* Nov. 9, 1858 = *PRBC* 2.28.

39 Urban Hicks 1893: 291-2.

40 *CD*, Nov. 9, 1858 = *PRBC* 2.28.

41 *CD*, Oct. 14, 1858 = *PRBC* 1.68.

42 *CD*, Dec. 14, 1858 = *PRBC* 2.45.

43 Slocumb's diary, Sept. 13, 1858.

44 Waddington 1858: 28.

45 *VG*, Nov. 20, 1858: 1.2-3.

46 *CEG* 9, dated Dec. 29, 1857; *CD*, July 1, 1858 = *PRBC* 1.20-1; and *VG*, June 30, 1858: 2.4.

47 *VG*, June 30, 1858: 2.3.

48 Waddington 1858: 37.

49 Urban Hicks 1893: 293-4.

50 Hill's Bar regulations: letter of May 21 received May 26 quoted in Douglas 1858: 59-60; miners' committees in Paul 1954: 169. Fort Yale Bar regulations: June 27, 1858, in *VG*, July 3, 1858: 2.4. Puget Sound Bar regulations: Beam's diary, Aug. 26-Sept. 20; Urban Hicks 1893: 288, 293-4.

51 *CD*, Aug. 30, 1858 = *PRBC* 1.30-2.

52 *CD*, Nov. 9, 1858, paragraph 4 = *PRBC* 2.28 noted that Prince Albert Flat "is reported to be extensive enough to give employment to 4,000 men."

53 *CD*, Aug. 30, 1858 = *PRBC* 1.30.

54 *CD*, Aug. 30, 1858 = *PRBC* 1.31. Miners ignored regulations: De Groot 1859: 20.

55 *CD*, Sept. 13, 1858 = *FPBC* 3. 51.

56 Boswell 2012.

57 Pain 1987: 36-8.

58 Eisler 2004: 164-5.

59 Carlson and McHalsie 2001: 93.

60 *NL*, Aug. 7, 1858: 2.1.

61 *DAC*, Aug. 8, 1858: 1.5.

62 *DEB*, Aug. 24, 1858: 2.3.

63 *VG*, Sept. 11, 1858: 2.3.

64 *VG*, Dec. 23, 1858: 2.2.

65 Begbie 1859: 242-3.

66 Boswell 2012.

67 Richards 1864: 105.

68 Richards 1864, annotation facing p. 105 in copy at UK Hydrographic Office, Taunton, England. Fraser River channel change: Hales 2000: 51-2.

69 Goldwater 1972: 37-8.

70 Veiga and Baker 2004.

71 Wheatley and Paradis 1995.

72 Google "Grassy Narrows" for recent news. "They can't talk": Poisson and Bruser 2016: pp. A1 and A8.

73 See, for example, successful clean up at Pinchi Lake mine (Donald and Marshland 2013); less successful at Baker Lake and Takla-Bralorne Mines (French 2008).

74 Prospecting on Lillooet River in 1858-9: Otis Parsons' diary, Aug. 9 and 30, 1858; De Groot 1859: 14; and "New Gold Fields," 1858: 176. Gold and mercury levels: Veiga and Meech 1995, with tables.

75 Carlson and McHalsie, 2001: 92.

76 Hales 2000: 123, 126.

CHAPTER 4: Indigenous Resistance to Displacement

1 *DAC*, Sept. 2, 1858: 1.4.

2 Laforet and York 1998; Teit 1900; Teit 1912. Anderson 1858: 19, comments that the northern "Nicoutameens" were named "Couteaux" (knives) by French voyageurs and "Saw-mee-nâ" by Indigenous people living farther west.

3 Laforet and York 1998: 67. The rest of the paragraph is based on Laforet and York 1998: 48, 66-8; Carlson and McHalsie 2001: 40-2, 48, 62-3; Teit 1912: 411-2.

4 "*Ranchería*": *The New Velázquez Spanish and English Dictionary* (Clinton NJ: New Win Publishing, 1999): 738.

5 This paragraph and the next are based on Laforet and York 1998: 3, 34, 44, 66-71; Carlson and McHalsie 2001: 58, 72-3, 120-1.

6 Indigenous people travelled by remembering landmarks in sequence. From memory in 1859, Chief Thiusoloc sketched lines representing rivers in the sequence of travel, but not to scale. Lake Chelan, Washington, is at the bottom, while Chilliwack Lake, B.C., is near the top. A U.S. border surveyor added the names. The one name still current is Noo-saák, the Nooksack River (centre left), flowing westward. Its source is correctly placed just past the peak Tuk-we-sállio (Mount Baker), which feeds Noohts-háh-tsum (Glacier Creek). To the south is Tsuk-éh-nüm (Skagit River). It turns abruptly north at unnamed Ruby Creek, where a twentieth-century dam created Ross Lake. Several straight lines on both sides of two circles indicate a foreshortened portage (probably

via unnamed Beaver Creek). It leads to the headwaters of Kle-hái-hu (Chilliwack River), which flows in and out of, S'háh-cha-ka (Chilliwack Lake). The top, including Páp-lashe-ko (either Cultus Lake or Sumas Lake) is sketchy. Skaá-pat at the bottom is Glacier Peak, with unnamed Lake Chelan to the right.

7   Mayne 1862: 30. George Slocumb's diary, pp. S63-S64; *DEB*, Aug. 1, 1858: 1.2.

8   Bowsfield 1979: 38-9, Douglas to Archibald Barclay, Secretary of the Hudson's Bay Company in London, on Sept. 3, 1849.

9   Begbie 1859: 242. Williams 1977 devotes chapter 7 to Begbie's wide-ranging relations with Indigenous people. Begbie learned some languages so he could question Indigenous people at trial. He acknowledged customs that had no place in English common law. He often threw their cases out of court because he felt that charges had been trumped up or that white people had made them drunk. He stood against a number of Dominion of Canada policies that affected Indigenous people negatively. Now he is chiefly remembered as an instrument of colonial oppression for executing five Tsilhqot'in chiefs. They murdered white intruders who were building a road from the head of Bute Inlet to the Interior.

10 Marshall 2018: 57-8, quoting Jason Allard, n.d.

11 Duff 1997: 72.

12 "Indian Territory," *Wikipedia*; Utley 1967; Yenne 2006.

13 For numbers Hurtado 2002: 95; for narrative Cook 1943: 1-98.

14 Belshaw 2009: 72-90. Page 73 illustrates the difficulty of interpreting surviving data: eighteenth-century population estimates for British Columbia range from 75,000 to 1,612,622.

15 Richards 1979; washingtonhistoryonline.org. Railroad: Urban Hicks 1892: 149. Mixed-race: Jackson 1995: 215-30.

16 Urban Hicks 1892; Marshall 2015c: 131, 134; Richards 1979; and Utley 1967: 175-210.

17 Stevens 1856: 155.

18 *DAC*, Aug. 18, 1858: 2.1.

19 *PSH*, Oct. 8, 1858: 2.2.

20 Burns 1947; Marshall 2018: 147; Richards 1979; Utley 1967: 175-210. "Yakima War": *Wikipedia*; historylink.org; In his diary on May 29, 1858, George Slocumb mentioned "the defeat of Regular Soldiers at or near

Walla Walla." The number 1,500 comes from Marshall 2015c: 134. *DEB*, Oct. 16, 1858, published the Sept. 6 "Official Report on the Indian War in the North" (p. 2.2) and "Letters from Camp in Washington Territory" (p. 2.3). The latter printed the terms of peace with the Coeur d'Alene, including the stipulation that "all white men should pass through their territory hereafter unmolested."

21 *CD*, July 15, 1857 = *CEG* 7; cf. *CD*, Oct. 29, 1856 = *CEG* 1858: 6.

22 *CD*, Nov. 8, 1855

23 American mining bar names appear on three maps: the manuscript "Copy of Reconnaissance Sketch of the Fraser River" (Sept. 1858); the published *Sketch of Part of British Columbia* (1859), and the recent map in Nelson and Kennedy 2011-12.

24 Hauka 2003: 79.

25 *DEB*, Dec. 30, 1858: 3.

26 *PSH*, June 4, 1858.

27 *DEB*, June 7, 1858: 2; Douglas 1858: 58-60.

28 *DAC*, Aug. 19, 1858: 1.4.

29 *CD*, June 15, 1858 = *PRBC* 1. 16-7.

30 On the Fraser Canyon War or Fraser River War of 1858 and events leading up to it, see *Canyon War* 2009; Hauka 2003: 77-104; Laforet and York 1998: 51-6; Marshall 2000: 199-259; Marshall 2002; Marshall 2015c; Marshall 2018: 144-86. The most important contemporary sources are (1) a letter of Aug. 17 by H.M. Snyder published in *VG*, Aug. 24, 1858: 3.1; (2) a description after the end of the expedition, based on H.M. Snyder and published in *VG*, Sept. 1, 1858: 3.1-3; (3) a letter of H.M. Snyder to Governor Douglas written Aug. 28, 1858, cited as Snyder 1858/1996; and (4) a much later memoir by a Hudson's Bay Company man who accompanied Snyder, William Yates 1904. My account is based on a fresh study of contemporary sources.

31 Reinhart 1962: 119-20.

32 *DAC*, July 9, 1858: 1.3. A self-identified American complained: "Thus far, only *one* side of the story has been heard. The Indians have robbed, murdered and mutilated the whites without cause or provocation" (*VG*, Sept. 1, 1858: 1.2).

33 *VG*, Aug. 24, 1858: 3.2. Further reports of miners killed by Indigenous people appeared in *VG*, July 30, 1858: 2.2; *DEB*, Aug. 11, 1858; *DAC*,

Aug. 19, 1858: 1.5; *DEB*, Aug. 24, 1858: 2.3; *SDU*, Aug. 26, 1858: 4.3; *CD*, Aug. 30, 1858; *DEB*, Sept. 1, 1858: 2.2; Stout 1910: 5.

34 Ned Stout, quoted in Laforet and York 1998: 53. See also Marshall 2002: 45-6, Stout 1910, Walkem 1914: 51-62 (interview).

35 *DAC*, Aug. 2, 1858: 1.3-4. The estimate of 10,000 Indigenous people on the river is close to a Hudson's Bay count during 1830 (Harris 1997: 25, 107).

36 *DAC*, Aug. 19, 1858: 1.4.

37 "Provisions": *SDU*, Aug. 4, 1858: 1.4. "The Indians enter": *DAC*, Aug. 8, 1858: 1.5.

38 Jason Allard, n.d.

39 *VG*, Aug. 24, 1858: 3.1.

40 *DEB*, Sept. 1, 1858: 2.2.

41 *DAC*, Sept. 3, 1858: 1.4 (in Swindle 2001: 238). Further on this incident: *DEB*, Aug. 24, 1858: 2.3; *DEB*, Sept. 1, 1858: 2.2; *VG*, Aug. 24, 2858: 3.1.

42 *Canyon War* 2009, around 27 minutes in.

43 *VG*, Aug. 20, 1858: 2.2, reprinted in *DAC*, Aug. 25, 1858: 1.1-2.

44 *DEB*, Aug. 24, 1858: 2.3.

45 *VG*, Aug. 24, 1858: 2.1.

46 *VG*, Aug. 24, 1858: 3.1.

47 *DEB*, Sept. 1, 1858: 2.2 (reprinted in Swindle 2001: 235).

48 *DEB*, Sept. 1, 1858: 2.2. Further on Rouse's campaign and return to Fort Yale: *VG*, Aug. 20, 158: 2.2; *VG*, Sept. 1, 1858: 3.1-2.

49 *VG*, Aug. 24, 1858: 3.1.

50 Capt. J. Sewall Reed's account, quoted and paraphrased in his funeral eulogy (Morison 1864: 25-6). Sewall wrote a detailed letter on the war, *DAC*, Sept. 3, 1858: 1.4.

51 *DEB*, Sept. 1, 1858 (reprinted in Swindle 2001: 235).

52 The name "Harry," the San Francisco origin, and the white flag appear in an Aug. 18 letter, *DEB*, Sept. 1, 1858: 2.2. Snyder's job is on p. 205 of *Colville's 1856-1857 San Francisco Directory*. Other sources call him H.M. Snyder. Snyder 1858/1996: 140-1 mentions "fifty-two men;" cf. *VG*, Sept. 1, 1858: 3.1, has fifty-one men; *DAC*, Sept. 3, 1858: 1.4 has seventy-one men. "For any one to start": Snyder's Aug. 6 letter in *DEB*, Aug. 18, 1858: 3.3.

53 *VG*, Sept. 1, 1858: 3.1 refers to John "Centras' 72 men." Most sources say they were mainly Frenchmen: *DAC*, Sept. 3, 1858: 1.4, "50 men;" *DEB*, Sept. 1, 1858: 2.2; *VG*, Aug. 24, 1858: 2.1, "a company of Frenchmen numbering 75 men;" Captain James Prevost of HMS *Satellite*—120 Frenchmen who had banded together to avenge the deaths of Le Croix and Sargoase (enclosure in *CD*, Oct. 15, 1858, Romaine to Under-Secretary of State, online only). The group was also called "the Italian guard, 50 men" (*DAC*, Sept. 3, 1858: 1.4) or the "Austrian company . . . eighty men" (Snyder 1858/1996: 140).

54 *DAC*, Sept. 3, 1858: 1.4 refers to "Whatcom Guard, 33 men." *VG*, Sept. 1, 1858: 3.1 mentions Graham's company, 20 men.

55 *DAC*, Sept. 3, 1858: 1.4 refers to "Madison Guard, 44 men." Ned McGowan wrote in his "Reminiscences" (*The Argonaut*, 2.21 [June 1, 1878]: 10) that his friend "Martin Gallagher was placed in command of one of the companies, and a man by the name of Snyder, an old San Franciscan, of the other."

56 *DAC*, Sept. 3, 1858: 1.4 refers to "Rough and Ready Rangers, Capt. Galloway, 24 men." *VG*, Sept. 1, 1858: 3.1 has Galloway's company, 20 men."

57 Snyder 1858/1996: 140.

58 On Ovid Allard, *DCBO*; Watson 2010: 1.148-9.

59 Snyder in *VG*, Aug. 24, 1858: 3.1.

60 Copals: *VG*, Aug. 24, 1858: 2.1. *DEB*, Sept. 1, 1858; "Taking with me the Chief from the head of the canion": Snyder 1858/1996: 143. Kowpelst's offer of himself: Teit 1900.

61 Snyder 1858/1996: 143 (quotation), 140 (plan to find an interpreter).

62 Yates 1904: 3. Further on Yates: Watson 2010: 3.992.

63 Snyder in *VG*, Sept. 1, 1858: 3.1.

64 Snyder 1858/1996: 140.

65 *VG*, Sept. 1, 1858: 3.1.

66 Snyder in *VG*, Aug. 24, 1858: 2.2. Further, p. 3.1.

67 Laforet and York 1998: 55.

68 Snyder 1858/1996: 141. Also Snyder in *VG*, Sept. 1, 1858: 3.1; chiefs' assistance: Laforet and York 1998: 55-6.

69 Snyder in *VG*, Sept. 1, 1858: 3.1.

70 Snyder 1858/1996: 141. Also Snyder *VG*, Sept. 1, 1858: 3.1. "Captains Graham and Galloway avow[ed] their intention to make it a 'war to the "knife," on men, women and children.'"

71 Ballou 1878: 6-7.

72 Snyder 1858/1996: 141.

73 Yates 1904: 13.

74 Snyder 1858/1996: 141.

75 Snyder 1858/1996: 141.

76 Snyder 1858/1996: 141. The Chinese presence on the river was often overlooked by whites: Chow 2015. The map in Nelson and Kennedy 2011-12 shows "China Bar 1863-1866" in the middle of the Fraser River south of Anderson River, where China Bar now lies. A Fort Hope correspondent called it the "Chinese Camp, above the Big Canyon" (Aug. 23 letter in *DEB*, Sept. 2, 1858: 3-4). There Snyder "notified the Chinees that they must leave their claims . . . until such times as pease was restored," but "their claims should be protected to them" (Snyder 1858/1996: 142). Some Americans suspected that Chinese people selling revolvers, rifles, powder and shot to Indigenous people (*VG*, Aug. 10, 1858: 1.2; *DEB*, Sept. 1, 1858: 2.2). However, the Chinese told Snyder that all their arms had been taken by the first company to pass through (Laforet and York 1998: 230, note 66).

77 Snyder in *VG*, Sept. 1, 1858: 3.1. Cf. *VG*, Aug. 24, 1858: 2.1 on the date Aug. 19).

78 Snyder's description in *VG*, Sept. 1, 1858: 3.2.

79 Snyder in *DEB*, Sept. 2, 1858: 3.4. Also *VG*, Sept. 1, 1858: 1.1; *DEB*, Sept. 6, 1858: 2.2.

80 Yates 1904: 13-4.

81 *DAC*, Sept. 3, 1858: 1.4.

82 Poison arrows: *Canyon War* 2009, about 24 minutes in.

83 Snyder 1858/1996: 143. His men laid down "some two or three rods from the rest."

84 Yates 1904: 14. The *Pocket Diary for 1858*, p. [10], has the first quarter moon on August 16 and full moon on August 24.

85 Event on Aug. 20: Snyder in *VG*, Sept. 1, 1858: 3.2; cf. physical mutilation of other men, *VG*, Aug. 25, 1858: 2.1.

86 Sewall Reed's Aug. 21 letter later published in *DAC* (reprinted in Swindle 2001: 238).

87 *VG*, Sept. 1, 1858: 3.1. Marshall 2002: 57-8 and n. 140 on p. 77 concludes that Nlaka'pamux shot Graham.

88 Snyder 1858/1996: 143.

89 Yates 1904: 14-15.

90 Laforet and York 1998: 54.

91 *VG*, Aug. 25, 1858: 2.1.

92 *VG*, Sept. 1: 1.1.

93 *VG*, Aug. 25, 1858: 2.1-2.

94 *VG* Aug. 26, 1858: 2.1.

95 *VG*, Aug. 27, 1858: 2.3

96 Ovid Allard wrote a letter to Douglas on Aug. 20, 1858 (BCA).

97 Snyder 1858/1996: 142.

98 McGowan June 1, 1878: 10.

99 *DEB*, Sept. 25, 1858: 2.2.

100 Snyder in *VG*, Sept. 1, 1858: 3.3.

101 *DAC*, Sept. 9, 1858: 4.1. For Kumsheen, see "Camchin," *Wikipedia*.

102 Snyder in *VG*, Sept. 1, 1858: 3.2.

103 Snyder 1858/1996: 142.

104 Peace with two thousand: Snyder in *VG*, Sept. 1, 1858: 3.3. "Every-thing . . . unmolested": *DEB*, Sept. 25, 1858: 2.2.

105 Teit 1912: 412. The oral memory of Mary Williams (1898-1986) appears in Hanna and Henry 1995: 130-1, 199.

106 Snyder 1858/1996: 143

107 "Were much impressed . . . left of them": Snyder in *VG*, Sept. 1, 1858: 3.2.

108 McIntyre, Gordon. 2018. "Descendants of Two Men Who Avoided a Battle That Could Have Led B.C. to Join U.S. Will Meet in Lytton for 160th Anniversary of Canyon War," *Vancouver Sun*, April 13, 2018.

109 *DEB*, Sept. 1, 1858: 3.2.

110 *CD*, Aug. 27, 1858 = *PRBC* 1.29.

111 *CD*, Oct. 12, 1858 = *PRBC* 2.4. Douglas's private diary dove even further into denial: "It appears from reports of miners who have lately returned from the upper country that the Indians are thievish and without being positively hostile plunder the miners in the most shameless manner. . . . Drew up a proclamation prohibiting the sale or gift of intoxicating drinks to Indians" (Douglas 1858: 64, Sept. 4, 1858, at Fort Hope).

112 *CD*, Oct. 12, 1858 = *PRBC* 2. 4.

113 Douglas 1858: 65. On the hostage taking of Allard: Hauka 2003: 78, 98, 106-7.

114 "A long conversation . . . have adopted": Snyder in *DEB*, Sept. 25, 1858: 2.1. George Beam's diary for Sept. 14 states that after Douglas's visit to Puget Sound Bar, miners were no longer allowed to hold more than one claim.

115 Douglas in Howay 1926: 1-2.

CHAPTER 5: George Slocumb's Failure

1 Passages in Slocumb's diary can be found under the dates mentioned in the text.

2 On the family: Slocumb 1882: 558-9. The diary notes his twenty-eighth birthday on Sept. 7, 1858.

3 On Sept. 7, 1860 (diary p. S83), Slocumb remembered spending his twenty-second birthday in 1852 trekking to California *"on the Humbolt"* River in the Utah Territory (now Nevada). On the trail, *Atlas of American History* 1984: 138-41; Eaton 1974.

4 In San Francisco, Slocumb met E.B. Boust, editor of the *Placer Courier*, published at Yankee Jim's, a rich mine southeast of Mountain Springs. See www.californiagenealogy.org/placer/newpapers.htm.

5 "Seventy": *DAC*, March 9, 1858: 2.2. "Victoria": *DAC*, April 4, 1858: 1.5. "Tell": *SDU*, April 5, 1858: 3.4-5.

6 River steamers: Chamberlain and Wells 1879: 107-11. Marysville to San Francisco fares were "passage—$12 cabin, $10 deck; freight, $15 per ton" (Bowers 1999: 203).

7 French M.A. Rassette operated a hotel at the corner of Bush and Sansome Streets (*San Francisco Directory for the Year 1858*: 231, 315).

8 *SDU*, April 19, 1858: 1.3.

9 Any drinking, gambling, or sexual taste could be slaked in the Barbary Coast, between Broadway, Montgomery, Washington, and Stockton Streets: see "Barbary Coast," *Wikipedia*; www.sfmuseum.org; Bowers 1999: 36-40. Later, Slocumb mentions saloons (diary, pp. S64, S83), his addiction to gambling (pp. S16, S84, S90, and S94), and a desire for "*Calicofornica*" (p. S50). "Calico" was slang for women (Lighter 1994: 1.348).

10 *Embarcador* is Spanish for "someone who embarks on a ship." "*Tight*" means both "faithful, constant" (*Webster*) and "close-fisted" with money (Partridge and Beale 1984: 1233). Though unnamed on diary p. S3,

Brown, Drew, and Kelly frequently crossed Slocumb's path: diary pp. S11, S16, S17, S44, S47, S48, S94, S95. In Victoria, he played quito with them "*and am loser $13.50 for Blankets purchased for them in San Francisco*" (diary, p. S16).

11 Jameson 2002: 222, "for the Euro-American men who succeeded in California, it became a . . . mark of pride to establish middle-class homes."

12 George Gordon, Lord Byron, *Child Harold's Pilgrimage*, Canto 1, lyric after stanza xiii, verse 9.

13 *MGSR*, April 27, 1858, lists *Commodore* cargo. *MGSR*, July 3, 1958, lists under the heading of "Drugs" these items: Alum, Balsam copalba, Bicarbonate of soda, Borax, Sulphur, Cream of Tartar, Castor oil, Epsom salts, Hydro Postass., Opium, Oil of annis, Mercury, Sal soda, Quinine, Tartaric acid, Sulphuric acid, Saltpetre, and Nitric acid.

14 Bowers 1999: 168, 178, 186.

15 Douglas's offer to African-Americans in California is treated by Adams 2001: 121 and Pilton 1951. Archy Lee was a Mississippi slave who escaped into the care of free African-Americans in California. On April 14, 1858, the Supreme Court of California declared him a free man (Lapp 2008).

16 On the 1856 Vigilance Committee, see www.sfmuseum.org/hist1/vigil56.html; Hauka 2003: 54-68; Lotchin 1974, ch. 9; Senkewicz 1985. On pp. S15, S42, S43, and S58, Slocumb mentions Billy Carr, Charley Duane, John Duane, Ned McGowan, and Yankee Sullivan. For Slocumb's dislike of the Irish and Democrats, see diary pp. S17-S19, and S37. On his preference for Republican Abraham Lincoln, see p. S94.

17 *PSH*, April 30, 1858: 2.2. "Buck" is "an American Indian man" (Lighter 1994: 1.281).

18 Letter of April 25 from Victoria, published in *DAC*, May 6, 1858: 1.3-4, reprinted in Swindle 2001: 44.

19 Bailey's bar was "presided over by Mr. J.C. Keenan, formerly of the FASHION SALOON, Sacramento" (advertisement in *VG*, June 30, 1858: 3.3).

20 The San Francisco *Daily Alta California* took its name from the Mexican territory "Upper California." In July, it sent W. Wallace and Dr. Henry De Groot north as special reporters, incurring a "heavy outlay from a desire to furnish the community with most reliable news" (*DAC*, Aug. 2, 1858: 1.6). The *Herald* was edited and published by notorious John

Nugent (Senkewicz 1985: 170, 174). Bowers 1999: 83, "just about everything in San Francisco seemed to start at 25¢."

21 *SDU*, May 22, 1858: 2.5; *SDU*, June 28, 1858: 1.6. Pilton 1951: 207-12 lists early African-American immigrants to Victoria, but not dates of arrival.

22 San Francisco boarding-house owner Mary Jane Megquier 1994: 120, in a letter of March 31, 1853.

23 Rohrbough 1997, ch. 17, examines "The Permanent Lure of Success, the Enduring Shame of Failure" in gold rush days.

24 On Port Townsend as starting point for the mines and its early property boom: Waddington 1858: 8. Land speculation and crash: *SDU*, Aug. 20: 1.4. The town was too exposed for many: "The wind blows a hurricane, cold from the mountains of snow all about, and the air is full of dust" (*DAC*, Aug. 22, 1858: 1.3).

25 *DAC*, Aug. 22, 1858: 1.3.

26 *P&D* May 7, 1858: 2.4.

27 *PSH*, April 30,1858: 2.2.

28 *SDU*, May 22, 1858: 2.5.

29 "Where ignorance is bliss, 'Tis folly to be wise": Thomas Gray, "Ode on a Distant Prospect of Eton College," lines 95-6 (*ODQ2*, p. 230, no. 30).

30 "Bung": Lighter 1994: 1.316, Partridge and Beale 1984: 157.

31 "Cloochman" or "Klutchman" is the word for "woman," in the Chinook jargon developed by nineteenth-century traders and Indigenous people, named after the Chinook First Nation at the mouth of the Columbia River (Gibbs 1863, Hibben 1871).

32 "Hiyu": Chinook for "much, plenty" (Gibbs 1863, Hibben 1871). "Root hog or die": The phrase, alluding to pigs digging for food with their snouts, indicates self-reliance with a touch of desperation, as in an 1858 gold miner's song: "Way out upon the Platte near Pike's Peak we were told | There by a little digging we could get a pile of gold, | So we bundled up our clothing, resolved at least to try | And tempt old Madam Fortune, root hog or die" (*Wikipedia*).

33 In Whatcom on Aug. 13, correspondent W. Wallace was surprised that people answered him "in Chinook" (*DAC*, Aug.22, 1858: 1.4).

34 "Horrors": Lighter 1997: 2.158, *OED*.

35 On May 1, Slocumb noted that he "*only Spent three bucks besides bord this week,*" suggesting that alcohol was not affordable.

36 De Groot 1859: 13.

37 *VG,* July 24, 1858: 1.4.

38 *DAC,* July 23, 1858: 1.5.

39 Slocumb added the biblical phrase "The Lord says," then cited the poem inaccurately from memory. The original reads: "You may break, you may shatter the vase, if you will, | But the scent of the roses will hang round it still" (Thomas Moore's poem, "Farewell! But Whenever You Welcome the Hour," in *ODQ2,* p. 356, no. 18).

40 Edson 1968: 75 notes that "There were no clearings ... so [people] pitched their tents on the beach—a line of camps extending from Chuckanut Bay to Squalicum Creek."

41 *P&D,* July 30, 1858: 3.1.

42 *PSH,* June 4, 1858: 2.3; Waddington 1858: 9-10; Hazlitt 1858: 219. Other denigrations in *DEB,* July 3, 1858: 2.3; *P&D,* Aug. 13, 1858: 1.2.

43 "Canvas tents": *PSH,* June 4, 1858: 2.3. "Timbers": *SDU,* June 28, 1858: 1.5-7. The rest of this paragraph is based on *SDU,* June 28, 1858: 3.3; *P&D,* July 2, 1858: 2.5; *NL,* July 3, 1858: 2.1; Urban Hicks 1893: 289-90. Slocumb's number "*600*" is on diary p. S52. A June 21 estimate was 2,000 (*SDU,* June 28, 1858: 1.7). Three thousand arrived the next week (*P&D,* July 2, 1858: 2.5). After departures to the mines, 4,000 were still left at the start of July (*SDU,* July 3, 1858: 1.4).

44 Until *NL* ceased publication on September 11, almost every issue praised the Whatcom trail, surveyed and built by Captain W.W. DeLacy. On the trail, see Reid 1927.

45 "Over twenty men": *SDU,* July 14: 1.5. "Waded through": *SDU,* July 26: 1.5. "Was asked": *DAC,* July 23: 1.5. "A trail from Bellingham": *PSH,* July 2, 1858: 2.1.

46 Everywhere on Puget Sound, a real estate boom was followed by an inevitable bust: De Groot 1859: 14. Removal of buildings to Victoria: Edson 1968: 93.

47 Waddington 1858: 9. See p. 16 on fall of Whatcom and growth of Victoria.

48 Whatcom's wharf: *NL,* July 3, 1858: 3.2. Sehome's wharf: *P&D,* May 14, 1858: 2.3-4.

49 *SDU,* June 16, 1858: 2.1.

50 *Resolute* arrived at Bellingham Bay on August 22 at 10 p.m., and at Semiahmoo on August 23 at 2 p.m. (*P&D,* Aug. 27, 1858: 2.4).

51 "Semiahmoo": www.historylink.org; Waddington 1858: 10; *VG*, August 13, 1858: 2.1 ("The Two Semiahmoos"). One village was built on the spit at Drayton Harbor. The other stood on a hill, the start of a "projected trail or wagon road, to connect the town with Fort Langley.

52 John Bull personifies the United Kingdom and Uncle Sam the USA. The surveyors camped just north of the forty-ninth parallel, at mouth of the Campbell River. That was the closest source of fresh water.

53 *DAC*, Aug. 21, 1858: 1.2.

54 Chinook vocabulary: *Boston man* American; *chicamin* gold; *clatana* go; *closy* good; *cultus* nothing; *halo* no; *hias* absolutely; *hiyu* much; *hyack* fast; *illeha* country; *kultus* nothing; *kuway* all; *mamoke* work; *nanish* see, look for *nika* I; *spose* if; *wake* no. Slocumb learned the jargon by ear, since his spelling varies from Anderson 1858: 25-31; Gibbs 1863; and Hibben 1871.

55 *OED*; Partridge and Beale 1984; *Webster*.

56 For the Vigilance Committee exiles on the Fraser River, see Slocumb diary pp. S58 and S60; *SDU*, May 25, 1858: 2.2-3; cf. *PSH*, June 11, 1858: 2.4; *SDU*, June 11,1858: 1.5-7; *SDU*, June 12, 1858: 3.2; *PSH*, June 18, 1858: 2.1; Hauka 2003: 54-68.

57 "Got fifty dollars . . . agreeable companions": McGowan, June 1, 1878: 10.

58 *VG*, Sept. 28, 1858: 1.2; cf. Sept. 29: 2.1.

59 *DAC*, July 23, 1858: 1.

60 *DEB*, Aug. 2, 1858: 1.2.

61 Lighter 1997: 2.64.

62 "Coming events": Thomas Campbell, "Lochiel's Warning" (*Poetical Works*, 1803), "'Tis the sunset of life gives me mystical lore, | And coming events cast their shadows before" (*ODQ2*, p. 122, no. 22).

63 George Beam on Puget Sound Bar noted claims sold for $75, $100, and $125 (diary, Sept. 22), $75 (Oct. 4), $120 (Oct. 5), $150 (Oct. 18), $500 (Oct. 25), $200 (Oct. 26), and $300 (Nov. 11). The anonymous Canadian sold his claim near Fountain on October 12 for $400.

64 William Shakespeare, *Hamlet*, act 5, scene 2, lines 10-11: "There's a divinity that shapes our ends, Rough-hew them how we will."

65 *Hamlet* 3.1.56-64.

66 Gold Run: The 1870 U.S. federal census lists Slocumb in Placer County, Township 4, page 24, lines 30-33 (Archive.org, "Population Schedules

of the Ninth Census of the United States, 1870," microfilm roll 76, downloaded PDF page 95). His wife Sarah C. was born in Illinois, and their son George was in California in 1864. George is the only sibling whose spouse is not named in Slocumb 1882: 558, possibly because of pre-marital conception.

67 Slocumb is listed in the California Voter's Register for 1873, San Francisco (ancestry.ca). The 1880 U.S. census gives his profession as "dealer in mining stocks" and lists five children living with him: Elizabeth C., fifteen (born 1865); Georgie, ten (a daughter, born 1870); Augusta, six (born 1874); Hall, three (a son, born 1877); and Clay (a son, born 1879). See Archive.org, 1880 census, California San Francisco ward 11, Enumeration District 147, page 20, lines 46-50, PDF p. 43. Slocum 1882: 558 sanitized his work by making him a "book-keeper in San Francisco." The 1878-1890 San Francisco city directories (archive.org) show him moving often from one rented property to another in the 400 to 600 blocks of Natoma and Minna Streets. On the San Francisco Stock and Exchange Board, see Fracchia 1969, especially pp. 4-6, 11, 15, and 16 (note 8). Slocumb's burial is recorded in the "Odd Fellows Cemetery Records," 1890. A table of the "Longevity of Persons" gave the average age of death in Massachusetts as forty-eight years, with few men living more than fifty years (*MGSR*, August 14, 1858). At the low end were clerks and teachers, at thirty-four years; farmers lived to sixty-four, judges to sixty-five, and bank officers to sixty-eight. According to McQuillan 1985: 32, average life expectancy for men during 1861 was just 41.84 years in Canada West (later Ontario).

CHAPTER 6: George Beam, Entrepreneur and American Expansionist

1 Beam 1858b, letter of Sept. 1, 1858, p. [3].

2 Beam's diary is at UWSC, accession 2409, vertical file 858.

3 Biographies: University of Washington Library, Seattle, online notes about George Wesley Beam and Winfield Scott Ebey; anonymous, undated manuscript biography of Beam in WSE, box 5, file 5. Sangamon: ilgenweb.net/1876/beam.htm (some details are inaccurate). Accessed on May 23, 2015. Ancestry.ca lists Beam's father and mother. David Beam was born on March 13, 1803, in Manchester, Adams County, Ohio, and died on February 28, 1853, in Sangamon County, Illinois. His marriage took place at Sangamon on December 7, 1830, to Rosanna Ebey, born

around 1814 near Columbus Ohio. She died in Sangamon on April 16, 1860. Ebey 1854/1997: 7-9 for Isaac's settling and quotation, "Whidbey's Island."; Meeker 1905: 73 on the location of his cabin on the coast of Whidbey Island facing Port Townsend; Ebey 1854/1997, p. 2 on the 1851-54 offer of 160-acre claims; Evans-Hatch 2005, pp. 67 and 81 on Jacob Ebey. Early farming on Whidbey is described in White 1980: 35-53.

4 Ebey 1854/1997.

5 Beam's claim on Protection Island: page [3] of his Sept. 1, 1858, letter; Wright, Almira, 1858. Isaac and the volunteers: Ebey 1852/1916: 242. Blockhouses: Crockett 1892: 249.

6 Background: Bancroft 1890: 137, Richardson 1967, and Weiser 2012. Isaac's murder: Crockett 1892: 248-9, Ebey 1854/1997: 221-5, Edson 1968: 63-70, and Evans-Hatch 2005: 90-2.

7 Morris 1857/1929: 139-40. Warriors from Haida Gwaii, just south of the Alaskan panhandle islands, may also have been in Puget Sound at the time (Weiser 2012), but Douglas's testimony points to an invasion from Russian America.

8 Edson 1968: 69.

9 "Between Fort Hope": *P&D*, March 5, 1858, quoted in Howay 1914: 2.14. "GOLD DISCOVERIES": *PSH*, March 26, 1858: 2.3. "In less than ninety": Prosch 1892: 275.

10 Ebey 1858, diary entries for March 20, April 6, May 9, May 11, and June 21, 1858.

11 Ebey 1858, diary for June 25 and July 1, 1858.

12 *P&D*, Aug. 13, 1858: 1.2.

13 *P&D*, Aug. 13, 1858: 1.2.

14 Urban Hicks 1893: 288. On Urban Hicks, see Bancroft 1890: 78, n. 18 (auditor of Thurston County); Urban Hicks 1892; Urban Hicks 1893.

15 "Hundred stores": *P&D*, Aug. 13, 1858: 1.2. "Badly busted": Urban Hicks 1893: 290.

16 "John" refers to a man in general, sometimes a new recruit (Lighter 1997: 2.299-300), and "cheer" refers to "high spirits, enthusiasm, courage, and optimism" (*Webster*).

17 Whatcom's *NL* advertised Point Roberts supply stores, in either tents or primitive shacks.

18 Urban Hicks 1893: 292.

19 Ibid.

20 *SDU*, Aug. 4, 1858: 1.4.

21 "Nearly 1,000 . . . 'grub' money": *SDU*, Aug. 4, 1858: 1.4.

22 *DAC*, Aug. 9, 1858: 1.3.

23 *DAC*, Aug. 19, 1858: 1.5.

24 *PSH*, Aug. 20: 2.3. Billy Ballou's Express, and J. Horace Kent and H.F. Smith's Express are mentioned at the end of Chapter 2.

25 Beam 1858b, letter, Sept. 1, 1858: [3].

26 Beam 1858b, letter, Aug. 20, 1858: [4].

27 Beam 1858b, letter, Aug. 20, 1858: [3]. This letter summarizes the Fraser Canyon War.

28 Beam 1858b, letter, Aug. 20, 1858: [4].

29 Dr. Richard Hyatt Lansdale (1811-1898), a native of Maryland, went to California in 1849, then continued north to Whidbey Island, where he took out a claim at Oak Harbor in 1851 and became the first Island County auditor (Bancroft 1890: 18, 29-30; Ebey 1852/1916: 241 and 246, note 11; Crockett 1892: 248). Eucre: diary, Nov. 4, 1858. Preaching: diary, Sept. 19.

30 Beam's diary, Sept. 10-11.

31 Ferguson "had his right thigh broken at the fourth fire" on August 21 by George Penn Johnson, editor of the *National*. Ferguson died on September 14 of complications after a leg amputation. See *DAC*, Sept. 6, 1858: 1.3; *DSJR*, Sept. 16, 1858: 2.2.

32 On Whidbey house construction, Evans-Hatch 2005: 94-97.

33 *P&D*, Oct. 1, 1858: 2.3.

34 Beam, Charles Powell, and Ben Powell worked on Aug. 11, 13, 16, 20, 26, 31, Sept. 1-4, 6-11, 13-18, and 20-24. Beam and Charles continued without Ben on Sept. 28-30, Oct. 1-2, 5-9, 11-16, 18, 20-23, 25-30, Nov. 2-6, and 8-10. Seven hired men were employed between Sept. 20 and Nov. 10, as indicated in a two-page wide table near the end of the diary. Sunday rest, *VG*, June 30, 1858: 2.4. On Sunday, Oct. 17, Charles "Powell retorted Some four hundred Dollars." Rising river levels proved problematic on Aug. 14, 17, 19, 20, 27-30, and Sept. 21. The river fell four and a half feet from Sept. 4 to 6 (*VG*, Sept. 14, 1858: 2.2) and continued down until "boulders on the out side of the bar begins to show" on Nov. 7. Downpours on Sept. 26-27, Oct. 4, 29, 24, and Nov. 1, 10, and 12 forced all to take cover.

35 *VG*, Sept. 15, 1858: 2.2.

36 Beam and his companions prospected occasionally on Aug. 6, 10, 11, Oct. 31, etc. Beam panned out on Oct. 13, 14, 20, 21, 25, 26, 28, and Nov. 2. On making and fixing rockers, see Beam's diary for Aug. 9, 10, 13-14, 16; and Sept. 25. Two rockers were working on Oct. 12 and 18, and three on Oct. 11, 13, 20, and Nov. 2. Urban Hicks 1893: 294 noted that "We took in another partner, which enabled us to hold five claims in one body."

37 Beam's diary: B99-B100 includes a table of days worked by hired men, with several unexplained fours and fives. Those numbers probably refer to wages paid to them. Urban Hicks paid similar wages to his hired men (Urban Hicks 1893: 293).

38 The government regulation appears in *VG*, June 30, 1858: 2.4-5. The local extension back into the hills is recorded by Urban Hicks 1893: 294.

39 Beam and Powell 1858c: 2, partnership agreement reads: "*George Beam furnishes Claim No. 4 up stream from centre stake on said Bar. And Charles E. Powell furnishes Claim No. 7. up stream from said centre stake. Also Claim No. 34 up stream from said stake.*"

40 "Alcaide," Urban Hicks' designation (1893: 293) for the bookkeeper, is a Spanish word used since the sixteenth century in southwest USA areas once under Mexican control. It described the commander of a fortress or warden of a prison (*Random House Dictionary of the English Language*).

41 Disputed, abandoned, and jumped claims: Beam's diary, Sept. 9, Aug. 12, 26-7, Sept. 1, 1858. See also Sept. 15: "*Other Claims have bin jumped today;*" and Sept. 14: "*T. Prater and a Frenchman had a row about a Claim.*"

42 Beam's diary, Aug. 26, 27, 29, 30, 1858, Beam and Powell 1858c: 2-3.

43 Claims from $75 to $500: Beam's diary for Sept. 21, 22; Oct. 4, 18, 25, 26; and Nov. 11.

44 A thousand dollars is an approximate figure supported by two sets of figures in the diary. Beam's diary (dated September 13, 1858) has the only specific list of daily earnings: $224.00 for Sept. 14-18, $132.50 for Sept. 20-24, and $137.50 for Sept. 28-Oct. 2. Do the figures $2,862 at the lower left of that page and the $1,989 at the lower right refer to gross earnings and the profit after expenses and wages to hired men? That would mean that each partner made around $1,000. Seven pages earlier (on a page that starts with "G.W. Beam account, Sept 25th") has the figure $2,092.95, minus the $293.93 expenses listed on the previous

page, which is $1,809.02. His partner Charles Powell took half, bringing Beam's share to $904.51. On November 10, Beam and Powell realized an additional $300 each through the sale of their claims. Again, the implication is that both men took away around $1,000. On Engle and Hill: Ebey 1852/1918: 52, n. 62, and 50-1, n. 60.

45 Almira Wright, 1858.

46 The final two paragraphs of the chapter are based on University of Washington Library, Seattle, online notes about George Wesley Beam; anonymous, undated manuscript biography of Beam in WSE, box 5, file 5; *Washington Find a Grave Index, 1821-2012*.

CHAPTER 7: Otis Parsons' Work on the Harrison-Lillooet Trail

1 In an interview of 1964, Arthur William A. Phair (1880-1967) of Lillooet said that he once owned a copy of Otis Parsons' diary on the road building, then gave it to the BC Archives (Budd 2010: 84). The original has not been located there or elsewhere.

2 *SDU*, Aug. 4, 1858: 1.4 stated, "The proprietors of the *Victoria Gazette* have dispatched Wm. V. Wells—formerly of the *Alta California*—up these rivers, as their special correspondent." His first report, dated August 8 at Little Harrison Lake, appeared in *VG*, Aug. 13, 1858: 1.1-2. City Editor Wells had originally been sent north by *DAC*, June 12, 1858: 2.2. According to *SDU*, Aug. 4. 1858: 2.5, Henry de "Groot, late of the San Francisco *Times*, accompanies the expedition as the special correspondent of the *Gazette*."

3 Anderson 1845 (with sketch), Anderson 1846: 61-70, Anderson 1878: 57-64, and Anderson 2011.

4 The "Harrison Lillooet route" was Douglas's name (*CD* 1858.4.6.2). It is shown on the *Map Showing the Different Routes* in Anderson 1858. Edwards 1978 and Syrette 2010 include photographs of later stages.

5 Modern maps used to calculate distances over lakes and the following sources for land distances: Anderson 1846; G. Epner's 1862 *Map of the Gold Regions of British Columbia*, with distances on improved wagon roads; Mayne 1859; Palmer 1859/1861: 236; *VG*, Sept. 29, 1858: 2.4; and *VG*, Oct. 7, 1858: 2.4; cf. Hou and others 1978. Modern distances, Mussio 2013.

6 *VG*, July 24, 1858: 1.4.

7 "A foot trail . . . hand-barrow across the": *VG*, July 28, 1858: 2.1.

8 *VG*, July 28, 1858: 1.1.

9 *DAC*, Sept. 8, 1858: 1.5.

10 *VG*, July 29, 1858: 1.1.

11 *CD* 1858.8.19.1 = *PRBC* 1.28.

12 "From four to six weeks . . . necessary": *VG*, July 31, 1858: 2.2. "Pack-trail . . . property of the miners," *VG*, Aug. 3, 1858: 2.2. On the size of the Hudson's Bay Company bateaux used west of the Rocky Mountains, Anderson 1858: 5; Dunn 1844: 60-2; Mackie 1997: 16-17, 61; and Wilkes 1845: 4.378, who calls the director a "padroon." That term appears related to Italian *padrone*, a term brought into English to describe the master of a vessel on the Mediterranean (*OED*).

13 Crockett 1892: 245, writing of 1851.

14 *VG*, July 31, 1858: 2.2; *VG*, Aug. 3, 1858: 2.2.

15 Waddington 1858: 25. His description on pp. 22-25 echoes Parsons' frustrations.

16 *VG*, Aug. 4, 1858: 2.1.

17 Hill 1987. 76 (road widths); "A Register of [62] Bridges Constructed on the Harrison's River Road," Douglas, *CD*, Nov. 9, 1858 = *PRBC* 1.32-3; *VG*, Aug. 27, 1858. 3.1-2 (jacks). Miners who used their own tools were compensated (*VG*. Aug. 6, 1858: 2.1).

18 The 1840 U.S. census places Parsons in Litchfield, Connecticut. The 1850 U.S. census lists him as nineteen years old in Tuolumne County, California. *Orizaba*'s arrival: *VG*, July 10, 1858: 3.3.

19 *VG*, Aug. 6, 1858: 2.2. The second group left on August 10: *VG*, Aug. 10, 1858: 3.1.

20 *VG*, Aug. 13, 1858: 1.2.

21 Chief surveyor Charles Bedford Young in *VG*, Aug. 17, 1858: 2.1.

22 *VG*, July 28, 1858: 1.3; Aug. 17, 1858: 2.2; Aug. 27, 1858: 3.2; Sept. 14, 1858: 1.2; Pojar and MacKinnon 2004.

23 Young in *VG*, Aug. 17, 1858: 2.1-2: Wells in *VG*, Aug. 27, 1858: 3.1-2.

24 For Sevastopol, Gibraltar Hill, the mile houses and other landmarks, see Table 4.

25 Palmer 1859/1861: 225.

26 Wells in *VG*, Aug. 27, 1858: 3.1

27 Young requisitioned twelve more surveyors according to *VG*, Aug. 17, 1858: 2.1.

28 Wells in *VG*, Aug. 27, 1858: 3.1.

29 Wells in *VG* Oct. 23, 1858: 2.3.

30 Young in *VG*, Aug. 17, 1858: 2.1. He is called government "agent" in *VG*, Sept. 30, 1858: 2.3 and "surveyor" in *VG*, Oct. 23, 1858. On his wharf: *VG*, Oct. 18, 1858: 3.1.

31 "About ten miles . . . mules": Wright in *VG*, Aug. 19, 1858: 2.1.

32 Wells in *VG*, Aug. 27, 1858: 3.2.

33 Palmer 1859/1861: 226.

34 *VG*, Aug. 14, 1858: 2.1 lists the provisions. Because such large quantities were involved, the Hudson's Bay Company may have chosen the lowest wholesale price per pound available at either San Francisco through a Victoria wholesaler (*PCSL* for Aug. 1858): flour 16¢, beans 2.5¢, onions 1.5¢, salt pork 15¢, tea 20¢, coffee 20¢, sugar 15¢, and rice 6¢; or Puget Sound through its trading post at Fort Nisqually (*PSH*, Aug. 20, 1858): flour 9¢, beans 10¢, salt pork 18¢, tea 75¢, coffee 20¢, and sugar 18¢. *CD* 1860.02.25.1 calculated the cost of freight from Victoria to Port Douglas at £25 ($125) per ton. Fifteen tons for ten more days arrived shortly after, according to *VG*, Aug. 19, 1858: 2.1. On that occasion, the *Umatilla* dropped the cargo at the mouth of the Harrison River, "to be forwarded from that point in bateaux to Port Douglas" at extra cost.

35 "Bridging two . . . total loss": Wells in *VG*, Aug. 27, 1858: 3.2.

36 Mr. Blessing: Wells reported differently in *VG*, Sept. 14, 1858: 1.1. On Aug. 23, Abraham Savil from Wisconsin "died on the road. . . . Upwards of five hundred dollars in specie were found on his body."

37 Wells in *VG*, Aug. 27, 1858: 3.2.

38 On the site of the rapids: "Skatin Nations" online at *First Peoples' Language Map of British Columbia*, node 455. Oblates: Syrette 2010: 17-9.

39 Tenas means "little" in Chinook, hence the two names "Tenas Lake" and "Little Lillooet Lake."

40 Young had offered 600 lbs. of flour for the boat, which was not forthcoming. Robert Dexter and Jefferson Siggins complained to Douglas in an unnumbered petition of Aug. 21, 1858.

41 Petition 95, Sept. 8, 1858.

42 The cost of mules, horses, and wagons is recorded in VICB 2, Sept. 16 and 17.

43 *PSH* often lists mules and horses in its weekly commodity prices.

44 *VG*, July 28, 1858: 1.3 noted that Harrison "lake is usually calm all night and until about noon, after which, until sunset, heavy gusts sweep down

the mountains and kick up quite a little sea—much too boisterous a one for deeply laden canoes." This description matches my experiences canoeing on the narrow lakes north east of Vancouver. Sept. 7, 1858, had a new moon (*Pocket Diary for 1858*). In September, the sun sets around 8:00 p.m. and rises around 6:30 a.m. in Vancouver (www.timeanddate. com).

45 For Lil'wat First Nation, see online *First Peoples' Language Map of British Columbia*, node 452. Mayne's 1859 *Sketch* map has "Scaalux," Palmer's 1859 *Plan* has "Mosquito." The current name "Gates" commemorates John Gates, who settled there around 1900 (Akrigg 1973: 69).

46 Wells on Sept. 5 in *VG*, Sept. 14, 1858: 1.2.

47 A.B. on Sept. 25 in *VG*, Sept. 30, 1858: 2.3.

48 Wells on Oct. 4 in *VG*, Oct. 23, 1858: 2.2.

49 Three hundred workers: A.B. on Sept. 23 in *VG*, Sept. 28, 1858: 2.3. A quarter packing for 20 miles: A.B. on Sept. 25 in *VG*, Sept. 30, 1858: 2.4. "Made pack animals" and "The Chinese Company:" Wells on Oct. 4 in *VG*, Oct. 23, 1858: 2.3.

50 Wells on Oct. 4 in *VG*, Oct. 23, 1858: 2.2.

51 A.B. on Sept. 25 in *VG*, Sept. 30, 1858: 2.3. A.B. praised Bryant's "activity and energy . . . [and] courteous and obliging conduct" on Sept. 30 in *VG*, Oct. 7, 1858: 2.4.

52 Wells on Oct. 4 in *VG*, Oct. 23, 1858: 2.2.

53 A.B. on Sept. 25 in *VG*, Sept. 30, 1858: 2.4.

54 A.B. on Sept. 28 in *VG*, Oct. 5, 1858: 1.2. On October 9, Wells and his working party "reached the *final terminus* of the Trail and brought four wagon mules with us. . . . The boats are now ready to transport others across these two lakes": *VG*, Oct. 23, 1858: 2.3.

55 "By an armed party" and "two bateaux": A.B. writing on Sept. 28, printed in *VG*, Oct. 5, 1858: 1.2. "A young man": A.B. writing on Sept. 25, printed in *VG*, Sept. 30, 1858: 2.4. "An old man": A.B. writing on Sept. 30, printed in *VG*, Oct. 7, 1858: 2.3.

56 In November, Petition 120 begged Governor Douglas for protection against attacks by Indigenous people near Port Douglas.

57 A.B. writing on Sept. 28, printed in *VG*, Oct. 5, 1858: 1.2.

58 "Parties": *VG*, Sept. 7: 2.3. "Much perplexed": A.B. on Sept. 23 in *VG*, Sept. 28, 1858: 2.4. "Fitted": A.B. on Sept. 25 in *VG*, Sept. 30, 1858: 2.3.

59 A.B. on Sept. 30 in *VG*, Oct. 7, 1858: 2.3.

60   A.B. on Sept. 25 in *VG*, Sept. 30, 1858: 2.3. The *Otter* spent Oct. 4 load-ing more "supplies . . . in compliance with the contract of the Govern-ment, agreeing to furnish each member of the part with $25 worth of provisions" (*VG*, Oct. 5, 1858: 2.4).

61   A.B. on Oct. 13 in *VG*, Oct. 23, 1858: 1.1-2. The figures of 4¢ and 20¢ a ton also appear there.

62   "Abandoned": A.B. on Sept. 30 in *VG*, Oct. 7, 1858: 2.3. "Refunded": A.B. on Oct. 13 in *VG*, Oct. 23, 1858: 1.1.

63   Petition 121, Oct. 18, 1858, p. 7. In *VG*, Dec. 7, 1858: 2.4, Anderson wrote to clear the name of Young, who had "been assailed in divers ways." On the Lillooet River, "his powers were not discretionary," but his report in Victoria led the government "to modify . . . the commuted allowance for transport."

64   "Competent parties": *VG*, Oct. 26, 1858: 3.1, offering 18¢. "Sum of $36.18 . . . liberality": *VG*, Nov. 2, 1858: 3.1.

65   Packing charge of 26¢: *VG*, Nov. 27, 1858: 2.2. Cost of barley and hay: A.B. on Dec. 20 in *VG*, Jan. 4, 1859: 2.3. Boat fares and cargo: Walter Moberly from Victoria on Feb. 14 in *VG*, Feb. 17, 1859: 1.1; $2 fare on Seton Lake according to the second page of Petition 119 of Dec. 4, 1858. Roadblock: *VG*, Nov. 27, 1858: 2.2. Douglas's condemnation: *VG*, Nov. 30, 1858: 2.3.

66   "Soon": *VG*, Nov. 11, 1858: 2.3. "Five": A.B. on Dec. 9 in *VG*, Dec. 21, 1858: 1.1.

67   *VG*, Aug. 3, 1858: 3.4; cf. *CD*, Aug. 19, 1858 = *PRBC* 1. 28.

68   Begbie 1859/1861: 244: "On two lakes we had favourable winds; on two we were delayed for 24 hours by contrary winds" that impeded "the row-boats now in use." Mayne (1859/1861: 218) crossed Seton Lake in four hours and Anderson Lake in five. On Sept. 5, 1858, at Lillooet Lake, J.W. McKay and his party, "hired a boat, . . . started at noon . . . [and] reached the head of the lake at sunset" (*PRBC* 2.31). In December 1858, John G. Hutchings from Essex, Robert H. Brown from Yorkshire, John McIntosh from Canada, and Patrick Everitt from Ireland asked for a two-year monopoly to prevent a new group of foreigners from ruining their ferry on Seaton Lake (Petition 119).

69   Palmer 1859/1861: 232; Begbie 1859/1861: 243.

70   $6,000 estimate in *VG*, July 29, 1858: 1.1; £10,000 ($50,000) in *CD*, Nov. 9, 1858 = *PRBC* 2.29; £14,000 ($70,000) in *CD*, April 8, 1859 =

FPBC 3.1. A.B. in *VG*, Oct. 7, 1858: 2.3 heard estimates from $75,000 to $100,000.

71 J.W. McKay on bridges in *PRBC* 2.31. Low Harrison River: A.B. on Sept. 23 in *VG*, Sept. 28, 1858: 2.2-3; *CD*, Nov. 30, 1858, no. 2 = *PRBC* 2.39.

72 Begbie 1859/1861: 246.

73 Palmer 1859/1861: 225.

74 Plans for 1859: *CD*, June 8, 1859, no. 1 = *FPBC* 3.17. Engineers and progress: *CD*, July 4, 1859, no. 6 = *FPBC* 3.29-30; *CD*, Jan. 27, 1860, no. 2. San Juan Island Pig War: *CD*, Aug. 23, 1859, no. 1 = *FPBC* 3.49; "Pig War," *Wikipedia*; Vouri 2008 and 2013. At *CD*, Aug. 18, 1859, no 206, the parliamentary minister wrote, "I have for some time thought that the labours of the Engineers make very little show!"

75 Request to Colonial Office for gifts and loans: *CD*, Nov. 26, 1858, no. 1 = *PRBC* 2.10; *CD*, Aug. 23, 1859, no. 1 = *FPBC* 3.49. Payment of first year's expenses: *CD*, Nov. 9, 1858, no. 3 = *PRBC* 2.29. "10 per cent": *CD*, July 4, 1859, no. 6 = *FPBC* 3.30. Later B.C. taxes: "Twelve shillings [$3] for every ton of wares, goods, and merchandise transported or taken from New Westminster to any place in British Columbia": *CD*, Dec. 22, 1859 = *FPBC* 3.78). "£1 Sterling [$5] upon all pack animals leaving Douglas and Yale": *CD*, February 25, 1860, no. 1. "a duty of one farthing (1/2¢) a pound on all goods carried inland from Douglas, Hope, and Yale": *CD*, Dec. 12, 1860, no. 1. new customs rates (same source). Bonds for the Harrison and other roads: *CD*, Nov. 15, 1861; *CD*, Aug. 28, 1860.

76 Newcastle: annotation to *CD*, Jan. 27, 1860, no. 2. Douglas: *CD*, April 23, 1860.

77 Embanking shoals and reconstructing part of Lillooet River road: *CD*, April 23, 1860 = *FPBC* 4.4-5. "Section of 6 miles": *CD*, April 23, 1860 = *FPBC* 4.5. Contractor Joseph W. Trutch: Reid 1942: 36. Costs in 1860: *CD*, 1861.1.26.1 = *FPBC* 4.43. Roads and bridges accounted for £18,935 of the year's expenditures of £44,124.

78 *CD*, Oct. 9, 1860 = *FPBC* 4.22-6; Edwards 1978: 133.

79 *CD*, April 23, 1860 = *FPBC* 4.5.

80 Begbie 1859/1861: 244.

81 Colonel Moody, always antagonistic to Douglas, demoted Duffy to sapper for leaving his surveying post in Cayoosh without his permission (Hill 1987: 76-8; www.royalengineers.ca/DuffyJ.html). The drop in

salary would have placed a strain on his marriage. The Cayoosh River route was finally developed as the Duffy Lake Road, now part of Highway 99. See also Harris 1980, with map; Howay 1910: 7.

82 Contract to Colquhoun: Reid 1942: 38, citing *Victoria Colonist*, Sept. 14, 1860. James Chapman, George Cox, and Robert Ritchie were the owners of the five-year lease on the Anderson to Seton Lake tramway according to Edwards 1978: 129. Gibraltar Hill: Howay 1910: 7-8. Goulding's Dam: Syrette 2010: 29.

83 In early 1858, cartage was £360 per ton, or 90¢ per pound ($1,800 divided by 2,000): *CD*, February 25, 1860. In November 1858, nine pence (18¢) per pound: *CD*, Nov. 9, 1858 = *PRBC* 2.29 (at the same time, cartage from Fort Yale to Lytton cost more than twice as much—1s 11 1/4 d., or 47¢). In July 1859, fell from a high of 37¢ during the winter to just 10¢: *CD*, July 4, 1859 = *FPBC* 3.29 (at the same time, freight from Victoria to Port Douglas dropped to 1-1/7¢ per pound). In 1860, £20 a ton, or 5¢ a pound ($100 divided by 2,000): *CD*, Oct. 9, 1860 = *FPBC* 4.23.

84 *CD*, April 23, 1860, paragraph 6 = *FPBC* 4.4.

85 Prices at Fountain in 1858: Canadian miner's diary for Oct. 10. Cayoosh/Bridge River: *VG*, Dec. 21, 1858: 1.2. Other two columns: Parsons's diary, p. P45.

86 "Burned out" and other quotations for two paragraphs: Phillips 1858/1932: 153-6.

87 Nelson was Parsons' business partner until at least 1863, when he is listed in *The British Columbian . . . Directory for 1863*: 195. Parsons does not appear at any B.C. city in the next directory, published in 1867.

88 In winter 1858-9, Mayne 1859/1861: 219 found "the Indians charging 5 cent per lb. from Port Douglas to Port Lilloet, when the mule-trains were charging 15 cents."

89 Merchants are mentioned on diary pp. P46 and P48. Robinson, *First Victoria Directory* (1860); Wright, *VG*, Sept. 28, 1858: 2.3; Dozier, *VG*, Sept. 16, 1858: 2.3; Palmer 1859/1861: 232; Hutchinson Sr. and Jr., *The British Columbian . . . Directory for 1863*.

90 Parsons' diary, p. P41. By contrast, Puget Sound resident Urban Hicks (1893: 296) was shortchanged. In December 1858 at Victoria he "disposed of my dust at $14.50 per ounce."

91 In April 1859, Begbie at French Bar found a "ferry recently granted by

Captain Travaillot to Aimable Bonnet and Calmel" for one year (Begbie 1859/1861: 242; cf. *CD*, 1859.04.12 = *FPBC* 3.6).

92 Parson's life in the 1860s and 1870s: Downs 1992: 36-7; Hacking 1947: 75-83. A table of the "Longevity of Persons" (*MGSR*, August 14, 1858) recorded few men who lived more than fifty years.

CHAPTER 8: A Canadian Miner's Success.

1 The diary and photo of the miner are currently owned by the author.

2 "Licence" appears once, on Sept. 19, 1858.

3 In his diary, American George Slocumb uses first or last names except for his banker, "Mr. Purkins" (Apr. 19, 1858). American George Beam refers to "Captains," "Sergeants" and "Misters" on July 25, Aug. 13, Aug. 26-9, Sept. 10, Oct. 9, 16, 17, 23, 25, and Nov. 14, 1858, but usually he wrote just surnames or given names.

4 The details in this paragraph are based on Nelson Landon's additions to the same diary that the anonymous Canadian miner used.

5 *VG*, July 14, 1858: 3.4 gives July 12 as the arrival date of the *Oregon*.

6 Prices of building supplies at Victoria, see Chapter 1, especially note 17.

7 Phillips 1858/1932: 153, diary for July 20-9, 1858.

8 Stinging nettle (*Urtica dioica*): Pojar and MacKinnon 2004: 309.

9 Thefts: *DEB*, July 9, 1858: 2.1; *VG*, July 10, 1858: 3.3; *VG*, July 17: 3.3; *VG*, July 17, 1858: 3.3.

10 The only "E." advertising in the July 14 issue of *VG* (p. 3) was temporary auctioneer E.S. Mendels. He did not have a "*shop*," but only a room on the second floor of Bayley's Hotel.

11 *VG*, July 14, 1858: 2.4 lists an auction by Fitch.

12 J.D. Carroll and P.C. Dart advertised regularly in *VG*, June 30, 1858: 3.3 to July 14, 1858: 3.4.

13 *CD*, July 1, 1858 = *PRBC* 1.19-21.

14 *VG*, July 14, 1858 (second issue on microfilm, with four pages): 3.1; 4.2; 2.3.

15 *VG*, July 21, 1858: 1.3-4.

16 *VG*, July 28, 1858: 2.3.

17 "2,000": *DAC*, Aug. 8, 1858: 2.3. "Idle": *DAC*, Aug. 19, 1858: 1.5.

18 *VG*, July 14, 1858 (second issue): 4.3.

19 Mayne 1859/1861: 214.

20 *VG*, Sept. 7, 1858: 2.2.

21 Kequeloose is now rendered as Ti'kwalus, Tikuiluc, or Teeqaloose (Harris 1997: 106).

22 Kwak-a-hum, the anonymous Canadian miner's spelling, is Quayome in most nineteenth-century sources, and Tqua-yowm in Anderson 1858: 7. Harris 1997: 106 has Koia'um, Tkkoeaum, or Tuck-Kwi-owh-um. Anderson 1858: 7 wrote that "A large cedar statue, of Indian workmanship, and a small enclosure, mark the spot" of the suicide's burial. Laforet and York 1998: 47 comment that it was made "in the manner of Nlaka'pamux graves at that time."

23 Anderson's 1858 *Map Showing the Different Routes* shows "Skâoose Vil." south of the "Great Fork" of the Fraser and Thompson Rivers, while Mayne's 1859 *Sketch* map shows an "Indian Village" in the valley north of Jackass Mountain. The survey produced by Royal Engineers Sapper James Turnbull in 1860 shows "SISKA FLAT Indian Reserve" and "M. Paillard's Garden". The map in Harris 1997: 106 calls the settlement Si'ska.

24 On the cost of sending letters, see the end of Chapter 2.

25 William Manson, around thirty years old, was the son of Chief Trader Donald Manson at northern Fort St. James ("Donald Manson," *DCBO*; Watson 2010: 2.618-9). The miner and Manson worked together from August 10 to 17. They returned to Forks on August 18. The Canyon War preoccupied Manson from August 17 to 25, especially when thousands of Indigenous people gathered near Forks to meet Snyder. In March 1858, Douglas ordered the construction of Hudson's Bay Company Fort Dallas at Forks, but the building stopped when miners moved north (*CEG* 1858: 12; *PSH*, April 30: 2.2; *CD*, July 1, 1858 = *PRBC* 1.20; Perry 2006: 32).

26 Izman Creek, 19 kilometres north of Lytton, is the only stream in the vicinity. Tailings in Kennedy 2008-9: 48. I found no trace of "Cowman Creek" in recent or older records.

27 Mormon Bar is "six miles above the junction of Thompson's River" (*First Victoria Directory* of 1860; *CD*, July 1, 1858 = *PRBC* 1.19). Tailings in Kennedy 2008-9: 47.

28 Anderson 1858: 24.

29 Fosters Bar: *First Victoria Directory* 1860: 68; Mayne's *Sketch of Part of British Columbia*, 1859.

30 Douglas in *CD*, June 10, 1858 = *PRBC* 1.13-4; Waddington in *VG*, July 21, 1858: 1.3-4; and Waddington 1858: 6. The Canadian mentions Frenchman's Bar on Sept. 20 (Kennedy 2008-9: 58, 51), and notes two new shacks at Fountain on Sept. 18.

31 Palmer 1859/1861: 235; cf. Mayne 1859/1861: 218 on prices upriver.

32 *DAC*, July 23, 1858: 1.5.

33 *VG*, Dec. 18, 1858: 1.2.

34 Many trout lakes in B.C. got renamed. Pavilion Lake is the only possibility around 29 kilometres (18 miles) from Fountain, as confirmed by Waddington in *VG*, July 21, 1858: 1.3: "above Bridge river coarse gold is found . . . on the second or middle stream to the east, ending with a small lake. At the junction of this stream is an Indian village called the Pavilion." Pavillon is French for a "flag" which once marked an Indigenous chief's grave. The English heard "Pavilion:" Akrigg 1973: 132.

35 From August 2 to October 12, the anonymous Canadian miner recorded many daily gold earnings, though some require interpretation. The crescent and figure 22 on August 2 have been ignored. Half the figures recorded for August 11 ($6, $18, $3, and $7) belonged to Manson; the lowest have been assigned to the Canadian. The "*Gold $125*" recorded on August 28 has been included, though it is unclear whether that is a running total including some earnings double counted from earlier days. On September 2 appears the entry "*small pannings $1-2*," plus an additional "*$3*"; I have tallied only one of those $3 amounts. The entry for September 3 could be either $50 or $5.0; the lower $5 is included here. Half the amounts for September 8-9 belong to Mr. Daly; $12 and $20 appear to belong to the Canadian. The earnings totaled include Aug. 10, $13 (average of $12-$14); Aug. 11, $6 and $3; Aug. 12, $20; Aug. 14-5, $22 and $19; Aug. 20, $23; Aug. 22, $15; Aug. 23, $12; Aug. 25, $22; Aug. 26, $6; Aug. 27, $25; Aug. 28, $125; Sept. 1, $0.75; Sept. 2, $3; Sept 3, $5; Sept. 4, $12; Sept. 5, $18; Sept. 8, $12; Sept. 9, $20; Sept. 16, $22.10; Sept. 17, $50; Sept. 20, $15; Sept. 23, $14; Sept. 24, $17; Sept. 25, $30; Sept. 28, $17; Sept. 29, $20; Sept. 30, $12; Oct. 1, $20; Oct. 2, $22; Oct. 3, $26; Oct. 4, $16.50; Oct. 5, $8; Oct. 6, $10; Oct. 7, $14; Oct. 8, $13; Oct. 11, $5; Oct. 12, claim sold to M. Samuelson Co., $400. The conservative total, excluding the possibly repeated $125 on Aug. 28 is $1,115.35.

CHAPTER 9: Perspectives beyond the End of 1858

1 Shakespeare, *The Tempest*, Act 5, scene 1, line 183-4. Miranda, daughter of the Caucasian Duke of Milan who was exiled on a remote island, speaks the line with enthusiastic optimism. Current interpretation often grapples with the colonizers' mistreatment of the island's pre-settlement inhabitant, Caliban.

2 *VG*, Nov. 25, 1858: 1.1-2. For the major figures at the installation, short biographies appear in *DCBO*. Begbie: Williams 1977.

3 Hauka 2003.

4 "The storekeepers" and "Eight": Waddington 1858: 38, 47.

5 Gardiner 1858/1937: 252.

6 *VG*, Dec. 9, 1858: 2.2.

7 *PRBC* 2.29.

8 Surveys for Old Fort Langley, Fort Hope, and Fort Yale: *CD*, Oct. 11, 1858 = *PRBC* 1.38. Illustrations of surveys for Yale, Langley, Douglas, Lytton, and Lillooet: Hayes 2012: 66, 69, 80-2. A sale of lots at Old Fort Langley raised £13,000: *CD*, Nov. 29, 1858 = *PRBC* 2.37. Other land sales: *CD*, June 10, 1858 = *PRBC* 1.14; Aug. 14, 1858 = *PRBC* 1.49; and Oct. 27, 1858 = *PRBC* 2.17.

9 De Groot 1859: 19.

10 The maps are listed in the bibliography under their titles. Illustrations appear in Hayes 1999 and Hayes 2012.

11 Richards 2011.

12 Three lighthouse charts were folded after p. 14 in *PRBC* 2. On the lighthouses: *CD*, Jan. 15, 1859 = *PRBC* 2.56; May 11, 1859 = *PRBC* 2.87.

13 Mayne's view of Yale: *Sketch of Part of British Columbia*: 146. Mayne 1859/1861; Mayne 1862; "Richard Charles Mayne," *Wikipedia*.

14 Palmer 1859/1861, Higuchi 2002, and Woodward 2003.

15 *British Columbia and Vancouver's Island* 1858 (with a map of a proposed railway route across British North America), Broun 1852, Broun 1858 (with a *Map of The Atlantic & Pacific Junction Railway*—illustration 9.14), MacDonell 1858, and *Project for the Construction of a Railroad to the Pacific* 1852.

16 De Groot 1859: 15.

17 *CD*, Feb. 25, 1860.

18 During the summer of 1860, the Royal Engineers replaced the Douglas Portage from Fort Yale to Spuzzum with a road blasted along the river

(Howay 1910: 7). The Similkameen was the brigade route after 1848. See *CD*, Aug. 28, 1860, no. 84, paragraph 5, and *DCBO* on Edgar Dewdney, whose road was named after him. Douglas described early Coquihalla work by Fort Hope residents on June 8, 1859 (*FPBC* 3.17). Lieutenant Arthur Reid Lemprière supervised: see his "Sketch of Trail from Hope to Boston Bar," ca. 1859 (at LTSBC 15T1 Roads & Trails). The trail was twenty miles longer than the Fraser Canyon and closed by heavy snow from October to June and constant slides along the Anderson River. See Harris 1979, with map.

19 "The best": *CD*, July 31, 1858 = *PRBC* 1.45. "Exercising": *CD*, March 14, 1859.
20 Duff 1969 and Duff 1997: 85.
21 *CD*, Oct. 12, 1858, paragraph 20 = *PRBC* 2.5.
22 *CD*, March 14, 1859 = *PRBC* 2.68-9.
23 *CD*, Oct. 9, 1860, paragraph 35 = *FPBC* 4.26.
24 Fisher 1992, Harris 1997, Harris 2002.
25 Fisher 1994.
26 Trutch 1875: 41.
27 Carlson and McHalsie 2001: 94-5 and Fisher 1981: 160, 164-5. On 40,000 acres, B.W. Pearse to Trutch, Oct. 21, 1868, in *BCPC*: 53.
28 Supreme Court Tsilhqot'in 2014: unedited introduction.

ACKNOWLEDGEMENTS
1 Kennedy 2008-9, Nelson and Kennedy 2011-12.

REFERENCES

Early maps are scarce and catalogued by libraries and archives differently. Here they are listed by title, with cross references to creators where known. To help readers locate copies, locations are provided.

Adams, John. 2001. *Old Square-Toes and His Lady: The Life of James and Amelia Douglas.* Victoria: Horsdal & Schubart.

Affleck, Edward L. 1992. *Affleck's List of Sternwheelers Plying the Inland Waters of British Columbia 1858-1980.* Vancouver: Alexander Nicolls Press.

Affleck, Edward L. 2000. *A Century of Paddlewheelers in the Pacific Northwest, the Yukon and Alaska.* Vancouver: Alexander Nicolls Press.

Akrigg, G.P.V., and Helen B. 1973. *1001 British Columbia Place Names.* 3rd ed., rev. Vancouver: Discovery Press.

Akrigg, G.P.V., and Helen B. 1977. *British Columbia Chronicle, 1847-1871: Gold and Colonists.* Vancouver: Discovery Press.

Albemarle, William Coutts Keppell, Earl of. 1858. "British Columbia and Vancouver's Island." *Fraser's Magazine for Town and Country* 58 (October): 493-504. Signed "Beta Mikron." CIHM 17961. UBCR attributes the article, based on "accounts" of others, to Albemarle.

Alden, James Madison, artist—see Stenzel 1975.

Allard, Jason O. n.d. "White Miners Saved Lives of B.C.'s First Chinese— Some Stories of Yale in the Gold Rush." UBCR, Howay-Reid Collection, box 21.4.

Anderson, Alexander Caulfield. 1845. "Suggestions for the Exploration of a New Route of Communication." Hudson's Bay Company report, February 1845, with map: "Proposed Horse Road . . . Harrison's R." Hudson's Bay Company Archives, Winnipeg, B.5/z/1.

Anderson, Alexander Caulfield. 1846. "Journal of an Expedition under Command of Alex C. Anderson of the Hudson's Bay Company, Undertaken with the View of Ascertaining the Practicability of a Communication with the Interior, for the Import of the Annual Supplies." Pemberton Museum Archives, MG 34/1/1.

Anderson, Alexander Caulfield. 1858. *Hand-Book and Map to the Gold Region of Frazer's and Thompson's Rivers. Price One Dollar and Fifty Cents.* San Francisco: J.J. Le Count. With *Map Showing the Different Routes of Communication.* Advertised as "just published" in *Daily Evening Bulletin.* San Francisco, California, newspaper. Microfilm at University of B.C., May 31, 1858: 2.5. Copies with map: LAC, TRL, Vancouver Public Library. Text printed in *PRBC* 1.79-83, with map.

Anderson, Alexander Caulfield. 1878. "History of the Northwest Coast by Alexander Caulfield Anderson of Rosebank, Victoria, B.C." Typescript at UBCR.

Anderson, Nancy Marguerite. 2011. *The Pathfinder: A.C. Anderson's Journeys in the West.* Vancouver: Heritage House.

Anonymous Canadian miner. 1858. Handwritten diary from July 12 to October 29, 1858. In *Pocket Diary for 1858.* New York: Philip J. Cozans. Author's collection.

Atlas of American History. 1984. 2nd rev. ed. New York: Scribner.

Ballantyne, Robert Michael, ed. 1858. *Handbook to the New Gold Fields.* Edinburgh: Alex. Strahan; London: Hamilton, Adams. With map. UBC.

Ballou, William T. 1878. "Adventures of William T. Ballou." Typed transcript of interview by Hubert Howe Bancroft at Seattle, Washington. Bancroft Library, University of California, Berkeley BANC MSS P-B 1.

"Ballou's Express." n.d. "Ballou's Express: The Man Who Never Failed to Deliver," in "Colourful characters in Historic Yale." Online at https://www.communitystories.ca.

Bancroft, Hubert Howe. 1887. *History of British Columbia, 1792-1887.* In his *Works,* vol. 32. San Francisco: History Company, Publishers.

Bancroft, Hubert Howe. 1890. *History of Washington, Idaho, and Montana, 1845-1889.* In his *Works,* vol. 31. San Francisco: History Company, Publishers.

Barman, Jean. 2007. *The West Beyond the West: A History of British Columbia.* 3rd ed. Toronto: Univ. of Toronto Press.

Bartlett, John. 1980. *Familiar Quotations*. 15th rev. ed. Ed. Emily M. Beck. Boston: Little, Brown.

Basque, Garnet. 1991. *Gold Panner's Manual*. Langley, B.C.: Stagecoach.

Beam, George Wesley. 1858a. Handwritten diary. University of Washington Library, Seattle. Special Collections, accession 2409, vertical file 858.

Beam, George Wesley. 1858b. Letters to Winfield Scott Ebey, Whidbey Island, dated Aug. 20, Sept. 1, and Oct. 8, 1858. WSE, box 2.

Beam, George Wesley, and Charles E. Powell. 1858c. A handwritten contract for their mining partnership on Puget Sound Bar, 25 September 1858. WSE, box 5, file 9.

Beard, Richard R. 1987. *Treating Gold Ores by Amalgamation*. State of Arizona Department of Mines and Mineral Resources Circular No. 27. Online.

Begbie, Matthew Baillie. 1859. "Journey into the Interior of British Columbia." *Journal of the Royal Geographical Society* 31 (March 28 to April 25): 237-48. CIHM 15086. Text also in *FPBC* 3.17-25.

Begg, Alexander. 1894. *History of British Columbia from its Earliest Discovery to the Present Time*. Toronto: William Briggs.

Belshaw, John Douglas. 2009. *Becoming British Columbia: A Population History*. Vancouver: UBC Press.

Bennett, Robert A. 1985. *A Small World of Our Own: Authentic Pioneer Stories of the Pacific Northwest from the Old Settlers Contest of 1892*. Walla Walla, WA: Pioneer Press Books.

Beta Mikron—see Albemarle, William Coutts Keppell, Earl of.

Borthwick, John David. 1857. *Three Years in California*. Edinburgh: Blackwood. Author's collection.

Boswell, Randy. 2012. "Old Mines Partly to Blame for Floods: Gravel from 19th- and Early 20th-Century Mines Helped Alter Fraser River's Flow," *Vancouver Sun*, June 25, 2012, B3.

Bowers, Q. David. 1999. *The Treasure Ship S.S. Brother Jonathan: Her Life and Loss, 1850-1865*. Wolfeboro, NH: Bowers and Merena Galleries.

Bowsfield, Hartwell, ed. 1979. *Fort Victoria Letters, 1846-1851*. Winnipeg: Hudson's Bay Record Society.

Bridge, Kathryn, ed. 2015. *New Perspectives on the Gold Rush*. Victoria: Royal B.C. Museum.

Brigantine Recovery, 2010. "Brigantine RECOVERY—Revenue Vessel of

the Fraser River," August 24, 2010, https://queenboroughrevenuestation.
wordpress.com/2010/08/24/brig-recovery-revenue-vessel-of-the-fraser-
river.

British Colonist newspaper, Victoria. Online at https://britishcolonist.ca.

British Columbia and Vancouver's Island. 1858. *British Columbia and Vancouver's Island: A Complete Hand-Book*. London: Effingham Wilson. With a
map of a proposed railway across the continent. CIHM 28106. Copies with
map: BCA, LAC, TRL.

British Columbian Directory. 1863. *The British Columbian and Victoria Guide
and Directory for 1863*. Victoria: F.P. Howard and G. Barnett.

British Columbia: New Westminster to Lillooet (map). 1861. *British Columbia:
New Westminster to Lillooet from a General Map in Preparation by the Royal
Engineers . . . Vancouver Island, the Gulf of Georgia & Part of Fraser River,
are from Surveys by Capt. Richards, R.N. and the Officers of H.M.S. Plumper.
Prepared under the Direction of Capt. Parsons R. Eng^{rs} New Westminster,
August 1861*. BCA CM_A1368; LAC digital e010859303 (facsimile from
NA); NA CO 700 British Columbia 11/3 (original with pen notations by
Col. R.C. Moody); UBCR (proof before the forty-ninth parallel border was
added).

Broun, Richard. 1852. *British and American Intercourse. Letter to the Rt. Hon.
The Earl of Derby on the Imperial Halifax and Quebec Railway and Anglo-
Asian Steam Transit Project*. London: T. Saunders.

Broun, Richard. 1858. *European and Asiatic Intercourse via British Columbia,
by Means of a Main Through Trunk Railway from the Atlantic to the Pacific*.
London: R. Hardwicke. Folded at end, a *Map of The Atlantic & Pacific
Junction Railway*. TRL. CIHM 16727.

Buchanan, Iva L. 1936. "Lumbering and Logging in the Puget Sound Region
in Territorial Days." *Pacific Northwest Quarterly*. 27:34-53.

Buck, Franklin A. 1930. *A Yankee Trader in the Gold Rush*. Boston: Houghton
Mifflin.

Budd, Robert. 2010. *Voices of British Columbia: Stories from Our Frontier*.
Vancouver: Douglas and McIntyre.

Buffum, E. Gould. 1850. *Six Months in the Gold Mines*. Philadelphia: Lea
and Blanchard.

Burns, Robert I. 1947. "Pere Joset's Account of the Indian War of 1858,"
Pacific Northwest Quarterly 38:285-314.

California Atlas. 2011. *California Atlas and Gazetteer*. 3rd ed. Yarmouth, ME: DeLorme.

Canadian Topographic Maps. 1988-2010. Natural Resources Canada. They have much more detail for the Harrison and Fraser Rivers north to Lillooet than Google maps. 92-G, 92-H, 92-I, and 92-J, available in scales 1:50,000 and 1:250,000.

Canyon War: The Untold Story. 2009. Directed by Eva Wunderman. 53 min. Wunderman Film Inc. Videorecording. Vancouver: Moving Images Distribution. Written by Donald J. Hauka, hosted by Daniel Marshall and Kevin Loring.

Carlson, Keith Thor, ed., and Albert (Sonny) McHalsie, cultural advisor. 2001. *A Stó:lō Coast Salish Historical Atlas*. Vancouver: Douglas & McIntyre.

Cartwright, Peggy. 1985. "The Royal Governor and the Black Militia." *British Columbia Historical News*. 19.1:14-7.

Cass, Lewis. 1858. *Letter from the Secretary of State, Asking an Appropriation to Defray Expenses for Transporting Destitute Americans from Victoria to San Francisco*. December 14, 1858. Washington, DC: House of Representatives, 35th Congress, 2nd Session, Executive Document no. 12.

Census of the United States. 1870. "Population Schedules of the Ninth Census of the United States, 1870." Manuscript returns online at archive.org.

Census of the United States. 1880. "10th Census, 1880 Manuscript returns online at archive.org.

Chamberlain, William H., and H.L. Wells. 1879. *History of Yuba County, California*. Oakland, CA: Thompson and West. Chapter 37, "Navigation:" pp. 107-10.

Chandler, Robert J., and Stephen J. Potash. 2007. *Gold, Silk, Pioneers & Mail: The Story of the Pacific Mail Steamship Company*. San Francisco: Friends of the San Francisco Maritime Museum Library.

Chinook Vocabularies—see Gibbs 1863 and Hibben 1871.

Chow, Lily. 2015. "Chinese Foot Prints in the Fraser Gold Rush (1858-60)." In Bridge 2015: 80-91.

Church, Michael—see Nelson, Andrew D., and Michael Church 2011-12.

Clarkson, Thomas W., and David O. Marsh. 1982. "Mercury Toxicity in Man." In *Clinical, Biochemical, and Nutritional Aspects of Trace Elements*, edited by Ananda S. Prasad. New York: Alan R. Liss.

Colledge, J.J. 1969. *Ships of the Royal Navy: An Historical Index.* Vol. 1, *Major Ships*. Newton Abbot, England: David and Charles.

Colonial Despatches—see abbreviation CD.

Cook, S.F. 1943. *The Conflict between the California Indian and White Civilization.* Vol. 3, *The American Invasion, 1848-1870.* Berkeley: Univ. of California Press.

Copies or Extracts of Correspondence . . . Gold—see abbreviation CEG.

Copy of Reconnaissance Sketch (manuscript map). 1858. "Copy of Reconnaissance Sketch of the Fraser River between Fort Hope and Fort Yale Taken on the 13th. and 14th. Sept. 1858." Survey by a Royal Engineers Sapper whose name was cut away. LTSBC 1 T 2 miscellaneous.

Cornwallis, Kinahan. 1858. *The New El Dorado; or, British Columbia, with a Map and Illustration by the Author.* London: T.C. Newby. Preface dated Sept. 4, 1858. UBC.

Correct Map of the Gold Diggings (map). 1858. *Correct Map of the Gold Diggings on Frasers and Thompsons Rivers, Compiled from Recent Surveys.* In *Hutching's California Magazine,* May 20, 1858: 46.

Correct Map of the Northern Coal & Gold Regions (map). 1858a. *A Correct Map of the Northern Coal & Gold Regions, Comprehending the Frazer River. Carefully Compiled from the Latest Data & Personal Observations by A. Waddington. San Francisco, April 1858.* Cambridge University Library, England. Maps.654.85.1.

Correct Map of the Northern Coal & Gold Regions (map). 1858b. *A Correct Map . . . 4th Edition Revised. San Francisco, May 1858.* BCA CM_A79.

Crockett, Hugh. 1892. "The beheading of Colonel I.N. Ebey." Reprint in Bennett 1985: 242-51.

Dawson, George M. 1889. *The Mineral Wealth of British Columbia.* Published as *Geological and Natural History Survey of Canada Annual Report, 1887-88,* new series, vol. 3, part 2, report R. Montreal: Dawson Brothers.

De Groot, Henry. 1859. *British Columbia; Its Condition and Prospects, Soil, Climate, and Mineral Resources, Considered.* San Francisco: Alta California Job Office. No map. Based on De Groot's 1858 reports in *Daily Alta California.* San Francisco, California, newspaper. Online at CDNC. CIHM 22786.

Deaville, Alfred Stanley. 1928. *The Colonial Postal Systems and Postage Stamps of Vancouver Island and British Columbia, 1849-1871.* Victoria: C.F. Banfield, King's Printer.

Delgado, James P. 1993. *The Beaver: First Steamship on the West Coast*. Victoria: Horsdal & Schubart.

Demand and Supply. 2022. "Demand and Supply," at www.gold.org, revised Jan. 28, 2022.

Dolnick, Edward. 2014. *The Rush: America's Fevered Quest for Fortune, 1848-1853*. New York: Little, Brown.

Domer, John (typographical error on title-page)—see Dower, John (correct on printed cover).

Donald, B., M. Unger, and Rob Marsland. 2013. "Decommissioning and Remediation of the Pinchi Lake Mine." *British Columbia Mine Reclamation Symposium*. Online.

Douglas, James. 1853, 1857, and 1859. Proclamations on gold mining—*printed in* Martin 1903: 536-8.

Douglas, James. 1858. "Diary of Gold Discovery on Fraser's River in 1858." In his "Private Papers, First Series," pp. 58-69. Abridged typescript by H.H. Bancroft in 1878 (original lost). BCA B/20/1858.

Douglas, James. 1859. Letter of September 20, on Harrison Lake trail. BCA GR 1180, file 21.

Dower, John. 1858. *New British Gold Fields. A Guide to British Columbia and Vancouver Island, with Coloured Map*. London: W.H. Angel. "Domer" on title-page. Copy with map: TRL.

Downs, Art. 1992. *British Columbia-Yukon Sternwheel Days*. Surrey, B.C.: Heritage House.

Duff, Wilson. 1969. "The Fort Victoria Treaties," *BC Studies* 3: 3-57.

Duff, Wilson. 1997. *The Indian History of British Columbia: The Impact of the White Man*. New ed. Victoria: Royal British Columbia Museum.

Duffus, Maureen. n.d. "James Yates Family." www.maureenduffus.com/james-yates.html.

Dunn, John. 1844. *History of the Oregon Territory and British North-American Fur Trade*. London: Edwards and Hughes.

Eaton, Herbert. 1974. *The Overland Trail to California in 1852*. New York: Putnam.

Ebey, Isaac Neff. 1852/1916. "Diary of Colonel and Mrs. I.N. Ebey," edited by Victor J. Farrar. *Washington Historical Quarterly* 7 (1916): 239-46, 307-21; 8 (1917): 40-62, 124-52.

Ebey, Winfield Scott. 1854/1997. *The 1854 Oregon Trail Diary of Winfield Scott Ebey*. Edited by Susan B. Doyle and Fred W. Dykes. Independence,

MO: Oregon-California Trails Association.

Ebey, Winfield Scott. 1858-1861. "Diary." January 1857-April 1858, WSE, box 1, file 7. April 1858-September 1861, WSE, box 9 oversize.

Edson, Lelah Jackson. 1968. *Fourth Corner: Highlights from the Early Northwest.* Bellingham, WA: Whatcom Museum of History and Art.

Edwards, Irene. 1978. *Short Portage to Lillooet and Other Tales and Trails.* Lillooet, B.C.: Edwards.

Eisler, Ronald. 2004. *Biogeochemical, Health, and Ecotoxicological Perspectives on Gold and Gold Mining.* Boca Raton, FL: CRC Press.

Encyclopedia of British Columbia—see abbreviation *EBC.*

Entrance of Esquimalt Harbour (chart). 1859. *Entrance of Esquimalt Harbour Showing the Proposed Site for a Light House on Fisguard Island. J. Arrowsmith Litho.* In *PRBC* 2.14.

Epner, Gustavus—see *Map of the Gold Regions.*

Esquimalt District—Official Map—1858 (manuscript map). "Esquimalt District—Official Map—1858," from Metchosin to Victoria, surveyed by Joseph Pemberton and Hermann Otto Tiedemann. BCA CM_C64; LTSBC 21T2 large tray, East Coast Vancouver Island.

Esquimalt Harbour. 1861. *Esquimalt Harbour Surveyed by Captn G.H. Richards & the Officers of H.M.S. Plumper 1858, the Interior from a Survey by J.D. Pemberton Esqre Surveyor General 1860.* London: Admiralty Chart 1897a. UKHO chart 1897a, series A, sequence no. 1.

Essex, Phil, and others. 2003. "An Owner's Guide to Tonnage Admeasurement," www.jensenmaritime.com.

European and Asiatic Intercourse—see Broun, Richard. 1858.

Evans, D. Morier. 1859. *The History of the Commercial Crisis, 1857-58, and the Stock Exchange Panic of 1859.* London: Groombridge.

Evans, Elwood. 1870/1965. *The Re-Annexation of British Columbia to the United States.* Olympia WA: E. Evans. Reprint Victoria: Adelphi Book Shop, 1965.

Evans, Elwood. 1878a. "Fraser River Excitement, 1858." 95 pages of handwritten notes and newspaper clippings at Yale University. Microfilm in *Western Americana: Frontier History of the Trans-Mississippi West, 1550-1900,* no. 1871.

Evans, Elwood. 1878b. "The Fraser River Excitement, 1858: Its Philosophy and Claims to Historical Notice." 26 leaves, handwritten at H.H. Bancroft's request in Olympia, Washington. Original at Bancroft Library, University of California, Berkeley; typed transcript at BCA I/GA/Ev4.

Evans-Hatch, Gail E.H., and Michael Evans-Hatch. 2005. *Ebey's Landing National Historical Reserve: Historic Resources Study*. Seattle: National Park Service.

First Victoria Directory. 1860. Victoria: E. Mallandaine. Other editions followed in 1863, 1868, 1869, 1871, 1874. See also *British Columbian . . . Directory* (1863) above. "British Columbia City Directories" online at Vancouver Public Library, https://www.vpl.ca/digital-library/british-columbia-city-directories

Fisher, Robin. 1981. "Joseph Trutch and Indian Land Policy." In *British Columbia: Historical Readings*, edited by Peter W. Ward. Vancouver: Douglas & McIntyre.

Fisher, Robin. 1992. *Contact and Conflict: Indian-European Relations in British Columbia, 1774-1890*. 2nd ed. Vancouver: UBC Press. 1st ed., 1977.

Fisher, Robin. 1994. "Trutch, Sir Joseph William," *Dictionary of Canadian Biography* Online

Forsythe, Mark, and Greg Dickson. 2007. *The Trail of 1858: British Columbia's Gold Rush Past*. Madeira Park, B.C.: Harbour Publishing.

Fracchia, Charles A. 1969. "The Founding of the San Francisco Mining Exchange." *California Historical Society Quarterly* 48.1:3-18.

Fraser, Donald. 1858-62. Articles on B.C. in the London *Times*, August 1858-August 1862. Typescript at BCA E/B/F86.

Fraser River and Burrard Inlet (chart). 1860. *Fraser River and Burrard Inlet, Surveyed by Captⁿ G.H. Richards, R.N., 1859-60*. London: Admiralty Chart 1922. BCA CM_B186; LAC online image MIKAN 3673912 (torn); UBCR; UKHO.

Fraser River and Burrard Inlet (chart). 1890. LAC digital e010675443.

Fraser River from a Drawing (chart). 1849. *Fraser River from a Drawing by Mr. Emelius Simpson in H.B.C. Schooner Cadbore [i.e. Cadboro], 1827*. London: Admiralty Chart *1922*. LAC online image MIKAN 3673909; UKHO chart 1922, series A, sequence no. 1.

Fraser River from a Drawing (chart). 1858. Reissue of the 1849 map with two vertical rectangles showing the *Continuation of River on a Diminished Scale. That portion of the River . . . above Fort Hope is taken from a sketch by an Indian communicated by Capt. G.H. Richards, R.N. 1858*. These additions resemble the map, *Reconnaissance of Fraser's River*. UKHO chart 1922, series A, sequence nos. 2 and 3.

Fraser River Gold Mines (map). 2012. *Fraser River Gold Mines and Their Place Names: A Map from Hope to Quesnel Forks. Data Compiled by Andrew Nelson and Michael Kennedy. Cartography by Eric Leinberger*. Folded in Nelson and Kennedy 2011-12.

The Frazer River Thermometer. 1858. San Francisco: Sterett & Butler. First sheet, "Great gold discoveries of 1858: the Frazer River gold mines and their history." Second sheet, "The Bubble Bursted!!" Copies: LAC digital e010800080 (sheet 2 only); UBCR (both sheets).

French, Margo. 2008. "New Approaches to Abandoned Mines in Takla's Territory." Takla Lake, B.C.: Takla Lake First Nation.

Fur Brigade Trails 1826 to 1860 (map). In Hou 2010: 2.

Further Papers Relative to the Affairs of BC—see abbreviations *FPBC* 3, *FPBC* 4.

Galbraith, John S. 1957. *The Hudson's Bay Company as an Imperial Factor, 1821-1869*. Toronto: Univ. of Toronto Press.

Gardiner, Charles Coulson. 1858/1937. "To the Fraser Mines in 1858: A Letter from C.C. Gardiner," edited by Robie L. Reid, *British Columbia Historical Quarterly* 1:243-54.

Gibbs, George. 1863. *Dictionary of the Chinook Jargon*. New York: Cramoisy Press.

Gibbs, Mifflin Wistar. 1902. *Shadow and Light: An Autobiography with Reminiscences of the Last and Present Century*. Washington, DC, 1902. Reprint, New York: Arno Press, 1968.

Globe, Alexander. 2019. "The Only Known Myers Express Cover," *Collectors Club Philatelist*, 98 (2019): 202-12.

Gold Fields Act of BC. 1859—*reprinted in* Martin 1903: 538-50.

Gold Mining Licences. 1858-72. Manuscript gold mining and ditch licences, Fort Yale area. BCA GR 252, vol. 1. Photocopy at UBC Rare Books, Frederick Howay collection, box 24, file 1.

Gold Mining Licences. 1858-64. Manuscript gold mining licences for the Fraser and Thompson Rivers. BCA GR-0224, box 21; GR-0252, vols. 12, 12a, 12b, 12c, 12d, 31, 31a, 31b, and 31c; GR-0833.

Goldwater, Leonard J. 1972. *Mercury: A History of Quicksilver*. Baltimore: York Press.

Goodman, David. 1994. *Gold Seeking: Victoria and California in the 1850s*.

Stanford: Stanford Univ. Press. Victoria in this book is the Australian state.

Grass, Jude, and Glennis Taylor. 1993. *The Inland Sentinel: Emory Creek Provincial Park.* [Victoria, B.C.]: B.C. Parks, 1993.

Gudde, Erwin G. 1975. *California Gold Camps: A Geographical and Historical Dictionary.* Berkeley: Univ. of California Press.

Guide Book to the Gold Regions of Frazer River—see Smith, Elias. 1858.

Hacking, Norman R. 1944. "Steamboat 'Round the Bend. American Steamers on the Fraser River in 1858." *British Columbia Historical Quarterly* 8:254-80.

Hacking, Norman R. 1946. "Steamboating on the Fraser in the 'Sixties." *British Columbia Historical Quarterly* 10:1-41.

Hacking, Norman R. 1947. "British Columbia Steamboat Days, 1870-1888." *British Columbia Historical Quarterly* 11:69-112.

Hales, Wendy J. 2000. "The Impact of Human Activity on Deltaic Sedimentation, Marshes of the Fraser River Delta, British Columbia." Ph.D. diss., University of British Columbia.

Hanna, Darwin, and Mamie Henry, eds. 1995. *Our Tellings: Interior Salish Stories of the Nlha7kápmx People.* Vancouver: UBC Press.

Haro and Rosario Straits (chart). 1859. *Haro and Rosario Straits, Surveyed by Captn. G.H. Richards & the Officers of H.M.S. Plumper, 1858-9.* London: Admiralty Chart 2689. LAC online MIKAN 3674012 (1866 issue); NA FO 925/1384; NA FO 925/1650, item 38 in San Juan Boundary Arbitration Atlas, sent to Berlin on June 12, 1872 (coloured 1868 issue).

Harris, Cole. 1997. *The Resettlement of British Columbia: Essays on Colonialism and Geographical Change.* Vancouver: UBC Press.

Harris, Cole. 2002. *Making Native Space: Colonialism, Resistance, and Reserves in British Columbia.* Vancouver: UBC Press.

Harris, R.C. 1979. "Old Trails and Routes in British Columbia: The Boston Bar Trail 1859-1860, Fort Hope to Boston Bar." *BC Historical News*, 12.3:13-15.

Harris, R.C. 1980. "Sapper Duffy's Exploration, Cayoosh Creek to Lillooet Lake, 1860." *BC Historical News.* 14.2:14-19.

Hauka, Donald J. 2003. *McGowan's War.* Vancouver: New Star Books.

Hauka, Donald J. 2009—see *Canyon War.*

Hayes, Derek. 1999. *Historical Atlas of British Columbia and the Pacific Northwest.* Vancouver: Cavendish Books.

Hayes, Derek. 2012. *British Columbia: A New Historical Atlas*. Vancouver: Douglas & McIntyre.

Hazlitt, William Carew. 1858. *British Columbia and Vancouver Island . . . with a Map*. London and New York: G. Routledge. Lithograph of miners on cover. UBC.

Helmcken, John Sebastian. 1975. *The Reminiscences*. Edited by D.B. Smith. Vancouver: UBC Press.

Heyl, Eric. 1953-69. *Early American Steamers*. 6 vols. Buffalo: Heyl.

Hibben, Thomas Napier. 1871. *Dictionary of the Chinook Jargon*. Victoria: Hibben. CIHM 14264.

Hicks, Urban E. 1892. "An Overview of the 1855-56 conflicts between the Indians and the Recent Arrivals Who Had Settled around Puget Sound." Reprint, Bennett 1985: 149-59.

Hicks, Urban E. 1893. "Mining in the Fifties: The Fraser River Boom Graphically Described by One Who Was There." Reprint, Bennett 1985: 288-96.

Higuchi, Jiro. 2002. *The Biography of Major-General Henry Spencer Palmer, R.E., F.R.A.S. (1838-1893)*. Tokyo: Mori Printing Office.

Hill, Beth. 1987. *Sappers: The Royal Engineers in British Columbia*. Ganges, B.C.: Horsdal & Schubart.

Hittell, John S. 1861. *Mining in the Pacific States of North America*. San Francisco: H.H. Bancroft. CIHM 16737.

Holliday, J.S. 1999. *Rush for Riches: Gold Fever and the Making of California*. Oakland, CA: Oakland Museum of California; Berkeley: Univ. of California Press.

Hou, Charles. 2009. *The HBC Fur Brigade-First Nations Trail of 1848-49*. Rev. ed. Vancouver: Moody's Lookout Press.

Hou, Charles, M. Morgan, and S. Bailey. 1978. *The Harrison-Lillooet Gold Rush Trail, 1858-1978*. No location [B.C.]: no publisher.

Howay, Frederic William. 1910. *The Work of the Royal Engineers in British Columbia, 1858 to 1863*. Victoria: Richard Wolfenden, King's Printer.

Howay, Frederic William. 1914. *British Columbia from the Earliest Times to the Present, Illustrated*. Vol. 2. Vancouver: S.J. Clarke Publishing Co.

Howay, Frederic William. 1926. *The Early History of the Fraser River Mines*. Archives of British Columbia, Memoir 6. Victoria, B.C.: Charles F. Banfield, King's Printer. Reprints letters.

Howe, Octavius T., and Frederick C. Matthews. 1926-7. *American Clipper Ships 1833-1858*. 2 vols. Publication 13. Salem MA: Marine Research Society. Reprinted 1986.

Hurtado, Albert L. 2002. "Clouded Legacy: California Indians and the Gold Rush." In *Riches for All: The California Gold Rush and the World*. Lincoln, Univ. of Nebraska Press.

Jackson, John C. 1995. *Children of the Fur Trade: Forgotten Métis of the Pacific Northwest*. Missoula, Montana: Mountain Press Publishing Company.

Jameson, Elizabeth. 2002. "Where Have All the Young Men Gone? The Social Legacy of the California Gold Rush." In *Riches for All: The California Gold Rush and the World*. Lincoln, Univ. of Nebraska Press.

Kennedy, Michael. 2008-9. "Fraser River Placer Mining Landscapes," *BC Studies* 160 (winter): 35-66.

Kennedy, Michael—see also Nelson, Andrew D., and Michael Kennedy, 2011-12.

Kilian, Crawford. 1978. *Go Do Some Great Thing: The Black Pioneers of British Columbia*. Vancouver: Douglas & McIntyre.

Laforet, Andrea, and Annie York. 1998. *Spuzzum: Fraser Canyon Histories, 1808-1939*. Vancouver: UBC Press.

L[amb], W.K. 1940. "The Census of Vancouver Island, 1855." *British Columbia Historical Quarterly* 4:51-58.

Lapp, Rudolph M. 2008. *Archy Lee*. Berkeley, CA: Heyday Books, Baytree Books.

Lemprière, Arthur Reid—see "Sketch of Trail from Hope to Boston Bar."

Lewis and Dryden's Marine History of the Pacific Northwest—see Wright, E.W.

Lighter, J.E. 1994, 1997. *Random House Historical Dictionary of American Slang*. Vols. 1, *A-G* and 2, *H-O*. New York: Random House.

Limbaugh, Ronald H. 1998-9. "Making Old Tools Work Better: Pragmatic Adaptation and Innovation in Gold-Rush Technology." *California History*. 77.4 (Winter 1998-9): 24-51.

Line of Route from Chapman's to Boston Bar (manuscript map). 1860. "Line of Route from Chapman's to Boston Bar by Sapper Turnbull, R.E. 1860 . . . Sapper Turnbull's sketches are handed to Serg^t McColl herewith." LTSBC 14 FT 1 Roads & Trails.

Liscombe, R. Windsor. 2003. "Tiedemann, Hermann Otto." *Dictionary of Canadian Biography Online*.

London *Times* articles—see Fraser, Donald.

Lotchin, Roger W. 1974. *San Francisco, 1846-1856: From Hamlet to City.* New York: Oxford Univ. Press.

Lovell's Canadian Directory. 1871. *Lovell's Canadian Dominion Directory for 1871.* Montreal: John Lovell.

Lowther, Barbara J. 1968. *A Bibliography of British Columbia: Laying the Foundations 1849-1899.* Victoria, B.C.: Social Sciences Research Centre, University of Victoria.

MacDonell, Allan. 1858. *The North-West Transportation, Navigation, and Railway Company: Its Objects.* Toronto: Lovell and Gibson.

Macfie, Matthew. 1865. *Vancouver Island and British Columbia.* London: Longman, Green.

MacGregor, David R. 1984. *Merchant Sailing Ships, 1850-1875: Heyday of Sail.* London: Conway Maritime Press.

MacKay, Douglas. 1937. *The Honourable Company: A History of The Hudson's Bay Company.* London: Cassell.

Mackie, Richard Somerset. 1992-3. "The Colonization of Vancouver Island, 1849-1858." *BC Studies* 96: 3-40.

Mackie, Richard Somerset. 1997. *Trading Beyond the Mountains: The British Fur Trade on the Pacific, 1793-1843.* Vancouver: UBC Press.

Map of a Portion of BC. 1860. *Map of a Portion of British Columbia, Compiled from the Surveys & Explorations of the Royal Navy & Royal Engineers, at the Camp New Westminster, Nov.ʳ 24th 1859.* London: John Arrowsmith. In *FPBC* 3: 78. Simplified in *FPBC* 4: 8.

Map of The Atlantic & Pacific Junction Railway. 1858. In Richard Broun, *European and Asiatic Intercourse via British Columbia.* TRL.

Map of the City of Victoria. 1858. *Map of the City of Victoria, V.I. Published by Alfred Waddington. Lith. By Drouaillet, San Francisco, Cal.* A BCA copy has a note by Waddington to Joseph Pemberton on the back: "The Original of this Map was copied by permission from the Official Map, in the Land Office, by Mr. Lamotte . . . on December 23rd 1858, and sent to San Francisco to be lithographed . . . December 24th." BCA CM_A497.

Map of the Districts of Victoria and Esquimalt. 1854. *Map of the Districts of Victoria and Esquimalt in Vancouver Island.* London: John Arrowsmith. Survey by Joseph Pemberton. NA CO 700/British Columbia 2.

Map of the Gold Regions in British Columbia. 1862. *Map of the Gold Regions in British Columbia, Compiled by Gust. Epner*. San Francisco: Britton & Co., lithographers. UBCR.

Map of the Harrison. 1858. *Map of the Harrison and Lillooet Route to the Upper Fraser*. In San Francisco *Daily Evening Bulletin*, August 2, 1858: 3.

Map Showing the Different Routes. 1858. *Map Showing the Different Routes of Communication with the Gold Region on Frasers River, Compiled from Original Notes by Alexander C. Anderson*. San Francisco: J.J. Lecount. In Anderson 1858. LAC digital e011157737.

Marshall, Daniel Patrick. 2000. "Claiming the Land: Indians, Goldseekers, and the Rush to British Columbia." Ph.D. diss., University of British Columbia.

Marshall, Daniel Patrick. 2002. "No Parallel: American Miner-Soldiers at War with the Nlaka'pamux of the Canadian West." In *Parallel Destinies: Canadian-American Relations West of the Rockies*. Edited by John Findlay. Seattle: Univ. of Washington Press.

Marshall, Daniel Patrick. 2009—see *Canyon War*.

Marshall, Daniel Patrick. 2015b. "The British Columbia Commonwealth: Gold Seekers and the Rush for Freedom." In *New Perspectives on the Gold Rush*. Victoria: Royal BC Museum.

Marshall, Daniel Patrick. 2015c. "Conflict in the New El Dorado." In *New Perspectives on the Gold Rush*. Victoria: Royal BC Museum.

Marshall, Daniel Patrick. 2018. *Claiming the Land: British Columbia and the Making of a New El Dorado*. Vancouver: Ronsdale Press.

Martin, Archer. 1903. *Reports of Mining Cases Decided by the Courts of British Columbia . . . ; with an Appendix of Mining Statues from 1853 to 1902*. Toronto: Carswell.

Mayne, Richard Charles. 1859. "Report on a Journey in British Columbia in the Districts Bordering on the Thompson, Fraser, and Harrison Rivers." *Journal of the Royal Geographical Society* 31 (April 23 to May 30, 1859): 213-23. Text also printed in *FPBC* 3.32-9.

Mayne, Richard Charles. 1862. *Four Years in British Columbia and Vancouver Island . . . with Map and Illustrations*. London: John Murray. Illustrated. CIHM 36542.

Mayne, Richard Charles—see also *Sketch of Part of British Columbia* (chart).

McGowan, D. 1859. *Map Exhibiting the Routes to Pike's Peak*. St. Louis, MO: Leopold Gast. Digital image: www.loc.gov/resource/g4050.rr001760/.

Illustration: Andrew M. Modelski, *Railroad Maps of North America* (Washington DC: Library of Congress, 1984), p. 62.

McGowan, Edward. 1857. *Narrative of Edward McGowan, Including a Full Account of the Author's Adventures and Perils While Persecuted by the San Francisco Vigilance Committee of 1856*. San Francisco: T.C. Russell.

McGowan, Edward. 1878. "Reminiscences: Unpublished Incidents in the Life of the 'Ubiquitous'" *The Argonaut*, 2.17 (May 4): 7; 2.18 (May 11): 4; 2.19 (May 18): 10; 2.20 (May 25): 3; 2.21 (June 1): 10; 2.22 (June 8): 10.

McKay, Joseph William. 1858. "Report of Journey through Part of the Fraser's River and Adjoining Districts." On the Harrison Lillooet trail. In *PRBC* 2.30-3.

McNeil, Samuel. 1850. *McNeil's Travels in 1849, to, through, and from the Gold Regions in California*. Columbus: Scott and Bascom.

McQuillan, Kevin. 1985. "Ontario Mortality Patterns, 1861-1921." *Canadian Studies in Population*. 12.1: 31-48.

Meeker, Ezra. 1905. *Pioneer Reminiscences of Puget Sound*. Seattle: Lowman & Hanford.

Megquier, Mary Jane. 1994. *Apron Full of Gold: The Letters of Mary Jane Megquier from San Francisco, 1849-1856*. Edited by Polly Welts Kaufman. Albuquerque: Univ. of New Mexico Press.

Meldahl, Keith Heyer. 2011. *Rough-Hewn Land: A Geologic Journey from California to the Rocky Mountains*. Berkeley: Univ. of California Press.

Mikron, Beta—see Albemarle, William Coutts Keppell, Earl of.

Milliken, Augustus St. Clair. 1963/2010. "I'll Sell It to You Cheap: Gus Milliken and the Hills Bar Claim (Recorded March 13, 1963)." In *Voices of British Columbia: Stories from Our Frontier*. Vancouver: Douglas and McIntyre.

Miners' Own Book. 1858. *The Miners' Own Book, Containing Correct Illustrations and Descriptions of the Various Modes of California Mining*. San Francisco: Hutchings & Rosenfield. Illustrations, by Charles Nahl, from *Hutchings' Illustrated California Magazine*, 1856-8.

Moody, Richard Clement. 1859. Letter about the road from Yale to Little Canyon. BCA GR 1180, file 17.

Moody, Richard Clement. 1859/1951. "First Impressions: Letter of Colonel Richard Clement Moody, R.E., to Arthur Blackwood, February 1, 1859." Edited by Willard E. Ireland. *British Columbia Historical Quarterly* 15: 85-107. The original is at BCA E/B/M77.

Moore, James. 1914/1939. "The Discovery of Hill's Bar in 1858," edited by W. Kaye Lamb, *British Columbia Historical Quarterly* 3:215-20.

Morison, John H. 1864. *Dying for Our Country: A Sermon on the Death of Capt. J. Sewall Reed.* Boston: John Wilson. CIHM 17162.

Morris, T. 1857/1928. "Army Officer's Report on Indian Wars and Treaties." *Washington Historical Quarterly* 19 (1928): 134-41.

Mouat, Jeremy. 2002. "After California: Later Gold Rushes of the Pacific Basin." In Owens 2002: 264-95.

Mussio, Russell. 2013. *Backroad Mapbook: Vancouver, Coast BC, & Mountains.* Coquitlam, B.C.: Mussio Ventures.

Nelson, Andrew D., and Michael Church. 2012. "Placer Mining Along the Fraser River, British Columbia: The Geomorphic Impact." *Geological Society of America Bulletin.* 124, nos. 7-8: 1212-28.

Nelson, Andrew D., and Michael Kennedy. 2011-12. "Fraser River Gold Mines and Their Place Names," *BC Studies* 172 (Winter 2011/12): 105-35. With large map of *Fraser River Gold Mines and Their Place Names.*

New El Dorado (map). 1858. *The New El Dorado. A Complete View of the Newly Discovered Gold Fields in British North America.* London: Read & Co. LAC digital e002140138.

"New Gold-Diggings." 1858. "The New Gold-Diggings, First Article" and "The New Gold-Diggings, Second Article." *Chambers's Journal*, Sept. 18: 182-5, 197-8.

"New Gold Fields." 1858. Letter from Pavilion, Upper Fraser River, November 28, 1858. *Journal of the Statistical Society of London*, 22 (1859): 176-7.

Newell, Gordon R. 1951. *Ships of the Inland Sea: The Story of the Puget Sound Steamboats.* Portland Ore.: Binfords and Mort.

North America: Map. [1858]. *North America: Map of Part of the British Possessions to the West of the Rocky Mountains ... under the Direction of Captⁿ Elphinstone.* London: Topographical Depot, War Department. Captain Howard C. Elphinstone left the War Department to become governor of Queen Victoria's third son, Prince Arthur, on January 15, 1859. NA CO 700 British Columbia 5; UBCR ARC 1677 1858.

Nugent, John. 1859. *Vancouver's Island and British Columbia. Message from the President of the United States, Communicating the Report of the Special Agent of the United States Recently Sent to Vancouver's Island and British Columbia.* United States House of Representatives. 35th Congress, 2nd Session. Executive Document No. 111. Washington, DC.

"Odd Fellows' Cemetery Records." 1890. Manuscript records of the San Francisco I.O.O.F. Cemetery, book 3, p. 287 for the record of George L. Slocumb's burial.

Official Map of the Town of Victoria. 1858. "Official Map of the Town of Victoria, 1858." Manuscript survey by Joseph Pemberton and Hermann Tiedemann. LTSBC 1 T 1 large tray, East Coast Vancouver Island.

Otter, Hudson's Bay Company steamship. Log book. Referred to as OtterL. Hudson's Bay Company Archives, Winnipeg. C. 1/625.

Owens, Kenneth N., ed. 2002. *Riches for All: The California Gold Rush and the World*. Lincoln: Univ. of Nebraska Press.

Pain, Stephanie. 1987. "After the Goldrush." *New Scientist*. 115 (Aug. 20, 1987): 36-40.

Palmer, Lieut. H. Spencer, R.E. 1859/1861. "Report on the Harrison and Lilloet Route, from the Junction of the Fraser and Harrison Rivers to the Junction of the Fraser and Kayosch Rivers, with Notes on the Country Beyond, As Far As Fountain." [May and June 1859], *Journal of the Royal Geographical Society* 31 (1861): 224-36. Also printed in *FPBC* 3.40-9.

Palmer, Lieut. H. Spencer, R.E.—see also *Plan of Route from New Westminster* (map). *Papers Relative to the Affairs of BC*—see abbreviations *PRBC* 1, *PRBC* 2, *FPBC* 3, and *FPBC* 4.

Papers Relative to the Affairs of BC—see abbreviations *PRBC* 1, *PRBC* 2, *FPBC* 3, and *FPBC* 4.

Parsons, Otis. 1858. Diary from January 1, 1856, in California, to early 1859 on the Fraser River. 50 pages. Microfilm at BCA, 24A (4).

Part of British Columbia (map). 1861. *Part of British Columbia to Illustrate the Papers of Mr. Justice Begbie, Com^r Mayne, R.N., Lt Palmer, R.E., & Mr. Downie*. London: J. Murray. Folded in Begbie 1859/1861, Mayne 1859/1861, and Palmer 1859/1861. LAC digital e010859305.

Partridge, Eric, and Paul Beale. 1984. *A Dictionary of Slang and Unconventional English*. 8th ed. London: Routledge and Kegan Paul.

Paterson, T.W. 1985. *Fraser Canyon*. Langley, B.C.: Sunfire Publications.

Paul, Rodman W. 1954. "'Old Californians' in British Gold Fields." *Huntington Library Quarterly*. 17: 161-72.

Pemberton, Joseph Despard. 1860. *Facts and Figures Relating to Vancouver Island and British Columbia*. London: Longman, Green. With map of *Vancouver Island and Gulf of Georgia*

Pemberton, Joseph Despard—see also "Esquimalt District," *Esquimalt Harbour*, *Map of the City of Victoria*, *Map of the Districts of Victoria and Esquimalt*, "Official Map of the Town of Victoria," "Plan of the Town of Victoria," and *Town of Victoria, Vancouver Island and Gulf of Georgia*, and "Victoria District."

Perry, Kenneth E. 2006. *Frontier Forts & Posts of the Hudson's Bay Company*. Surrey, B.C.: Hancock House.

Pethick, Derek. 1969. *James Douglas: Servant of Two Empires*. Vancouver: Mitchell Press.

Petition. 1858. "Petition of the Undersigned Robert Dexter and Jefferson Siggins, Miners," August 21, 1858. BCA GR 1372, file 1342, microfilm B1354.

Petition 95. 1858. "Petition: Mules Required to Assist in Making Harrison River Trail, 8 September 1858." BCA GR 1372, file 1342, microfilm B1354.

Petition 116. 1858. "Petition: for Gold Escort in Fraser River, 22 November 1858." BCA GR 1372, file 1342, microfilm B1354.

Petition 119. 1858. "Petition: Right of Ferry on Lake Seaton, 4th December 1858." BCA GR 1372, file 1342, microfilm B1354.

Petition 120. 1858. "Petition Requesting Protection against the Indians. Douglas, November 1858." BCA GR 1372, file 1342, microfilm B1354.

Petition 121. 1858. "Petition: Harrison River Trail Grievances, 18th October 1858." BCA GR 1372, file 1342, microfilm B1354.

Petition 122. 1858. "Ft. Yale Petition, 22nd October 1858. To Assist Mr. George." BCA GR 1372, file 1342, microfilm B1354.

Petition 134. 1858. "Petition from the Miners of Fort Yale to Mr. Hincks to Be Presented to Govr. Douglas—dated Fort Yale December 8, 1858." BCA GR 1372, file 1342, microfilm B1354.

Phair, Arthur William A. 1964/2010. "Gold Was Lying on Top of the Ground: Artie Phair and the Lillooet Gold Rush." In *Voices of British Columbia: Stories from Our Frontier*. Vancouver: Douglas and McIntyre.

Phillips, Cyrus Olin. 1858/1932. "To the Fraser River! The Diary and Letters," edited by F.W. Howay. *California Historical Society Quarterly*, 11.2: 150-6. With Phillips' manuscript map.

Pilton, James W. 1951. "Negro Settlement in British Columbia, 1858-1871." Master's thesis, University of British Columbia.

Plan of Part of Fraser's River (chart). 1859. *Plan of Part of Frasers River*

Shewing the Character of the Ground from the Entrance to the Site of Old Fort Langley. London: John Arrowsmith. At end of *PRBC* 2.

Plan of Route (map). 1859. *Plan of Route from New Westminster to Fountain in British Columbia by Lieut^t. H.S. Palmer R.E.* London: Topographical Depot, War Office. BCA (photostat); NA, CO 700/ BRITISH COLUMBIA 8/1 (original); LAC digital e010859300 (lithographed copy, 1934).

Plan of the Town of Victoria (manuscript map). 1852. "A Plan of the Town of Victoria Shewing Proposed Improvements." By Joseph Despard Pemberton. LTSBC 7 locker 9.

Pocket Diary for 1858, for Registering Events of Past or Present Occurrence. New York: Philip J. Cozans. The anonymous Canadian miner wrote his Fraser River account in a copy.

Poisson, Jayme, and David Bruser. 2016. "Grassy Narrows' Babies at Risk for Years." *Toronto Star*, July 18, 2016, pp. A1 and A8.

Pojar, Jim, and Andy MacKinnon. 2004. *Plants of the Pacific Northwest Coast*. Vancouver: Lone Pine Publishing.

Proclamations on gold mining by Governor Douglas, 1853, 1857, and 1859—*printed in* Martin 1903: 536-40.

Project for the Construction of a Railroad to the Pacific. 1852. *Project for the Construction of a Railroad to the Pacific, through British Territories; with Report of the Committee of the Legislative Assembly of Canada.* Toronto: Lovell and Gibson.

Prosch, Charles. 1892. "He was the first to receive and publish news of the Fraser River gold boom." In Bennett 1985: 265-75.

Provinces of British Columbia (map). 1859. *The Provinces of British Columbia and Vancouver Island.* London: John Arrowsmith. At end of *PRBC* 2 and sold separately.

Race Islands (chart). 1859. *Race Islands, Showing Proposed Site for a Light House.* London: John Arrowsmith. After p. 14 of *PRBC* 2.

Random House Historical Dictionary of American Slang—see Lighter, J.E.

Reconnaissance of Fraser's River (map). 1858. *Reconnaissance of Fraser's River from Fort Hope to the Forks.* Based on Alexander Anderson's survey and "a sketch by an Indian communicated by Capt. G.H. Richards," according to the 1858 ed. of the chart *Fraser River from a Drawing.* In *CEG* 1858: 10.

Record of American Shipping. 1871. *Record of American and Foreign Shipping from Surveys Made and Compiled under the Direction of the American Ship-*

masters' Association, with the Sanction of the New York Board of Underwriters. New York.

Reid, J.H. Stewart. 1942. "The Road to Cariboo." Master's thesis, University of British Columbia.

Reid, Robbie L. 1927. "The Whatcom Trails to the Fraser River Mines in 1858," *Washington Historical Quarterly* 18:199-206, 271-6.

Reid, Robbie L. 1944. "John Nugent: The Impertinent Envoy," *British Columbia Historical Quarterly* 8:53-76.

Reinhart, Herman Francis. 1962. *The Golden Frontier: The Recollections of Herman Francis Reinhart, 1851-1869.* Edited by Doyce B. Nunis, Jr. Austin: Univ. of Texas Press. Written from memory in 1887.

Report Hudson's Bay. 1857. *Report from the Select Committee on the Hudson's Bay Company.* London: Ordered by The House of Commons to be Printed. 3 maps. CIHM 48795.

Report of the Royal Commission. 1889. *Report of the Royal Commission on the Relations of Labor and Capital in Canada.* Ottawa: A. Senecal. CIHM 9_08109 online.

Richards, George Henry. 1864. *The Vancouver Island Pilot.* London: Hydrographic Office, Admiralty. No maps.

Richards, George Henry. 2011. *The Private Journal of Captain G.H. Richards: The Vancouver Island Survey (1860-1862).* Ed. Linda Dorricott and Deidre Cullon. Vancouver: Ronsdale Press.

Richards, George Henry—see also *Fraser River and Burrard Inlet* (chart); *Haro and Rosario Straits* (chart); *Reconnaissance of Fraser's River* (chart); and *Sketch of the Upper Part of the Fraser River* (chart).

Richards, Kent D. 1979. *Isaac I. Stevens: Young Man in a Hurry.* Provo, UT: Brigham Young Univ. Press.

Richardson, David. 1967. "The Port Gamble Incident," *Seattle Times,* 2 April.

Rohrbough, Malcolm J. 1997. *Days of Gold: The California Gold Rush and the American Nation.* Berkeley: Univ. of California Press.

Rough Diagram (manuscript map). 1864. "A Rough Diagram Shewing the Position of the reserves Laid Off for Government Purposes &c on the Fraser, Chillukweyak, Sumas & Masquee Rivers." Survey of fourteen Indigenous reserves by Royal Engineers Sergeant William McColl, May 16, 1864. LTSBC 31 T 1 Land Reserves.

Rough Sketch Showing Line (manuscript map). 1860. "Rough Sketch

Showing Line of Waggon Road from Lytton in Direction of Boston Bar. Surveyed & Drawn by James Turnbull, Sap^r R.E." Five manuscript sheets. LTSBC 14 T 1 Roads & Trails.

Senkewicz, Robert M. 1985. *Vigilantes in Gold Rush San Francisco.* Stanford: Stanford Univ. Press.

Sketch Map of Part of BC (manuscript map). 1860. "Sketch Map of Part of British Columbia Shewing Trails and Routes of Communication." Sent by Royal Engineers Col. R.C. Moody to Governor Douglas. LTSBC 17 T 1 Roads & Trails.

Sketch of Fraser River (map). 1858. *Sketch of Fraser River and the New Gold Fields.* In San Francisco *Daily Evening Bulletin,* June 7, 1858, p. 3.

Sketch of Line of Waggon Road from Boston Bar to Yale (manuscript map). 1862. "Sketch of Line of Waggon Road from Boston Bar to Yale. W. McColl, Srg. Royal Engineers." Six sheets of surveys for the Cariboo wagon road. LTSBC 16 T 1 Roads & Trails.

Sketch of Part of British Columbia (map). 1859. *Sketch of Part of British Columbia by Lieut^{nt} R.C. Mayne, R.N. of H.M.S. Plumper.* London: Topographical Depot, War Office. BCA CM_C187 (photostat); NA, CO 700 / BRITISH COLUMBIA 8/2 (original); LAC digital e006609994 (lithographed copy, 1935).

Sketch of the Upper Part of the Fraser River (chart). 1859. *Sketch of the Upper Part of the Fraser River from Langley to Yale by Lieut. Mayne R.N. of H.M.S. Plumper—Capt. Richards and the Honble. M.B. Begbie Judge in British Columbia.* London: Admiralty Chart 2666. BCA CM_B184; UKHO OCB 2666 A1.

Sketch of Trail from Hope (manuscript map). 1859. "Sketch of Trail from Hope to Boston Bar by Lt. Lempriere, R.E." LTSBC 15 T 1 Roads & Trails.

Sketch to Accompany Dr. Forbes (map). 1861. *Sketch to Accompany Dr. Forbes' Geological Sections on Harrison Lake & Lillooet River.* Folded in *FPBC* 4.32.

Slocum, Charles Elihu. 1882. *A Short History of the Slocums, Slocumbs and Slocombs of America . . . from 1637 to 1881.* Syracuse: the author.

Slocumb, George Leach. 1858. Diary, 1858-63. Bancroft Library, University of California, Berkeley BANC MSS 2006/111 v. 1.

Smith, Elias. 1858. *Guide Book to the Gold Regions of Fraser River, with a Map.* New York: Wynkoop. With map (only copy at Yale).

Smyth, William Henry. 1867. *The Sailor's Word-Book: An Alphabetical Digest of Nautical Terms.* London: Blackie.

Snyder, H.M. 1858/1996. Letter of August 28, 1858, to Governor James Douglas, on the Fraser River War, edited by Daniel P. Marshall. *Native Studies Review*, 11.1: 139-45. Original at BCA GR 1372: 1617.

South East Part of Vancouver Island. 1859. *South East Part of Vancouver Island Showing the Proposed Sites for Light Houses on the Great Race Rock and Fisgard Island*. London: John Arrowsmith. Folded after p. 14 of *PRBC* 2.

Stenzel, Franz. 1975. *James Madison Alden: Yankee Artist of the Pacific Coast, 1854-1860*. Fort Worth, TX: Amon Carter Museum.

Stevens, Isaac Ingalls. 1856. "Fellow Citizens of the Legislative Assembly," Jan. 21, 1856. In *Journal of the House of Representatives of the Territory of Washington, Being the Third Session of the Legislative Assembly, Begun and Held at Olympia, December 3d, 1855*. Olympia: Geo. B. Goudy.

Stopford, Woodhall. 1979. "Industrial Exposure to Mercury." In *The Biogeochemistry of Mercury in the Environment*, edited by J.O. Nriagu. Amsterdam: Elsevier/North-Holland Biomedical Press.

Stout, Edward. 1910. "Edward Stout, Pioneer prospector and Miner Tells a Great Story, Was a Survivor of the Indian Massacre along the Banks of the Fraser River in 1858—Crossed Plains in '49." *Nicola Valley News, 22* April: 4-5, 17. Online.

Supreme Court Tsilhqot'in. 2014. Supreme Court of Canada. *Tsilhqot'in Nation v. British Columbia, 2014 SCC 44*. Docket 34986. Ottawa: Supreme Court of Canada, June 26.

Swindle, Lewis J. 2001. *A Gold Rush Adventure. The Fraser River Gold rush of 1858 As Reported by the California Newspapers of 1858*. Victoria: Trafford.

Syrette, Sharon E. 2010. *Traveller's Guide: Cultural and Historic Landscapes of the Harrison to Lillooet Lake Gold Rush Trail*. [Mission, B.C.]: Ama Liisaos Heritage Trust Society.

Teit, James. 1900. *The Thompson Indians of British Columbia*. Memoirs of the American Museum of Natural History, vol. 2. [New York: American Museum of Natural History].

Teit, James. 1912. *Mythology of the Thompson Indians*. Memoir of the American Museum of Natural History, New York, vol. 8, no. 2. New York: G.E. Stechert; Leiden: E.J. Brill.

Thiusoloc, Chief. 1859. Map of the Skagit and Chilliwack Rivers for the US Boundary Commission. National Archives of the United States, RG 76, series 69, map 26.

Thoreau, Henry David. 1995. *Walden: An Annotated Edition*. Edited by

Walter Harding. Boston: Houghton Mifflin. First edition at Boston: Ticknor and Fields, 1854.

Town of Victoria (map). 1861. *Town of Victoria, Vancouver Island, from the Official Map, J. Despard Pemberton, Surveyor General.* London: John Arrowsmith.

Trutch, Joseph William. 1875. "Lower Fraser River Indian Reserves." In *British Columbia. Papers Connected with the Indian Land Question, 1850-1875.* Victoria: Richard Wolfenden.

Turnbull, James—see "Rough Sketch Showing Line."

Utley, Robert M. 1967. *Frontiersmen in Blue: The United States Army and the Indian, 1848-1865.* New York: Macmillan.

Vancouver Island and Gulf of Georgia (map). 1860. *Vancouver Island and Gulf of Georgia*, facing title of Joseph D. Pemberton, *Facts and Figures.* LAC digital e010800083.

Veiga, Marcello, and Randy Baker. 2004. *Protocols for Environmental and Health Assessment of Mercury Released by Artisinal and Small-Scale Gold Miners.* Vienna: Global Mercury Project, UNIDO in collaboration with University of BC, Department of Mining Engineering.

Veiga, Marcello M. and John A. Meech. 1995. "A Brief History of Amalgamation Practices in the Americas." In *Proceedings of the 16th Brazilian Symposium on Ore Processing and Hydrometallurgy, Rio de Janeiro, Sept. 3-6, 1995.* Ed. Dutra, Luz, and Torem. Vol. 1, pp. 581-94. http://www.jmeech. mining.ubc.ca/briefhi2.htm

Victoria District (manuscript map). 1858. "Victoria District—Official Map—1858." Surveyed by Joseph Pemberton and Hermann Tiedemann. LTSBC 37 T 2 large tray, East Coast Vancouver Island.

Victoria Harbour. 1861. *Victoria Harbour, Surveyed by Captain G.H. Richards & the Officers of H.M.S. Plumper, 1859.* London: Admiralty Chart 1897b. LAC online digital MIKAN 3673605; UBCR; UKHO. BCA CM_B173 has the manuscript survey.

Vouri, Mike. 2008. *The Pig War: Images of America.* San Francisco: Arcadia Publishing.

Vouri, Mike. 2013. *The Pig War: Standoff at Griffin Bay.* Seattle: Discover Your Northwest.

Waddington, Alfred Penderill. 1858. *The Fraser Mines Vindicated; or, The History of Four Months. Price, Fifty Cents.* Victoria: Printed by P. de Garro,

Wharf Street. Preface dated "Victoria, Nov. 15, 1858." No map. CIHM 42693.

Waddington, Alfred Penderill—see also *A Correct Map of the Northern Coal and Gold Regions*.

Walkem, W. Wymond. 1914. *Stories of Early British Columbia*. Vancouver: News-Advertiser.

Walske, Steven C. 2006. "Postal Rates on Mail from British Columbia and Vancouver Island via San Francisco, 1858-1870." *The Chronicle of the U.S. Classic Postal Issues*, 58 (2006): 289-97.

Washington Atlas. 1992. *Washington Atlas & Gazetteer*. 2nd ed. Freeport, Maine: DeLorme Mapping.

Watson, Bruce McIntyre. 2010. *Lives Lived West of the Divide: A Biographical Dictionary of Fur Traders Working West of the Rockies, 1793-1858*. 3 vols. Kelowna, B.C.: UBC Press.

Way, Franklin. 1860. Manuscript sketch of gold mining bars on the Fraser River from Spuzzum "Ferry House" (which Way operated) to "Boston Bar." BCA CM_B471, aaaa6064.

Weiser, Kathy. 2012. "Washington Indian Wars—Page 6. Battle of Port Gamble (November 20-21, 1856)." www.legendsofamerica.com/wa-indianconflicts6.html.

Wellburn, Gerald. 1970. "Ballou's Fraser River Express," *BNA Topics*, no. 295: 292-3.

Wellburn, Gerald. 1987. *The Postage Stamps & Postal History of Colonial Vancouver Island & British Columbia, 1849-1871: The Gerald Wellburn Collection*. Edited by Daniel L. Eaton and Jack Wallace. [Vancouver: D.L. Eaton]. For editors and date, see pp. 5, 7, and 164.

Wheatley, Brian, and Sylvain Paradis. 1995. "Exposure of Canadian Aboriginal Peoples to Methylmercury." *Water, Air, and Soil Pollution*. 80: 3-11.

White, Richard. 1980. *Land Use, Environment, and Social Change: The Shaping of Island County, Washington*. Seattle: Univ. of Washington Press.

Wilkes, Charles. 1845. *Narrative of the United States Exploring Expedition During the Years 1838, 1839, 1840, 1841, 1842*. 5 vols. Philadelphia: Lea and Blanchard.

Williams, David R. 1977. *"The Man for a New Country": Sir Matthew Baillie*. Sidney, B.C.: Gray's Publishing.

Wilson, Eugene B. 1918. *Hydraulic and Placer Mining*. 3rd, rev. ed. New York:

Wiley; London: Chapman and Hall.

Woodward, Frances M. 1974-5. "The Influence of the Royal Engineers on the Development of British Columbia." *BC Studies* 24 (Winter 1974-75): 3-51.

Woodward, Frances M. 2003. "Palmer, Henry Spencer," *Dictionary of Canadian Biography Online.*

Wright, Almira Neff. 1858. Letter of October 16, 1858, from Whidbey Island to George W. Beam on Puget Sound Bar. WSE, box 5, file 6.

Wright, E.W., ed. 1895. *Lewis and Dryden's Marine History of the Pacific Northwest.* Portland, Ore.: Lewis and Dryden Printing Co.

Wunderman, Eva. 2009—see *Canyon War.*

Yates, William. 1904. "Reminiscences of a Hudson's Bay trader before and during the 1858 Fraser gold rush." Typescript at BCA E/E/Y2.

Yenne, Bill. 2006. *Indian Wars: The Campaign for the American West.* Yardley Pa.: Westholme.

Young, William. 1859. Letter of Sept. 15, 1859, on the Harrison pack trail. BCA GR 1180, file 16.

ABOUT THE AUTHOR

Alexander Globe is a professor emeritus of English and Comparative Literature at the University of British Columbia. He enjoys the interplay of texts, illustrations, and history from antiquity to the present through studies of Sumerian poetry, seventeenth-century English engraving, Catharine Parr Trail's *Canadian Wild Flowers* (Canada's first illustrated book on botany), and the development of early Canadian air mail. He is the author of *Peter Stent, London Printseller circa 1642-1665: A Catalogue Raisonné of His Engraved Prints and Books, with an Historical and Bibliographical Introduction.*

INDEX

Citations of photographs are in bold.
Citations of tables are indicated by the letter t.

Melbourne, 2, 39-40, 244

Mercantile Gazette and Shipping Register, 234, 236-37

mercury, 51, 55, 58, 69, **70**, 71-72, 80-81, 149, 151-52, 204

Mexicans, 19, 93

Mexico, 28, 39, 228

Mickie, A., 148

mining licence, 22, 24, 72, **73**, 75t, 142, 184, 187, 192, 209, 247

mining recorder, 77t, 148, 155

mining equipment. *See* long tom; pan of prospector; rocker; sluice; water wheel

Montreal, 219, 226

Moody, Richard Clement, 185, **186**, 216, 224-25

Moore, Colonel, 96

Moore, James, 18

Mormon Bar, 77, 89, 197, 205

Mosquito Creek, 178

Mount Baker, **85**, 113, 199, **200**

Mount Currie. *See* Port Pemberton

Mountain Springs, 108, 121, 124

Musqueam First Nation, 230

Nanaimo, 16, 118, **219**

Napier, Lord (Francis), 19

New British Gold Fields, 53

New Brunswick Bar, 103

New Caledonia. See Caledonia

New El Dorado, 53

New Westminster, **59**, 60, 216, 220, 225, 240, 243, 247

New York Bar, 89, 127

New York City, 34, 39, 40, 193, 239, 240, 241, 244, 245, 246, 248, 250

New York Herald, 29

New York Times, 29

Newcastle, Duke of (Henry Pelham-Clinton), 184

Nicaragua, 28, 30, 39, 127, 241, 245, 248

Nisqually, 27

Nlaka'pamux, 10, 83, 92-93, 96-101, 103

North America: Map of Part of the British Possessions to the West of the Rocky Mountains, 224

Northern Light, 21, 79, 123, 234

Nugent, John, **29**, 30

Official Map of the Town of Victoria, 221

Ohio Bar 89

Okanagan Lake, 91

Olympia, 48, 141, 234

Oregon, 16, 18, 22, 27, 45, 58, 88, 91, 209, 238, 241-42, 249

Oregon, 40, 194, **195**, 244

Orestes, 40, 244

Orizaba, 171, 237, 245

Otter, HBC, 8, 44, **46**, 47, 114, 126, 169, 171, 174, 177, 220, 233-34, 244-45

Pacific, 26, 133, 189, 223, 242, 245

Pacific Mail Steamship Company, 29, 240-41, 244, 246

Palmer, Henry Spencer, 162, 165t, 172-73, 183-84, 207, **225**, 226